INFORMolution

by Dr. Ken Hildebrandt

"We live entangled in webs of endless deceit,
in a highly indoctrinated society where elementary truths are easily buried."

\- Professor Noam Chomsky

This book aims to unearth several of the grandest buried truths most people will find shocking. What's presented will at times seem outright unbelievable. However, the evidence is what it is.

How on earth can a minority fool a majority at the height of the Information Age? It seems so unlikely. All I ask of anyone is to take a look at the evidence I've gathered for over a decade and a half and presented in as simple manner as I could. Please don't believe anything I say or write. I'm just asking for you to look at my findings and think things through for yourself. Unless you like living with harmful lies and don't mind not knowing the truth, I don't think you'll be disappointed. Besides, the world needs you. As it stands now we're all losing as you'll soon see, even those who are the roots of these problems, for they too live in a far more dangerous and sickening world than need be.

Everyone counts one way or the other and make no mistake about it, we're all making history right now. Will an INFORMolution happen with this book? I honestly don't know. What I do know is that it should and I have done my best to give you the reasons why. I hope my best is good enough. There is far too much inefficiency, misery and danger to ignore. I wrote to Professor Chomsky last year and said I felt as if we're all living in a giant insane asylum. He wrote me back saying that case was easy to make. We need to stop the insanity together as soon as possible. Please read on.

Table of Contents

Part I - ELECTION SPOILERS

INTRODUCTION - 4

Chapter 1 – Telling it like it is: Ken's talk for Ralph Nader at the University of Texas in 2004 9

Chapter 2 – The Greatest Weapon 12

Chapter 3 – Confirming Reality using the Internet 18

Chapter 4 – The Package and the Cage: Easy Setups for Non-Crimes 24

Chapter 5 – A Way Out: Informing Others and Voting 30

Chapter 6 – Ken asks Presidential candidate detailed question at Press Conference in 2004 32

Chapter 7 – Media-censored U.S. Senatorial Candidate Arrested 36

Chapter 8 – In Memory of Doug Friedline, former Minnesota Governor Jesse Ventura's campaign manager 40

Chapter 9 – The Journalist Who 'Covered' a Censored Debate 44

Chapter 10 – The Not-so-great Escape of Former U.S. Senator Robert (Bob) Torricelli 47

Chapter 11 – Another Censored Candidate Discusses Wind, Hemp, and More 52

Chapter 12 – A Corporate Country Club for Democrats 58

Chapter 13 – More Candidate Censorship Compliments of The Corporate Media 62

Chapter 14 – Corporate Power 66

Chapter 15 – Media-Censored Presidential Elections Metastasizes to the Republican & Democratic Parties 69

Chapter 16 – The Military-Industrial Complex 72

Chapter 17 – On the Eve of the 2008 New Hampshire Primary with Professor Noam Chomsky 77

Chapter 18 – 2010 Skype interview with California Governor Candidate, Laura Wells 79

Chapter 19 – 2012 Interview with Highly Censored Presidential Candidate, Jill Stein, M.D. 82

Chapter 20 – Conclusion of Part I 86

Part II – Down the Rabbit Hole 89

Chapter 1 – Guns and Children 90

Chapter 2 – The Absurdity of Racism – from the Charlottesville, VA League of Women Voters' 2014 US Congressional Candidate Forum 91

Chapter 3 – Achieving Peace in Israel/Palestine 92

Chapter 4 – Historic Mainstream Coverage of the VA, US Congressional District 5, 2012 Election 94

Chapter 5 – Elaine and Ken's "spotlight videos" for the 2014 Election 104

Chapter 6 – Historic Introduction of the US Congressional Candidate Forum sponsored by the League of Women Voters in Charlottesville, Virginia, on October 30, 2014 107

Chapter 7 – "The Secret Government" is not a conspiracy theory, nor is weather modification 109

Chapter 8 – Downed Extraterrestrial Craft Near Nuclear Base in 1947 112

Chapter 9 – The UFO issue expanded markedly during WWII with what were called "foo fighters." By 1947 UFOs were acknowledged as real, though they were called "flying saucers" until the early 1950s..114

Chapter 10 – Key Testimony regarding a UFO interfering with US Nuclear Weapons 115

Chapter 11 – UFOs and nukes go way to July 1947, outside Roswell, New Mexico, home of the 509th, the ones who bombed Hiroshima and Nagasaki 119

Chapter 12 – Nuclear physicist/UFO researcher Stanton Friedman gives testimony at the Citizen Hearing on Disclosure regarding Roswell and more 121

Chapter 13 – Roswell witness Colonel Jesse Marcel, Jr., MD gives testimony at the Citizen Hearing on Disclosure.....124

Chapter 14 – Denice Marcel, granddaughter of Jesse Marcel and daughter of Col. Jesse Marcel, Jr., MD gives testimony at the Citizen Hearing on Disclosure 126

Chapter 15 – Jesse Marcel III, grandson of Jesse Marcel and son of Col. Jesse Marcel, Jr., MD, gives testimony at the Citizen Hearing on Disclosure 129

Chapter 16 – Testimony of Roswell investigator Dr. Kevin Randle at the Citizen Hearing..131

Chapter 17 – Further Testimony from Col. Jesse Marcel, Jr., MD at the Citizen Hearting..135

Chapter 18 – Testimony of Linda Moulton Howe at the Citizen Hearing 137

Chapter 19 – More testimony of Linda Moulton Howe at the Citizen Hearing 139

Chapter 20 – We're in deep #@*&! Where do we go from here? 141

Chapter 21 – Discussing the US Libertarian Party with Noam Chomsky 144

Chapter 22 – Conclusion 153

Addendum – 160

Index – 163

Part I –
ELECTION SPOILERS

Introduction

The following are three quotes (in addition to the Noam Chomsky one above regarding the buried elementary truths) to always keep in mind when reading this book.

"The fact that an opinion has been widely held is no evidence whatever that it is not utterly absurd. Indeed, in view of the silliness of the majority of mankind, a widespread belief is more likely to be foolish than sensible."

- Bertrand Russell, 20th century philosopher,
pictured to the left and behind Professor Noam Chomsky in the photo below with Ken from 2003

"See, in my line of work you got to keep repeating things over and over again for the truth to sink in, to kind of catapult the propaganda."

- George W. Bush, (photo below from Ken's February 2001 "proxy" interview with the president,
in which the Iraq War was brought up over two years before it began)

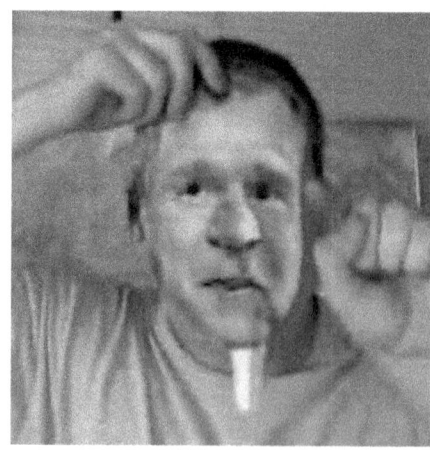

"Science is the search for the truth--it is not a game in which one tries to beat his opponent, to do harm to others. We need to have the spirit of science in international affairs, to make the conduct of international affairs the effort to find the right solution, the just solution of international problems, and not an effort by each nation to get the better of other nations, to do harm to them when it is possible. I believe in morality, in justice, in humanitarianism."

- Linus Pauling

This should also apply to national affairs too of course.

WHATEVER ITS ORIGINAL SOURCE IS, our five billion year old solar system has given birth to us all, no doubt. In reality we share this moment of time together on this planet and have the ability to communicate worldwide like never before in history.

Recalling that the Sumerians were able to transmit thought via writing millennia ago; cannot we at the height of the Information Age spread censored critical news to enough to matter in time? If you keep reading you'll soon see who your worst enemies are and how you can legally, morally, and effectively defend yourself and everyone else you care about against them. The widely held belief that people are basically divided into two political camps "conservative" or "liberal" is but a media manufactured distortion of reality likely developed simply to divide the people amongst themselves. I'm not claiming neither has its gripes. I am saying that we're all getting royally scammed to such a point the very survival of our species is at stake right now and their complaints pale in comparison to that and the other concerns discussed herein. Neither side can reasonably be considered conservative or liberal, as is presented repetitively by multiple sources throughout this book. A rational person would think these matters would dominate discussion, and hopefully this will soon be the case.

Possibilities vs. Impossibilities

Surely most will agree that no matter what anyone does, the Earth will still be spinning around the Sun, making a complete revolution in just over 365 days. That much won't change. What *might* change is how we treat the problem of our ailing atmosphere, which we as humans need not be harming, though we clearly are, thus putting at considerable risk the continued survival of our very species within this century.* That just doesn't make sense, does it? It happens because most people don't know a handful or so of irrefutable truths, and they vote in disfavor of themselves and their world by choosing those whose interests lie in the gluttony of a disproportionate few over the survival of humankind. *The Information Age* could very well be called *The Age of Ignorance,* which, I'm hoping, with your help, will soon come to a close. It's time to stop complaining about our society and become honorable participants in its governing at the highest of levels. If you, along with others including me, put forth the effort to inform others, and ask them to ask others to do the same, we have a chance of getting out of this mess. Otherwise, we don't. Each of us could very well be the deciding factor. Please think about that.

* See, *Planet's Future At Stake, U.N. Report Says,* as reported in the *Toronto Star,* though originating from London and available now at, **http://www.roadtopeace.org/research.php?itemid=437**, a little more than halfway down the page.

The United Nations is in the United States, so how come we have to find out paramount concerns such as the above via Canada and England? At least with the internet it's easy to do.

A handful of media-censored topics are primarily discussed in Part I, those being:

1) The media's open distortion of elections;

2) The mass caging of known innocents at taxpayers' and children's expense, while leaving more real criminals at large in society as a result;

3) The royal tax scam;

4) We could be growing our own oil;

and...

5) The way out of this mess, should enough of us make the effort of our lives as if our lives depended on it-as is surely the case-and as if the fate of humankind was in our hands, as it is.
What's here is elementary, profound, censored, and luckily also easily verifiable. Never "believe" anything I say or write. My goal is for people to understand things, not believe.

Part II gets into the seemingly surreal as well as presenting both my wife Elaine's and my experiences when running for US Congress in 2014, for Virginia's 5th and 6th districts, in which we both received media attention, but neither a televised debate unfortunately. That's all we're pushing for, but at least we made progress over 2012 when only I ran and was excluded from the one and only debate there was, televised or not.

We made Virginia history and I believe we were the second married couple to run for US Congress ever in the entire US. Part II also discusses other things that I think adults or even children can handle, yet judging from the mainstream you'd think they're science fiction. Of course that's fine because I never want anyone to believe anything I say or write. I do hope enough examine the evidence presented and check things out for themselves. Sometimes the mainstream media leak something out they ordinarily hide, and when that happens I cite it. In other words when possible, what Noam Chomsky refers to as "the occasional nugget" in *MANUFACTURING CONSENT: NOAM CHOMSKY AND THE MEDIA,* is used. They're good to have memorized when debating others about what's really happening.

Our best chance lies in enough getting informed in time; otherwise we can expect a downward spiral in several life impacting ways.

For those with short attention spans, consider reading just the Introduction and the Conclusion of Part I, and then pick and choose what you find of interest in between, which consists mostly of the evidence supporting what's written at the beginning and end.

Book II is perhaps a bit more scary, and therefore of interest to many, but I recommend going over the basics first, meaning at least come away with an idea of what I'm trying to get across in Book I, since it is the foundation of it all. If we didn't have puppets of the elite as representatives instead of people, we wouldn't be in near the mess we're in now.

There are quotes at every chapter's beginning, and enough to keep most interested I'm hoping, especially since what's in this book is about profound censored news at your expense. It's the kind of book one can skip around while reading. Everything here is easy to understand and most is alarming. These are fixable political problems, so long as each reasonable person out there does what he or she can in a quick decisive vote in favor of themselves, and by informing as many as possible, asking them to ask others to do likewise. Informing others is the key, so if for one reason or another you can't vote yourself, don't worry about it. Either you'll let others know what's going on, or what's going on will continue to get worse at everyone's expense. Old myths die hard, though if you take your life seriously as well as the lives of those around you, you'll do what you can, I'm hoping. If enough try, things will change.

Our leaders, nearly without exception, at the congressional, senatorial, gubernatorial, vice presidential and presidential levels, clearly stand against us, in one way or another. An opinion is an opinion, and facts are facts, and the fact is that our elected leaders are almost exclusively known-proven by their actions-supporters of unnecessary and unjust suffering, misery and death, all to benefit the criminal gluttony of a disproportionate few who finance their elections.

A disproportionate few are misguiding most. Their immorality and lack of concern for you and your loved ones is unfathomable, especially when they smile in your face on television. Don't take my word for any of this. All I'm asking is for you take a look at the evidence. No research project required here, just a brief review of one that's already been done.

Is there something we can do now?

Yes, become informed regarding these basics mentioned above and discussed below, and once you understand yourself, tell others. None of this is complicated, it's just censored. It's all straightforward and easy to verify I trust you'll find. Our elections are misguided is the main point to understand here. Like a chain letter spread the news, post it on social media, discuss it with your friends, etc. The message to spread is that, as one can clearly see from reading this book as well as checking for oneself, the media misguide the masses by either marginalizing candidates or censoring them completely, especially from debates and candidate forums and this censorship results in our nation and world being misguided in terribly destructive ways. We also need to let those know in office that we realize how we're all being scammed in the manners discussed herein and it's time they stopped.

The media call those who challenge their corporate backed puppet candidates "spoilers," when in reality it's the censors who are the spoilers as you'll soon see. We are calling for fair debates in which all ballot qualified candidates, or in the case of the presidency if they're on enough ballots to win, are included and given equal time on television. Is that too much to ask? How can we call our country a democracy when, as happened when we covered the alternate debate for vice-president in 2004 in Cleveland, two people debated on corporate television and three others debated at another venue the mainstream media ignored across town? That's the norm not the exception. Third party candidates are kept from televised debates by force if deemed necessary, right here in the US. What do you suppose former President Jimmy Carter, who has been called to monitor elections in East Timor, would say of such a thing? If someone sees him and has the opportunity please ask.

The "545 People" Charlie Reese discussed in his famous article* are steering our ship here in the most influential nation on Earth, and we elect all but 9 of them. It's about time we started making decisions based on reason, not who's put in our faces and spend beaucoup bucks to fool us into making insane choices.

* http://articles.orlandosentinel.com/1984-02-03/news/os-ed-charley-reese-545-people-1984-073111_1_tax-code-president-vetoes-con-game

After first meeting with Noam Chomsky on October 25, 2002, regarding our findings exposing media-censored elections, he said to us on camera upon leaving what's quoted below.

"Terrific. You bring it to others."

When reading this book you'll see that spaces exist between paragraphs instead of the standard book style of using indentations. No doubt I'll receive criticism of this due to the increased use of paper, unless I explain myself I'm hoping. I think leaving spaces like this will make it more appealing since this is how we're used to reading things on the web these days. I also want this book to attract people who generally don't read books, hence so many photos, quotes and skipped paragraphs making it easier for people to take a rest pretty much anywhere. Lastly, industrial hemp's legalization will have an enormous impact on the saving of trees, incomparable to adding a few pages to a single book.

Chapter 1

Telling it like it is: Ken's talk for Ralph Nader at the University of Texas in 2004

"If liberty means anything at all, it means the right to tell people what they do not want to hear."

- George Orwell

Ken's speech for Presidential candidate Ralph Nader at the University of Texas on April 30, 2004

Ken: Dr. Ken Hildebrandt is the name. (The moment I was handed the microphone, the Twelve O'clock bell started going off at the top of the tower just behind me.)

Man who introduced Ken by another name completely: That's even better.

Ken: I want to turn this thing around a little bit and just talk about some basic things, some basic reality, which (most) people are not aware of. This campaign coming up is about, basically, life or death if you want to look at it. A couple years ago a thousand scientists submitted a report to the U.N. saying that basically our environment is at such a point that we need to turn it around *now* or we're in dire straits.* How come that wasn't on the front page of the news? In fact it was hardly even reported here in the United States. Now isn't that, (pointing up to the sky), that we're all breathing, don't we all need to be concerned about that?

* See, *Planet's Future At Stake, U.N. Report Says*, as reported in the *Toronto Star*, though originating from London and available now at, **http://www.roadtopeace.org/research.php?itemid=437**, a little more than halfway down the page.

Well, in this upcoming presidential election, we can choose a man who had more executions than any governor in the history of the United States, or we can choose a man who's not much better than him, or we can choose a man who is responsible for our cars having seat belts and air bags. I mean this is so cut and dried.

If you were going to choose a doctor... OK, if you were going to choose a doctor, which doctor of three you were presented with would you pick? Would you pick a doctor who had lost many many patients, and really shown open contempt for 90% of them? Or another doctor who was the same, but yet these doctors were portrayed by the TV, the news, and all the other sources. Yet you found out from your friend with this life-threatening illness you had, that there was an alternative of somebody who had saved hundreds of thousands of lives. Now who would you pick? I mean, this whole thing about Nader being a spoiler is a media-manufactured myth.

The United States, the Land of Liberty, has more incarcerates per capita than any civilization on planet Earth...

Check it out yourself, there were three quarters of a million* of our own people who were cuffed and caged last year for possession of a plant, leaving by default more pedophiles, rapists, murderers, extortionists, you name it, more criminals at large...

* See, **http://norml.org/aboutmarijuana**

Now, that's (pointing toward the sky) endangered, A); B), we have more incarcerates than anyone else, and C), our top crime is a non-crime...

You know, if you can't refute what I'm saying, just look at what I'm saying, because the stuff that I'm talking about is definitely making you look at your world like this, (topsy-turvy gesture with arm). But let it soak in, and if it feels right to you and you want to do something about it, then get these signatures so we can vote for a viable candidate... I mean, (do) you think the mass media is going to portray the guy who's responsible for seat belts and air bags? You think they're going to give him fair time? Why do you think Nader was eliminated from the debates last time? Because he's a rational candidate. Would've won hand's down. Oh jeez... ah... do you want this guy who supports death, misery and suffering of Americans, or do you want this guy who stands for death, suffering and misery of Americans, or do you want this guy who stands for Americans and has for four decades? It's time to bury the myth about him being a spoiler...

We just invaded another country because of what they are supposedly doing to their citizens (and their manufactured threat against others too of course). Meanwhile, we have 13-million hungry kids today, here, and we just heard back from a probe from Mars! Now that's insane. Can't you see that? Is there any excuse for that? (President) Wilson... saw that we could eradicate poverty by the end of the century.

And yet...(a heckler interrupts) Hey... are 13-million hungry kids real to you? You know? I hope so. No, I'm not going to back off... I mean, you're supporting death and suffering and you're telling me to back off, and you're for Christ? ...Would Christ have voted for one of two candidates who was for caging of innocent Americans for no reason? Jeez.

Alright, now let's talk about the tax structure. Alright, when I was a kid a man worked in a hardware store in the fishing department and he raised his whole family, and his wife didn't have to work outside the home. It should have gotten easier in the last four decades but it got worse, in spite of four decades of technological advancement. Now why is that? Well, (in no small part), because the rich in the year 1960 were taxed 91% on their most superfluous of income. Sounds like a lot but it takes other people to make that money. Now the rich are taxed 35% with earnings to infinity. So, if you look at the billionaire stats last year, Mr. Gates and the Wal-Mart crew (not referring to the workers of course), they made more money last year. What a surprise?

The superfluities of a few over the necessities of the many. Bottom line is, in the presidency, the House, and the Senate we don't have one person who doesn't stand for unnecessary human suffering and pain and unnecessary American suffering and pain. I was a physician for 13 years and... I either got them better or I didn't. I was a manual medicine physician, my hands and my brain. That was it. I practiced in New Jersey and was never sued, which is almost a miracle. But the point is, is that, we need to start looking at these as real life and death issues. We're talking about caging our own people for no reason, leaving by default more criminals... The tax structure I talked about how it was 91%... in the year 1960. The other day Nader said, he said, 'Listen, we'll revert it back to what it was in the 60's and the deficit is gone, instantly.' Oh jeez, he's the spoiler if he was given a fair shot... I mean he wants to revert (it) back. We don't need 13-million hungry kids everyday...

Let me tell you the last thing. We could be growing our own oil. Hemp oil ran cars; it's decades-old technology... Anyone (who) has a problem with anything I've said about cannabis or hemp can go to

JackHerer.com and refute it with Jack... (that shuts them up real fast), you know, because he's got a $100,000 challenge. The bottom line is, we could be growing our own oil...

So, we got the most addicting substance known to man supporting our president's campaigns, and we got the top crime being a non-crime. Now, both Kerry and Bush stand for that... and the tax structure, remember which... is all the way down to 35%... Those issues alone will really show you where you're at...

So, I'm jumping up and down, running out of, not running out of steam, it's just that this is not only about me. You know, that's our atmosphere, (pointing up toward the sky). It could be way better for us. I've shown you that in a short period of time. That all we have to do when we go to vote... we could shoot that way, that way, or that way. You know, just because the elite display the other two candidates, you got to be kind of foolish to pick them...

Here we are, to give you perspective, (holding up a poster of the earth rotating around the sun with one division marked for each of the 365 days), spinning through space, living under delusion at the height of the Information Age, while people *who claim* they're followers of the Prince of Peace heckle what I'm talking about, with millions of people being hungry, little innocent children right here.* That's what it is. For those of you who want to do something about it... go to votenader.org, and get these signatures. You need 64 thousand signatures. Get other people to get signatures, and let's get him on...**

* *"A single death is a tragedy, a million deaths is a statistic."*

– Joseph Stalin

** Note: Nader made it on 34 state ballots and DC in 2004. In 2008, he made it on 45 states and DC, as well as a write-in for four other states. Oklahoma was the only state where people did not have the option of voting for Ralph Nader that year.

Last time around, (meaning Election 2000) my wife (Elaine) ...she called... the head of a major U.S. newspaper and he said that he would post, he would actually print my editorial, six sentences long, until he saw it, and then he even called her back, and he denied that he got it, but he wouldn't print it. And yet three days later (an estimate), he found front page space to compare Bush and Gore to the makes of automobiles...*

* Note: This was the key point for me to realize that we the people could not ever expect the elite-owned-and-operated media to print the truth regarding paramount hidden concerns, especially regarding elections, but we now had the tool of the internet to overcome the media myths and thus fight the liars who have convinced the lion to submit to the lamb, at the expense of millions and now to the point of risking the ability for our species to continue to survive.

I'm in this because we're all in this together. I mean we're all endangered right now. Our atmosphere is heating up while (proclaimed) followers of the Prince of Peace are gabbing about whatever. Sorry, I don't mean to criticize anyone but it's just that we're all in this together. It's like Flight 93 has been hijacked, and I'm up here bashing on the cockpit door. We both got arrested, incarcerated in the Land of Liberty for doing this, and other people are playing pinochle and they've got the nerve to criticize or just chat about nonsense, while we're trying to get through the cockpit door... So, if you want to do something constructive... (tell others).

Chapter 2

The Greatest Weapon

"The greatest weapon in the hands of the oppressor is the mind of the oppressed."

- Steve Biko

Above, former US Congresswoman and Green Party Presidential candidate, Cynthia McKinney, shortly after speaking with me at the 2008 march for Mumia Abu-Jamal, who's been incarcerated for decades for the murder of a police officer, when in fact there's testimonial evidence demonstrating that he's not guilty beyond a reasonable doubt. At least two witnesses claimed they had been manipulated by police to testify against Mumia. One faced quite a long sentence by coming forward, but she couldn't continue on living knowing an innocent man had been framed and she had been a part of it. Another was a Vietnam veteran who was told to just forget about the fact that he knew an innocent man was, at that time, on death row. He was unable to forget and later told the truth. According to him, it sounded as if Abu-Jamal had approached the fallen officer after he'd been shot in a clear attempt to assist him after the real shooter had already fled the scene.

When I first envisioned this book, I wanted to put a section about Mumia Abu-Jamal in it, and I'm finally doing that just before it goes to print. I had no photo for this chapter, so figured I'd use the one of Cynthia McKinney above (which I used to have amongst half a dozen photos at the introduction to the book as it appeared on various websites through the years) and I saw my opening.

The person who murdered Officer Daniel Faulkner has never been charged for so doing and an innocent man remains in a human cage for nothing, no longer on death row, and no longer in solitary confinement, but away from his right to roam the earth quite likely due to his skill as a reporter.

I've said he's the United States' answer to South Africa's now deceased Nelson Mandela, only now he's been in there for a much longer time than even Mandela. Wouldn't it be nice if President Obama was pressured to have this man pardoned before he leaves office? At this point a presidential pardon is his only chance of having freedom again. And it should be explained just why he's being released, so he'll be safe.

For reasons beyond my ken, there are people, mostly police or former police, who want this man to rot in prison, since they didn't get their way in having him put to death. They just don't seem to be looking at the case with the most elementary of reason. It baffles me. I mean what do they have? They have the testimony of a police officer who said months afterwards that Abu-Jamal said, "I shot the m-f'er and I hope he dies," yet in his police report of the incident he made no such statement. Instead he said something along the lines of 'The negro male made no comment.'

Mumia Abu-Jamal needs to be pardoned by President Obama, along with Leonard Peltier, who fully expected to be released by Clinton, and no doubt a host of others whose stories should be known. Imagine Mumia Abu-Jamal pardoned by President Obama, and then running for President of the United States and winning in 2020. There's a thought, huh?

Getting back to the focus of our* book, in order to help demonstrate how long I've been trying to get my basic message about our openly ridiculously unfair elections in the US, the following commentary was published on *Znet interActive* in early October 2000.

If you're on Earth, this book's about you. We're all in this together spinning through space tens of millions of miles every single day on the crust of the same rock.

Observations of a Concerned Citizen

I am absolutely appalled that not only was Ralph Nader not allowed to participate in the first presidential debate, but was blocked by the police Gestapo outside when he arrived with a valid ticket to sit in the viewing audience. This truly represents just how far our democracy has deteriorated. It is reminiscent of the tyranny that we were all taught happened in communist countries, which in turn made us abhor those political entities. How can anyone of sane mind still feel that we are free as Americans under these conditions? A presidential debate committee that can ignore a candidate, who has received nearly 100,000 signatures in an online petition for his inclusion, is far from just and representative of the people. We are talking about a decision about who is going to get the most important job in America. I think, we, as citizens, deserve more than having to pick between "the least of the worst," as Mr. Nader has rightfully termed our bipartisan choices. It must be borne in mind that the arbitrary 15% inclusionary rule was not present when the debates were run by the League of Women Voters and has only been present for eleven years. Besides that, recent polls have indicated that the majority of Americans would like to see Ralph Nader in the debates. If diverse opinions are not allowed, then why have a debate at all? If Vice President Al Gore is seriously concerned about the plight of middle class Americans and the environment, then how can he support the WTO, which clearly does not? You won't get an answer to that question from a Bush-Gore debate because both support the WTO. Nader does not, and don't we as Americans deserve to hear this topic discussed? After all, the protests in Seattle last year over this issue were the largest seen in America since the Vietnam War days. I would like to hear the opinion of this issue from a man that has done more as private citizen for the benefit of the people in this country than both Bush and Gore have done while holding public office. Ralph Nader is a man who has always stood for the people over big business, which is the antithesis of the Republican and Democratic candidates, both of whom have obtained wealth via corporate welfare from the tax-paying public. If we allow ourselves to be dominated by the interests of the wealthy to such an extent that we are not even given a fair chance of choosing a president, then we can no longer claim that we live in anything even remotely resembling a democracy.

End of first 2000 commentary

Like it or not, we're all in this together and the media are harming all, even those who work within same, though they don't realize this is the case obviously enough. All are in the same predicament, dependent upon the same atmosphere for survival, and whether the media accurately portray our mutual situation or not, reality remains reality. Those of us living in the U.S. live in the most influential and powerful nation in the world, and in spite of it being the height of the Information Age, we are allowing ourselves to be deluded to such a point the continued survival of humankind is at stake within this very century, all to satisfy the murderous greed of a disproportionate few, thanks to those who misguide the mass media and thus the majority of Americans, in spite of the internet's ability to overcome the media.

It's hard to believe that the majority of Americans would allow themselves "*…to be deluded and manipulated by* *the system,"** to use the words of the most quoted living author, Professor Noam Chomsky, who's all but completely censored by the U.S. corporate media giants, most notably in my view the major television networks, since televised footage gains more attention than print news** and is arguably a stronger medium to transmit information, yet that's clearly the case. Most are duped, big time.

* See, *MANUFACTURING CONSENT: NOAM CHOMSKY AND THE MEDIA*, a documentary by Mark Achbar& Peter Wintonick

** See, **http://www.pbs.org/wgbh/pages/frontline/newswar/part3/stats.html**

Professor Chomsky has been described in the *New York Times* as being, "*... arguably the most important intellectual alive,*"* and as stated he *is* the most quoted living author,** so why do you suppose he's not invited as a guest on any of these numerous television political talk shows we have nowadays on the major networks?

* See, *MANUFACTURING CONSENT: NOAM CHOMSKY AND THE MEDIA*, a documentary by Mark Achbar& Peter Wintonick

** See, *CHOMSKY FOR BEGINNERS*, by David Cogswell, page 1

As a matter of fact, Professor Chomsky has lambasted the *New York Times** for burying important information, one example being East Timor in the late 1970s, where a slaughter of innocent human beings occurred, yet received very little coverage, and the coverage it did receive was primarily from the view of the aggressors. So, it wasn't like this comment about him being, "*...arguably the most important intellectual alive,*" was put on their front page. It was in what the Professor referred to as a "*publisher's blurb*" and he further stated that "*...and you always got to watch those things. Because if you go back to the original you'll find that that sentence is there, this is in the* New York Times*, but the next sentence is; 'Since that's the case, how can he write such terrible things about American foreign policy?'* (laughs, Chomsky and audience) *And they never quote that part. But in fact if it wasn't for that second sentence I would begin to think that I'm doing something wrong, and I'm not joking about that.*"

* Discussed in the second October 2000 commentary, *The Daily Paper - No Longer an Essential News Source*

I usually stick with the fact that in spite of the U.S. corporate media strongly censoring him he's still the most quoted living author. That's a fact. Don't you think he ought to at least be heard?

Chomsky tells people there's no reason they should "believe" anything he says, and I echo those sentiments wholeheartedly. All I'm asking is for people to consider what's presented here, especially in relation to elections, unknown tax facts, and a war against innocent people that the citizens have sponsored, and for each person to decide what he or she feels is right in relation to same in terms of who they vote for and/or encourage others to vote for in our high office elections. The media have and are continuing to censor significant realities that impact your life. Everything here is elementary. It's merely hidden. Cannot the internet help bring it into plain view for enough to see to matter in time? Suffice it to say one way or another we're all making history right now. In time we'll find out and one way or another whether we made it or not, won't we?

The Daily Paper - No Longer an Essential News Source

by Dr. Ken Hildebrandt

(published on *ZNet* on or before October 20, 2000)

At the end of last year Johann Gutenberg was the first one listed among "The Most Important People of the Millennium" by *TIME* Magazine, for his invention of the printing press in the 15th century. This was likely a good call because his invention enabled mass communication for the first time in history. Unfortunately for most people however, the power of the press fell into too few hands and enabled the greedy to write history as they saw fit for their own gains. As the population of the planet continued to grow, so did the amount of human suffering therein as a consequence. *The Prosperous Few and The Restless Many*, a book title by the great linguist Noam Chomsky, is a concise way of stating the resultant status quo. It takes only one example to clearly illustrate just how immoral those in power became, that being of the genocide that occurred in East Timor in the late 1970s.

Although the United States supplied 90% of the arms used by Indonesia to slaughter an estimated 200,000 innocent human beings, there was virtually no awareness of the issue at all in the land of justice and freedom. *The New York Times*, who boast their contents to contain "All the News, That's Fit to Print," didn't report the story at all in the peak killing year of 1979. No news, no outcry, was unfortunately the fate for the East Timorese, whose women were sent back to the barracks of the Indonesian soldiers for their "use."

It must also be clearly stated that almost all of this was during the Jimmy Carter era, the so called, "man of integrity" being personally responsible himself for vast amounts of human suffering and death. This truly illustrates how "elementary truths" are easily withheld from the people and additionally that the controlling powers of *The New York Times,* along with the rest of the US media actually had "complicity in genocide in this case," as Chomsky pointed out. All of this occurred, yet just last year when Timor atrocities were covered in the American press, the U.S. was depicted as benevolent death camp liberators, a status both of our top two presidential candidates still maintain. It is an outrage that this kind of lying can go unchecked. We should be sending vast amounts of aid to that country, along with an open apology, for what was done to them. How do you think those who survived in Timor look at our country, with our leading two presidential contenders asserting they are decent human beings worthy of such a high office? I would assume that they would think we're pretty simple-minded, immoral, or both.

We must put an end to this kind of nonsensical behavior, getting our information from such consistently unreliable and inaccurate sources when we no longer need to due to the internet. *Associated Press* wires are available as they happen from a variety of sources on the net, as are non-corporate sponsored news websites that help prevent truly newsworthy material from slipping through the cracks. We don't need the newspapers anymore, at least not to get our news. All we have to do is spread the word, completely boycott these most undeserving institutions, and devise ways to bring computer access and skills to those who don't have them. There are many people who are working hard to remove the barriers that still exist in bringing the truth to the people in our country. The emancipation has begun, so let's enjoy it!

End of second 2000 commentary

Below: *TIME* magazine web post by the author as reposted on *Znet interActive* in October of 2000 under the category of "IRAQI EMBARGO," though it also deals with the Drug War.

Of note, to clarify what's stated in the introductory "NOTE," the last I had checked just prior to writing was that out of over a million respondents, Mr. Nader had received 58.77% of the votes in the referred online *TIME* magazine poll.

At Children's Expense!

NOTE: The following was originally an e-mail in response to posted message at TIME.com, to one, Dave, who I assume was the moderator. I have a feeling there's more than one person over there who regrets they had this online election thing, in retrospect. I mean, one could interpret these findings (they had over 100,000 respondents the last time I checked and Nader had 58.77%, Bush about half that, and Gore in the single digits) as evidence that even conservatives would vote for Nader over Bush and Gore combined, if they gave moderate effort at becoming informed. Dave concluded his statement about people demonizing the corporate candidates

with a quote from Charlie Brown, "Good Grief!"

"Good grief!" Dave, come out of the *Peanuts* cartoon and get with reality. Your Mom &/or Dad were unlikely to have been sent to jail for years during your childhood, due to an unjust drug war that singled them out for the color of their skin. The prison population in the United States has grown 600% in the last 20 years, Dave. The rich are now floating bonds to build more prisons and capitalize on the suffering of others by depriving them of freedom for years of their lives. It kind of sounds like slavery to me, Dave. Oh yeah, I forgot to mention that major corporations have discovered that they can hire the inmates at slave labor wages because they are not entitled to the same rights as citizens. I'm talking about 50 cents an hour, right here at home, without setting up operations overseas. Solutions to the problems for the rich abound in our land of opportunity. Did anyone in power bother to think about the inmates' children, Dave? Do they deserve to be so insufficiently supported during their upbringing? What did they do to deserve this punishment, Dave? Haven't you thought about these issues, or don't they concern you because it's not your pain? They're dehumanizing children, Dave, little innocent children! The corporations involved in these affairs are nothing less than greed-motivated, serial-child-abuse offenders. They steal children's childhoods for money, Dave. Think about it, serial-child-abusers build prisons for people who use seemingly arbitrarily chosen substance illegalities. After all, the most destructive drug, alcohol, and the most addicting, nicotine, are both legal. The others are not though, with extreme human consequences of pain and suffering. Those are not just words Dave; I'm talking about real pain and real suffering. Suffering meted out to satisfy the superfluous desires of the wealthy. If they were sent to rehabs it would be far more effective than prisons in every way, including cost, according to UNICEF and other legitimate studies on the issue. Giving children more potential for happiness would actually cost us less money. Rich people would be the only losers here. In a just society, they would be put in their own prisons, for their sickening crimes against humanity. "Good" grief? No way! There is no such thing as "good" grief, Dave.

I didn't have to go through these kinds of things in my childhood to understand and care about what's going on. Does it not violate your internal sense of justice that hurting children has not only been in essence legalized, but it is a profitable enterprise as well? The evidence is widely available, albeit sparingly in your publication, that clearly demonizes the top two contenders. You so hypocritically demand the non-use of offensive language at your site so as to not disturb the more fortunate families, while you simultaneously endorse campaigns that actually starve children to death. I'm claiming that you endorse these immoral endeavors because you have attempted to *defend them* from being called the names that best suit supporters of these policies.

While we're on the topic of how politics affect children, let's look at the embargo against Iraq that kills between 4 and 5 thousand children a month via starvation and malnutrition. Elementary logic clearly discloses two guilty parties here, in that if either would stop its torturous behavior, the children would be saved from starvation, literally from starvation! Wake up, please, anyone who doesn't get that! Nazi Germany was involved in the starvation of innocent people. This policy, likewise, results in the starvation of innocent people. If the end product is the slow death of starvation, to anyone, notwithstanding innocent children, it is not a moral option for us. It is clearly wrong. The Iraqi embargo has killed about a million children under the age of Elian, since it began nearly a decade ago. Please explain the difference between each one of those children and Elian, Dave. Both Bush and Gore boast of their commitment to punish Saddam, killing the women and children in the country that he dominates. How grotesquely absurd and simpleminded can human's become? This embargo is nothing other than a sustained act of the worst form of terrorism known to man, starvation. Bush and Gore are demonized because they deserve to be. I assume that you rationalize the starving to death of children, because if you didn't, you wouldn't retort with such nonsense to such truly justified descriptions of our leading two candidates.

Why don't you come to Harlem with me someday, or go out in the middle of the night with me and talk to some homeless people? I meet a lot of homeless people who are confined to wheelchairs

Dave. Let's go talk to them together, and maybe the time will come when we can both tell them that we're fighting the system that has allowed their situation to reach this level of despair. The only way you're still a jerk is if you continue to act like one, Dave, and anyone else for that matter. So jump on board and start putting some real use to your life on this planet and stop denying the reality of other breathing human being's pain! The invite is sincere, you have my e-mail address and I'd love to show you why those two examples of "personified ineptitude" who are running for president deserve to be demonized in a big way. See for yourself why they have been demonized, by obtaining easily found examples of real people, Dave, who have been victimized by the perverse actions that these two incompetent candidates wholeheartedly support. I'll likely publish this letter to you in an open format and I'm looking forward to hearing from you soon.

End of third 2000 commentary

Chapter 3

Confirming Reality using the Internet

"First they ignore you, then they laugh at you, then they fight you, then you win."

- Mahatma Gandhi

Above: Journalists who traveled from Japan to cover the New Hampshire Primary in 2008 and interviewed Senator Mike Gravel on the sidewalk.

THANKS TO THE INTERNET, ONE CAN EASILY CONFIRM REALITY, especially regarding basic, yet profound concerns, such as the platforms and histories of all the candidates who are ballot qualified in US federal elections, meaning those running and able to win presidential (2 people, one president and one vice president), congressional (435 people, one member of congress to represent each voting district), and senate seats (100 people, two senators per state), for a grand total of 537 people, who basically run the show, or a big part of it anyway. And all of them are freely elected. Of note is that when I first wrote this paragraph I was not yet familiar with Charlie Reese's famous article entitled *545 People*, in which he leaves out the vice president and adds the Supreme Court.

These people not only guide the direction of over 320 million Americans, but being the leaders of the dominant nation on planet Earth, and the clear military leader, 'admittedly' spending nearly half the rest of the entire world combined, in addition to environmental and atmospheric dangers that are now threatening all life on Earth, one would think choosing who these people are should be more than a haphazard choice, not a decision based on people whom it can readily be demonstrated withhold and/or distort reality into fiction regarding our world, time after time.

As perplexing as it is, in the face of hard evidence and facts many adults are seemingly incapable of letting go of their "beliefs." This is unfortunate and luckily does not apply to all. If it applied to all we'd be in trouble and there would certainly be no point in my writing this book discussing amongst the most profound yet buried elementary truths the media have been distorting in relation to our federal and state elections, and some key ramifications of same. If a third* understand then it would seem rational people would finally have a fair shot of electing far more reasonable candidates for high political offices in spite of the media's all-out efforts to have the people choose representatives whom it can be readily proven do not represent them with respect to their very lives as well as the lives of others, but instead prioritize greed, power and death over "*...Life, Liberty, and the pursuit of Happiness.*"

* An approximate figure, since even in the hotly contested 2004 election, over a third of eligible voters didn't vote. So, we need half of two thirds, i.e., about a third. For stat verification see, **http://www.census.gov/Press-Release/www/releases/archives/voting/004986.html**. Please remember effort in informing others is far more potent than just a single vote.

The founders of this country, flaws and all, would likely be disgusted beyond comprehension as to what we've allowed to happen due to deception and apathy, all the while hanging out our flags as if we actually should be proud for not standing up for ourselves or others. The very future survival of our species is at stake here, and yet the many are still letting the few run the course full steam ahead at the height of the so-called Information Age*. "*Truth is stranger than fiction…*," Mark Twain observed. Does this not appear to be the case right here right now, whilst Americans gather around their propaganda boxes weekly glued to *American 'Idle'*, or whatever it's called, yet have not the foggiest idea that the survival of their species is in unnecessary jeopardy* simply to satisfy the gluttonous wants of a disproportionate few because they're "*…allowing themselves to be deluded and manipulated by the system*?"

* See, *Planet's Future At Stake, U.N. Report Says*, as reported in the *Toronto Star*, though originating from London and available now at, **http://www.roadtopeace.org/research.php?itemid=437**, a little more than halfway down the page, for an article originally published in the *Toronto Star*, about a report submitted to the U.N. regarding our global situation. Remember, the U.N. is in New York. Why do we need to find out what's happening in the United States via Canada, in relation to profound implications that affect the entire world? Should not a story like this be front page news and top headlines?

Once I discovered in 2000 that the capability was there to put things in video format on the internet, I thought the days of television, magazine, and newspaper dominance were numbered. Perhaps I was correct, just not in timing. In the fall of 2000, I posted at a prominent web site not of my creation, and tried to get others who already had video on their websites to hear me out as to what I thought they could do to help in their elections, since that is what their websites were about - they were political in nature.

So, since 2000 I've been trying to put what I wanted to say out there on the internet, all free of charge. I learned a lot about human apathy along the way, something Professor Chomsky has claimed horrifies him more than the occasional Hitler or LeMay who crops up in history, because without the backing of the people, individuals such as Hitler would be powerless. People simply are not living to their human potential if they knowingly submit their very lives to others based on false pretenses, especially when it's been explained that their very tax dollars directly fund mass human suffering and misery whilst millions of children worldwide die of neglect each year for what just a fraction of the Pentagon budget could easily prevent. In other words, these children die horrible deaths simply because they're dehumanized.* And please don't buy the malarkey that we're giving a high proportion of our money for the good of those elsewhere. Though over 20 industrialized nations of the United Nations including the United States agreed to allocating 0.7% of their Gross National Product in 1970, it's a standard that's yet to be consistently met by anyone 45 years after its birth.**

* See, **http://thehungersite.com**, where it's been stated that someone dies of hunger every 3.6 seconds; 75% are under the age of five. Their lives are deemed meaningless. And that's from hunger alone.

** See, **http://www.globalissues.org/TradeRelated/Debt/USAid.asp**

Although I was far from a technological whiz, I managed to learn how to have my own video website in early 2001, mostly due to the Winter 2000 edition of *Videomaker's Guide to PC Video*, in which Matthew York, its editor and publisher, stated at the conclusion of the Editor's Letter, "*Now, even you, can make a television program!*" I realized that the corporate media could be beat, if only an organized effort to inform the masses was made by enough caring people to matter in time.

Here it is years later, and I finally heard the 2008 U.S. presidential election called the "YouTube Election," after the internet site YouTube.com, where people can upload their videos for all to see. As stated, this technology was available at least in 2000, perhaps before. In my humble opinion internet video should have had a profound impact on the presidential election in 2000. Had it done so we would likely be living in a much more sane, reasonable, fair world today. It didn't and thus we're not.

When Paul Revere (everyone knows it wasn't him alone, but that's not the point here) made his ride he didn't yell, "*I think the British are coming*," did he? Then why do we not yell, or at least tell others about how much the media have painted a fictitious view of our very reality at the height of the Information Age, making the 2008 presidential contest a bout between warmongering John McCain, who finished 894th out of 899 in the Naval Academy (arguably a potential threat to George W. Bush as the likely all-time cerebrally challenged president), and Barack Obama, who does not oppose the domestic and international Drug Wars, even though he admitted to doing drugs himself, with the people quickly forgiving him since deep down everyone knows it's really not a crime to do drugs?

I'm not claiming it's smart to do drugs; just that stupidity is not a crime in itself. Eating junk food isn't wise either, though it's not illegal. It's not like Obama robbed a bank, murdered or raped someone or something. If he had done any of those things and admitted it he would've been history long ago, don't you think? So why does he support the caging of those who've done the same thing?

The 'Land of the Free' now has more prisoners than any nation on Earth, both per capita and in total, ranking second only to Nazi Germany in the recorded history of humankind. Though comprising some five percent of the world's population, we house a full quarter of the world's slightly less than 10-million inmates. Over half of the U.S. prisoners have harmed no one, they've merely disobeyed in a land where one is supposed to be guaranteed the right to "...*Life, Liberty, and the pursuit of Happiness*," and then were put in harm's way in a cage. If you live in the U.S. you most likely directly funded this mass assault not only against innocent people, but everyone, really, since law enforcement personnel were ordered to waste their time chasing non-criminals at the expense of fighting crime. Doesn't that make you the least bit angry? Governments wouldn't be able to treat their citizens and others with contempt were it not for mass thoughtlessness as well as the lack of objection by most.

Although Part I of this book is primarily concerned with censored elections, as well as our direct funding of unnecessary mass human suffering and death as a result of the Drug War, and tax inequality, it should be pointed out that of course this is not all that's censored, since the U.S. media shape the news in their direction for other usually obvious reasons likewise. Remember, the ultra-wealthy own and thus run the major media outlets, so in whose interests do you suppose they'll be slanting reality? Whether they're censoring to guide an election or censoring to keep dissenters at a minimum regarding war, their scams are not that difficult to see if one spends the time and looks. For example, prior to September 11, 2001, there was extensive mainstream coverage regarding Heather Mercer and Dayna Curry, two female U.S. Christian aid workers who had been taken into custody by the Taliban and were being held in Kabul, yet as the days led up to Bush's forces bombing Kabul, not knowing where exactly these women were being held, I could find nothing regarding the two of them. It was as if they vanished into thin air, though in the weeks leading up to 9-11 they were given marked media coverage. Why do you suppose the media took them out of the limelight when U.S. forces were bombing the city in which they were held captive?

At one point I did read or hear on television that one of the fathers was protesting the bombing saying something along the lines of, 'They're bombing the hell out of Kabul and daughter's in there,' but that was just once! Not until they were luckily rescued did they become substantially newsworthy anew. By the way it wasn't American troops who rescued the aid workers - they were Afghanis.

One shouldn't get the wrong impression of the Taliban's foe, the Northern Alliance, as if this group was a bunch of freedom- loving peacemakers. Many will recall that picture of the man begging for his life on his knees, and the subsequent photo of the same man with his pants pulled down, lying on his back apparently dead, with blood that can be seen that had splattered on his lower shirt, as a member of the Northern Alliance took one more gunshot at him with the utmost of anger visible in his face, as two others likewise took shots at his now corpse. In one prominent periodical I read that he had begged for his life but was not granted his wish. In another I read that he had begged for his life, was humiliated, and was killed. Months later I read an article from the U.K. describing the photo and stating that his pants had been pulled down and then his gentiles, or part of his genitals, were cut off with a knife before he was shot to death. Unfortunately as of this writing I've been unable to confirm that source, though I do recall reading it and it was unmistakably describing this horrendous event. Did they tell the truth here in the U.S.? Sure they did, though they left out a major detail didn't they? Can't even trust them with a photograph can you?

I remember having a brief conversation with a young mother of three somewhere between 2000 and 2002 who worked in a convenience store. She said, "*I know exactly what you mean,*" regarding how if the media don't report something it's not known. This struggling single mother had lived in a neighborhood in which a young boy was murdered by a teenager when the boy was going door to door selling something or other for school or Scouts as I recall. If anyone didn't hear of this horrific event, particularly in this area, then they must've been living in a cave. People were outraged. The woman stated that those who lived in the neighborhood at the time knew the accused murderer had been captured, but the media withheld the information for fear of what the public might do if they realized he was captive in the local jail, so basically outside of the neighborhood no one knew. With social media that kind of local information would unlikely be successfully contained today but advances need to not be contained to just local events but must spread nationally and internationally.

In spite of the internet being comparably accessible as television, and the potential to have streaming and downloading video is possible, even just using a phone modem is enough in relation to download video from the net if its producer chooses to make his or her material in reasonable sizes available for downloading, years later vital information is still successfully repressed so that not enough people know to matter. Is this not shameful beyond comprehension?

Internet video was used at presidential candidate Ralph Nader's site in 2000, though it was not passed on by enough to matter. The video he had was easily accessible to those with dial-up service, which was predominant at the time.

Were it not for media distorted elections, we'd likely live in an entirely different world, a far more reasonable efficient world with much less cruelty. Who wants wealthy un-elected censors, many of whom are even unknown? Well, that's what we're getting and that's why the choices are so bad that many, and in the midterm elections - most, don't even bother voting at all. There is a way to get back, and that's in finding one's information about the candidates via their websites primarily, comparing platforms and histories and voting according to common sense, decency and reason.

In the U.S. presidential elections of 2004 and 2008 there were six candidates on enough state ballots to win the presidency, though only two were permitted in the televised debates. Who are these un-elected people who are censoring our elections to this profound degree? What Constitutional Amendment gives them this awesome power? Considering the seriousness of the highly censored realities at least two of the censored candidates were bringing up, the election was a farce resulting in casualties by the millions at least, a farce perhaps coming at the cost of the continued survival of our species on this planet within this century.*

* See, *Planet's Future At Stake, U.N. Report*
Says at, **http://www.roadtopeace.org/research.php?itemid=437**, a little more than halfway down the page.

Thanks to the media's deception and the public's general inability to recognize this grandest of scams, there was nearly a split decision amongst two unreasonable choices, George W. Bush, the who had and still has the national record of the most executions of any governor in the history of the United States, who started two wars in less than two years, though he made sure he didn't go to Vietnam himself, and John Kerry, so bad himself he was unable to decisively defeat someone as knowingly horrible as Bush.

Unless one thinks unnecessary human suffering, pain, misery and death are perfectly acceptable to be inflicted upon innocent people, all to benefit a disproportionate few, then we have a problem here.

I'm confident you'll see things clearly if you take the time to review the evidence presented throughout this book, no small part of which can be checked with video documentation for all to see. At the height of the Information Age there's a lot the American people are not aware of regarding the world in which they live.

As stated in my speech for Nader in Austin, Texas back in April of 2004, the U.S. houses a full quarter of the world's prisoners,* many, if not most, of whom have harmed no one but merely disobeyed laws against their rights to "...*Life, Liberty and the pursuit of Happiness*?" Chomsky has stated that we live in a society that's so highly indoctrinated that "...*elementary truths are easily buried.*"** The prison population when Ronald Reagan took office was somewhere in the neighborhood of 500,000. Now we have roughly 2.3 million prisoners, meaning it's more than quadrupled since 1980. Are we any safer? Of course not. Law enforcement can't do two things at once. According to this article*** from the Economist in 1965 the percentage of solved national homicides in the US was "around" 90%, but now it's just 64%. In other words, in spite of decades of technological advancement half a century ago only one out of ten got away with murder. Now it's more than one out of three.

* See, http://billmoyers.com/2013/12/16/land-of-the-free-us-has-5-of-the-worlds-population-and-25-of-its-prisoners/

      http://www.politifact.com/virginia/statements/2014/dec/15/jim-webb/webb-says-us-has-5-percent-worlds-population-25-pe/

      http://www.washingtonpost.com/blogs/fact-checker/wp/2015/04/30/does-the-united-states-really-have-five-percent-of-worlds-population-and-one-quarter-of-the-worlds-prisoners/

      http://www.washingtonpost.com/blogs/fact-checker/wp/2015/04/30/does-the-united-states-really-have-five-percent-of-worlds-population-and-one-quarter-of-the-worlds-prisoners/

** See segment of interview with Bill Moyers in, *MANUFACTURING CONSENT: NOAM CHOMSKY AND THE MEDIA*, a documentary by Mark Achbar& Peter Wintonick

*** - See, http://www.economist.com/news/united-states/21656725-police-fail-make-arrest-more-third-nations-killings-getting-away

The increases in prisoners have in no small part been due to the Drug War, yet one of the most addicting drugs, nicotine, which accounts for the deaths of some 400,000 Americans each year and 5,000,000 deaths each year worldwide, is perfectly legal. Likewise, alcohol, which impairs judgment as well as muscle and motor control, is also legal. Sending people to live in cages ought to be for valid reasons, and cruel and unusual punishments such as beatings and rape should not be tolerated as per the Eighth Amendment of the Bill of Rights of our Constitution, yet said punishments, which harm people for life, are even joked about routinely by so-called "comics," in spite of the fact that most of our prisoners have physically harmed no one themselves, nor ever ordered harm to anyone. How can a sane reasonable society accept such punishments as being the norm, and even laugh about it?

A relatively recent article released by the Associated Press disclosed that one out of every 136 U.S. citizens was behind bars as of the summer of 2005.* If one thinks that by obeying the law they'll be fine, think again. With drugs, it's easy to have them planted on "suspects," and indeed is reported to happen far too often. That's another problem with arresting people for non-crimes - the evidence becomes the law officer's word versus the defendant's.** Since no crime was in fact committed, the usual standards of collecting incriminating evidence are discarded, meaning more innocent people will be torturously punished for sustained periods of time. That's simple deductive reasoning. If our law enforcement personnel are being used to jail people who've committed no crime, then that leaves more real criminals as a result. Part of the reason this likely happens is because people, for the most part anyway, don't see who's being punished for what, unlike the days of the pillories of old, (see picture of pillory below). Oh sure, they read about this or that person being sentenced to prison in the newspaper, but how often do they report what happens inside those prisons? There was more transparency in the days of the pillory, you have to give them that much.

* See, http://www.prisontalk.com/forums/showthread.php?t=203449

** For example, see Chapter 4

Above: The pillory - At least in some ways it was a more open society then, unlike our prisons today where people are mostly punished who've harmed no one, hidden from the general public, and they're incarcerated at a number and rate higher than any nation on Earth. Imagine that, the Land of the Free.

Professor Chomsky has noted that if one has access to a wide variety of mainstream media sources one might find the "occasional nugget" of truth concerning a mostly censored topic. No doubt those nuggets are easier to obtain now thanks to the internet. I cite the mainstream whenever I can because when they admit something there's no going back. I try to cite sources that don't offend anyone if possible, though it must be remembered none of us would be here were it not for sex and that we're the only animal in the Animal Kingdom that doesn't generally present itself as-is, unless we're shooting a probe into outer space announcing who we are as per the famous NASA Pioneer Plaques sent into space in the 1970s, in which case the female's genitalia are absent and the male's present though both are presented in the nude.* What's that say about our species? We're not even honest about who we are.

* See, http://www.nasa.gov/centers/ames/images/content/72418main_plaque.jpg

It's astonishing that the Taliban were rightly criticized for not allowing women to show their faces, though men could, yet here in the U.S. men can show their chests but it's illegal for women to do the same. So, while we eliminate the very body part we nearly all came from in an image sent into outer space to introduce ourselves to any intelligent life form that may encounter the message, we live by double standards we largely don't even recognize and fail to realize how stupid we must look. To send something like that to who would almost certainly by odds be far more advanced than our primitive society with but little more than a handful of millennia of recorded history at our disposal and truly in the historic infancy of the Age of Technology is to openly demonstrate our mass absurdity does it not?

After reading the next chapter you'll likely think twice about signing for a package for the people next door, or for anyone other than yourself or a completely trusted friend or family member for that matter. This is about a man right here in the U.S. who was sentenced to 15 years for signing for a package, and a retired judge stepped out of his way and into my camera's lens to publicly declare his concern that this innocent person was living his life in a cage away from his family.

Chapter 4

The Package and the Cage:Easy Setups for Non-Crimes

"They who have put out the people's eyes reproach them of their blindness."

- John Milton – 1642

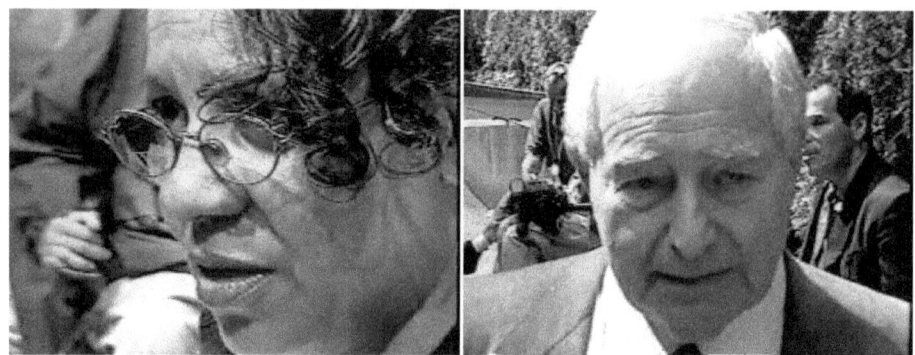

Above: Wanda Best, and an unidentified retired judge who walked into the picture as I was filming and began commenting on behalf of Wanda Best's husband, Darrel Best.

REGARDING A MAN WHO WAS SENTENCED TO 15 YEARS SIMPLY FOR SIGNING FOR A NEIGHBOR'S PACKAGE, the following is nearly the complete transcript, though some parts were inaudible. Someone walked up and he's the one who asked most of the questions, and since he didn't indentify himself and I didn't ask him who he was, for now he's referred to as the "Interviewer."

Interviewer: Oh this is an old picture?

Wanda Best: This is an old picture, right.

Interviewer: Oh, OK.

Wanda Best: This one, (pointing to a young girl in the family picture), today's her senior prom. She's getting ready to go to college...

Interviewer: Oh wow.

Wanda Best: And now, daddy won't be there.

Interviewer: Wow. Is he fighting it, is he a...?

Wanda Best: Of course, he was fighting it but, you know...

Interviewer: But what, um....

Wanda Best: Unfortunately, what happened to his case was right after 9/11, so everybody thought the cops wouldn't lie, they were heroes. So they just took the word of the cops and they didn't believe anything else. My husband had witnesses and everything.

Interviewer: What happened to the guys that gave him the package, can't you... (pause) ...get them... to help? These were the guys who gave him the package (?)... undercover cops...

Wanda Best: Federal Express. Yeah, the whole truck, the uniforms, everything…

Interviewer: Oh God!

Wanda Best: My husband…

Interviewer: Why did he…? What… was he rushing him or something?

Wanda Best: He needed glasses and the guy pressured him, you know, and when my husband was um… The defense attorney asked him: "Well, do you have a wire (or permission) or did you videotape it… Did you wire the conversation?" You see, so he lied. The cops lied, the jury bit… but he pressured him.

Interviewer: He has no record, this man has no record?

Wanda Best: No.

Interviewer: Based on a testimony, a cop's testimony?

Wanda Best: Solely on the testimony.

Interviewer: What kind of jury was this? How could…

Wanda Best: …I guess because, I don't know, I don't know why they believed him, but they believed him. Like I said, it happened right after 9/11.

Interviewer: What was the cop's testimony? What was his defense testimony?

Wanda Best: He didn't have any. He just said that my husband signed for the package. And then they took something my husband said and just twisted it, just like I just told you. He was up there trying to make money to (support) you know, buy his daughter's books. My husband told the cops that and the cop said; "Well he was up here trying to make extra money to support his five daughters, or his four daughters" - which was true, but he wasn't selling drugs, he was fixing my uncle's awning.

Interviewer: Right…

Wanda Best: You know…

Interviewer: But what went through his mind, what was in the package when he signed? What… what…

Wanda Best: He thought it was for the neighbor.

Interviewer: For the neighbor… He was signing something for the neighbor?

Wanda Best: Haven't you done that? I've done that.

Interviewer: Yeah!

Wanda Best: I don't do it anymore.

Interviewer: But if the guy tells me ahead of time…

Dr. Ken Hildebrandt: No, I guess not.

Interviewer: If he tells me ahead of time... This is the name on the package. Would you like to sign here?

Wanda Best: Well, it had his uptown address, but it had the last name of the neighbor. So he thought maybe they... cause he was like, it's a private home. Instead of 1019, it was like 1020.

Interviewer: OK, OK now, my next question. He made a mistake. The name wasn't in his, his ... ah ... it was somebody else's name? Why would they arrest you for signing for somebody else's package?

Wanda Best: You tell me why. That's why I'm here today.

Interviewer: Why, because I mail drugs to your house?

Wanda Best: Yeah, if I sign for it.

Interviewer: If I mail drugs to your house and you sign it by mistake, they arrest you?

Wanda Best: Oh yeah!

Ken: The potential for set-up is amazing. I've talked about this numerous times on my website, I mean.

Passer by: ...Federal Express... I've used it all the time for the people, never again. It happened to Patty Hearst. She got a big box. She signed for it. Fed agents got on it. Did she go to jail? No.

Interviewer: This is ... ah ...

Wanda Best: My husband? Yeah.

Judge: (inaudible)

Interviewer: It is, it is.

Wanda Best: He was at my husband's trial. He knows... nothing... He was good.

Interviewer: You had a good lawyer too?

Judge: Yeah, yeah, one of the best, but, um, I don't know...

Wanda Best: Who knows what the jury was thinking? Like I said...

Judge: Jurors have no idea, I'm sure, what the penalty is. They don't know what he was facing.

Interviewer: What was the amount? What was the amount? Do you know?

Wanda Best: I think it was...

Judge: Two pounds, wasn't it?

Wanda Best: A pound.

Interviewer: A pound?

Wanda Best: ...they were off ...

Judge: …one and a half years … there's a thirteen and a half year spread because he didn't plead guilty.

Wanda Best: They told him he could…

Interviewer: …what was... Oh, eight months?

Ken: Who are you? Sir, I'm sorry.

Judge: (inaudible) I'm a retired judge.

Ken: Oh, how are you doing? (The judge and I shake hands.)

Ken: Kenny Hildebrandt from NowWe'reTalking.TV.

Interviewer: So, he didn't take the conviction?

Judge: He didn't take the plea.

Interviewer: The plea. He didn't take the plea, which they wanted, so now they're making him spend money and drag this thing on? You gonna get hit with ... ah ...

Wanda Best: My husband's father, his life's savings. He's retired now...

Interviewer: Spent to helping him?

Wanda Best: $20,000 for lawyers.

Interviewer: Really?

Wanda Best: It's gone. My husband's still gone.

Ken: Wow.

Questioner: He's in...

Wanda Best: Of course now... You know the sad thing about, for my husband, being a big-time drug dealer. The day he was convicted I came home and I didn't have food to feed his daughters.

Interviewer: You didn't?

Wanda Best: You know ...we didn't have any money, we didn't have any money, you know, what can I tell you? This is why we're here, for justice.

Interviewer: I heard about this. I heard from the judge...

Judge: This is a strange case, in many respects. If he was willing to plead guilty... because he knew that... year... he was going to jail...

Interviewer: (inaudible)… he was going to cop...

Wanda Best: Yes, but no contest.

Judge: But he wouldn't… to plead guilty. Then the judge is going to ask you questions. Did you order this...

Interviewer: That he wouldn't accept, right?

Judge: Now some judges will accept that. They call that an Alford plea. It's … kind of plea that somebody figures: "Well I'm innocent but they're gonna have witnesses against me and I can't beat this and I'm facing all this heavy time. Forget it, I'll plead guilty." And that's what he tried to do but the judge wouldn't accept that.

Interviewer: He would not?

Judge: He wouldn't, no.

Wanda Best: …He was gonna plead for no contest.

Interviewer: He would accept the plea of no contest meaning that he…

Wanda Best: It means he's not guilty, he's not innocent, he's just accepting the plea.

Judge: But he wouldn't admit that he was guilty.

Wanda Best: He wouldn't admit that he was guilty.

Interviewer: He wouldn't admit that... this package...

Wanda Best: Why would he? He didn't do it.

Interviewer: But he wanted him to?

Judge: If this man was guilty he would've taken one and a half years.

Interviewer: Of course! He would have took that.

Judge: He'd have to be crazy not to...

Wanda Best: They told him that he didn't have to. This happened just before Christmas. They said you could spend the holidays with your children. You won't even have to go to jail until January. I mean, they sweetened this pot like you would not.... They said in eight months you'll be out. But he couldn't do it. We told our children, don't lie. How's he gonna lie and then be branded a drug dealer?

Interviewer: Actually right, be branded…

Wanda Best: But he still is branded a drug dealer.

Interviewer: He's branded as a drug dealer.

Wanda Best: And it still happened. But we fought it. We weren't gonna go down without a fight.

Interviewer: Whoa, what a shame. What a shame, man. Wow, sorry to hear that.

Unidentified person: (I have a feeling) I hope there's, you know, I hope there's a chance...

Wanda Best: Yeah.

Unidentified person: Horrible.

Wanda Best: It is, it is.

Interviewer: Whoa, sorry to hear that.

Ken: Occasionally (one can) get clemency, you know, like the woman back there. We'll hope for that.*

Wanda Best: Judge Michael Gross. He was devastated. He wanted to...

Judge: He wanted to... but by law you got to do it.

Wanda Best: That's what he said... He wished to God...

Ken: Exactly ...by the law.

Interviewer: The law, the law states 15 to life.

Wanda Best: 15 minimum, minimum, 15 to life.

Ken: Sentencing guidelines.

Judge: Anything over two ounces (selling?) or you possess over four, same as murder, 15 to 25 to life.

* Mr. Best was the sole person to receive clemency in the state of New York in 2005 by Governor George Pataki, though
the New York Times article hardly pointed out the main facts surrounding the case. –
See, http://www.nytimes.com/2005/12/25/nyregion/25clemency.html?_r=1&oref=slogin

As this book goes to print we're awaiting the outcome of a similar incident happening to two friends of ours. It seems likely the case will eventually be dismissed but the two of them have gone through hell for the last two and a half years because of it and there's no end in sight yet. The prosecutor refuses to let go, even though he has nothing. They were mailed a pound of a dead plant, cannabis. The woman was familiar with this chapter due to her boyfriend who read an earlier version of this book I had posted on the web. She said she didn't know anything about the package so didn't want it. He reportedly replied, "OK, then sign this," and acted as if he was rushed due to the light rain that was starting. Of note she had never seen this person before. Whether it's FedEx, UPS or the US Postal Service, if you don't recognize the person delivering you the package, it gives you all the more reason to be suspicious.

Chapter 5

A Way Out: Informing Others and Voting

"Every election cycle more lethally vicious regressives are victorious, crushing common sense and human rights in tandem, moving the country further in the direction of mindless fascism."

- Dr. David Michael Green, political science instructor at Hofstra University, New York, July 12, 2010

There have been presidential, vice presidential, senatorial, congressional and gubernatorial candidates who have been against the Drug War, particularly against cannabis, which accounts for approximately one of every twenty U.S. arrests. These candidates have been greatly marginalized by the major media. Is it not a waste of resources to arrest people for violations of their right to liberty? How many pedophiles, rapists, thieves and killers remain at large whilst so many of our law enforcement officers are spending their time harming innocent people as per their orders? No one knows for sure yet simple deductive reasoning indicates that whatever the number is it's totally unacceptable, unless one doesn't mind having more pedophiles, rapists, thieves and murderers on the loose than need be.

Yes, we live in a terribly inefficient cruel society, though the parameters have been set up for us such that it needn't be this way. We, as a society, have allowed ourselves "*...to be deluded and manipulated by the system,*" as Professor Noam Chomsky of MIT has pointed out long ago. At the height of the so-called Information Age, the statement still holds true today, though I must admit that's beyond my ken. That's "*ken*" with a small "*k*," meaning one's range of understanding, for those who aren't familiar with the word and were wondering what I meant. Nothing to do with my name, just my range of understanding, and it's beyond mine that at the height of the Information Age most are deluded, particularly in regard to elections in which they're picking known sponsors of mass misery and murder by voting for the media's puppets in lieu of the third party and independent candidates who in some cases do in fact stand for the people over big business, unlike nearly all in power today. Just because the others advertise more is no reason to pick one of them, is it?

If you were choosing a doctor and knew that two of the six or so you were considering heavily advertised yet could be shown to sometimes demonstrate complete contempt for human life, would you pick her or him as a doctor? Or would you go to someone who, it could be readily ascertained, genuinely cared about human life, though she or he didn't have as much money to advertise as a result of taking more time caring for her or his patients?

Media deception regarding elections is arguably the most important of truths successfully withheld due to its direct influence on how we are governed, what laws rule the land, whether or not said laws are fair and rational vs. immoral, cruel, completely unjust and irrational, and whether or not the superfluities of a highly disproportionate few should come at the expense of some 12-million real children feeling hunger pains right here in the U.S. on a daily basis, whilst allowing some eight September 11th Attacks'-worth of real live children to unnecessarily die each day of completely preventable causes for what just a fraction of the Pentagon budget could easily prevent,* in actuality, all due to neglect. If one does the math, one quickly arrives at the figure of some 6-million children dying worldwide every 250 days for no reason whatsoever - none justified, anyway. That's a holocaust of real children every 250 days. These aren't Cabbage Patch Kids or something.

* See, *Bad News When Madmen Lead the Blind*, by Norman Soloman, at, **http://www.fair.org/index.php?page=2164**

and, **http://thehungersite.com**

People can easily see that there are more than two candidates on their voting ballots, yet only two are displayed in televised public debates - practically without exception - for nearly every major political office available. Why? And why aren't more people asking why? What is it these other candidates have to say that is either A) so unimportant as to not be newsworthy, or B) newsworthy enough to send shockwaves throughout our democratic system? Who are the people withholding these candidates from public view? Have any of these censors been elected to do this kind of profound censoring? Did they have to go through any kind of public scrutiny to get their "jobs?" These are the kinds of questions thinking people ought to be asking, one would think.

We'll take a look at some of the repercussions of thoughtlessness and media dominance over people's thought, particularly here in the United States, where we have the guidelines set up to have a self-governing body in the interests of the common people. We've collectively allowed ourselves "...*to be deluded and manipulated by the system*," as Professor Chomsky has stated. Instead, we have a system designed to feed the wants of a disproportionate few over the necessities of many, if not most.

IS THERE A WAY OUT OF THIS? Yes, a simple vote would bring us well on our way to improvement, but it would involve the effort and recruitment of many to overcome the wealthy liars who censor our news. With the internet at people's disposal it is surely something that is doable. Along with the internet, our right to assemble would have to also be employed to gather like-minded caring people to do what we can by sharing the information learned from one another, using pamphlets, audios and videos as seen appropriate to help spread some basic, factual, easy-to-explain elementary truths to others. Nothing speculative need be discussed, since that would only leave rational caring people with weak points to attack. There are no conspiracy theories in asserting facts.

When Professor Chomsky debated the Dutch Minister of Defense years ago, the Minister was compelled to excuse himself out of humiliation. It's tough to argue against facts regarding human justice. Anyone who tries to do so will look foolish and/or cruel. That is almost surely the reason the powers that be do not want anyone outside the two corporate-controlled parties in major political debates.

"At this stage of history, either one of two things is possible, either the general population will take control of its own destiny and concern itself with community interests, guided by values of solidarity and sympathy and concern for others, or alternatively, there will be no destiny for anyone to control."

– Noam Chomsky

Time is indeed running short to do so.

Chapter 6

Ken asks Presidential candidate detailed question at Press Conference in 2004

"A single death is a tragedy; a million deaths is a statistic."

- Joseph Stalin

The following is the transcript of my question to presidential candidate Ralph Nader, from late October of 2004 in Iowa, accompanied by his answer in a room of journalists with their cameras running. The above picture of Mr. Nader is from election eve on Wall Street, 2004.

Ralph Nader: Yes... (pointing toward me).

Dr. Ken Hildebrandt: Mr. Nader, Ken Hildebrandt from MajorMediaBypass.com. Just briefly... a small amount of people who were not elected kept you out of the debates and therefore we didn't hear about the real risk of global warming, the fact that we could be using hemp to grow our oil right now, that our top crime is a non-crime and that we house a quarter of the world's incarcerates. These are all real issues and what I'm asking that you do is speak to the American people and ask them to vote their conscience and to take a look at these real issues, which people who were not elected kept from us. And, would you be willing to talk to us about this?

Ralph Nader: Well, of course. There's no time to go into our reform of the criminal injustice system, but being in Iowa I do want to emphasize that we have long favored the legalization of industrial hemp which has 5,000 known products, can reduce our reliance on oil, produce food, fiber like Patagonia clothing, and which reduces the need to cut down trees because it provides material for good paper and produces a source of food.

And farmers in this country are prohibited by law from growing industrial hemp even though it's legal for us to import it from Canada, France, Romania and China. That's because it's on the DEA proscribed list, a residue of medieval thinking that somehow it's connected with marijuana. The only connection it has with marijuana, other than 1/3 of 1% THC, is if it is planted near a marijuana plot it will cross-pollinate and dilute the marijuana crop to the chagrin of the marijuana crops growers. They don't want any industrial hemp anywhere near them.

So we have petitioned with a whole array of farm groups and state legislators, and even in international papers twice, to get it off the DEA proscribed list - once under Clinton and once under Bush. Both times our detailed petition was denied. It would be nice to have the two candidates talk about the multi-billion-dollar crop that would advance our national security by reducing our reliance on foreign oil as well as provide environmentally benign crops and income for hard-pressed farmers. Thank you.

Carl Mayer: OK Ralph, gotta go.

WE ARE LIVING IN A NATION THAT PRIDES ITSELF AS THE GREATEST DEMOCRACY ON THE PLANET yet a small amount of people who were not elected kept him out of the debates. Is that a democracy? What if former President Jimmy Carter was monitoring an outside nation's democratic elections, as he's been known to do in the case of East Timor, what would he say if the nation's mainstream televised media eliminated four out of six candidates who were on enough state ballots to win the election? Would he give the thumbs-up on such an election? I doubt it.

In 2000, Mr. Nader was physically blocked from even viewing one of the presidential debates, even though he had obtained a valid General Admission Pass to attend. He ended up suing and winning the case, to the tune of somewhere in the twenty thousand dollar range as I recall, which is next to nothing when one considers all that's at stake here. Mr. Nader has never been known to interfere with a television broadcast, so why was he prevented from even viewing something he should've been a part of? As we'll discuss later on, physical blocking of ballot-qualified candidates is not just confined to presidential elections here in the U.S. In other cases in which the would-be participants do not have such recognizable names as Mr. Nader, candidates are arrested for either A) demanding inclusion in public debates they should by right be participating in, or for B) simply demanding to view said debates. Examples of both will be given in awhile, but for now let's get back to Mr. Nader's question, and his answer.

Back to my question: "*...therefore we didn't hear about the real risk of global warming...*" Remember, this was 2004, and though the major media had by that time begun to bring up the issue, was it discussed with any seriousness by either Bush or Kerry in any of the debates? Some scientists had already called it the greatest threat to the human race by that time. We'll get more into global warming in Part II, discussing that humans have already likely taken steps to counter it artificially, a part of the argument you just won't hear discussed in the media as those in the know shake our heads in bewilderment. Mr. Nader did bring up that hemp was "*environmentally benign*" and that it "*would advance our national security by reducing our reliance on foreign oil.*" I realize that here in 2016 the question of whether or not the earth is heating up due to humankind is being debated without either side discussing the impact of proliferating jet trails and whether it's helping or hurting, as discussed in Part II.

Ralph Nader also mentioned that the growing of hemp "*reduces the need to cut down trees.*" So, he hit on some major points with that question for sure. Though I was disappointed about what he had said about the other two candidates at the time, in 2008 he was on 45 state ballots and as a write-in for four others. He had a much better chance in 2008. He just needed help. Not all could give dollars but all could give help.

Growing our own oil alone could've arguably won him the presidency, don't you think? Decreased terrorism and decreasing our reliance on foreign oil... Did the others offer any of this? Have they ever? We'll see later on that the ones who have, in spite of being in mainstream parties, were likewise excluded from televised presidential debates.*

* See, Chapter 15 - Media-censored Presidential Elections Metastasizes to the Republican and Democratic Mainstream Parties; Chapter 16 - The Military-Industrial-Media Complex; and Chapter 17 - On the Eve of the New Hampshire Primary with Professor Noam Chomsky

I also mentioned in my question to Mr. Nader, "*...that our top crime is a non-crime and that we house a quarter of the world's incarcerates.*" What I meant by our top crime being a non-crime is that drug violations account for more citizen arrests than anything else.* Again, if nicotine is legal, as is alcohol, why should other substances be deemed illegal in a nation that prides itself on people having the right to "*...Life, Liberty, and the pursuit of Happiness*?" And yes, though the Land of the Free comprises but 5% of the world's population, our imprisoned account for a full 25% of the world's prison inmates.

* See the third chart from the bottom at http://www.drugwarfacts.org/cms/Crime#sthash.LdDyX0b1.dpbs
Prison for many, if not most, means the end of their lives as they know it. Once one is a victim of a violent

crime, one's life is never the same afterwards. Being cuffed, strip-searched, and thrown into a locked cage is a violent crime in and of itself. Yes, we really do live in a barbaric society, and "...*elementary truths are easily buried*," as Chomsky has maintained.

After looking at Mr. Nader's platform since 2000 and realizing that if Americans actually understood that people's lives were at stake here by the millions - we're polluting the environment when this environmentally benign form of energy is available to us and the tax structures are scamming all but the very wealthiest of income earners - I figured he'd be elected hands down if people were just informed. Surely a short quality video could be made that would be impossible for the media to ignore and which Americans could pass onto one another via the internet. That's still true.

I learned something very important one day when I was in Harlem in 2000 passing out some of Mr. Nader's literature, as well as talking with anyone and everyone I could, when one passerby who was obviously in a rush bluntly stated to me: "*I don't want to see anything else other than his platform. I'm not interested in anything else you have. Show me his platform,*" before heading across the street. Though I had copies earlier in the day, as I frantically looked to find a copy, I saw that I had run out. The best I could do was run after him and give him something containing a partial list of some of the positions Mr. Nader stood for on a few issues, which the man accepted though he was obviously not fully satisfied.

That individual I met on the northwest corner of Martin Luther King and Malcolm X Boulevards hit the nail on the head as far as what was the most important thing about any candidate, i.e., her or his platform. It was something I'll never forget, and hope you never do either, because it really is one of, if not the single most important thing about a candidate, revealing, if one looks carefully enough, where one stands regarding human life and death. These things are not discussed, for the most part, by the media's puppet candidates.

Also looking back to 2000, I remember when it was announced on C-SPAN that George W. Bush had in fact won the election, and they were taking callers to express their thoughts regarding their newly-elected president. It seemed that every third caller or so viewed it as if Hitler himself had been elected.*

* Side note: At the time, those who had headsets and web cams were actually pictured making their comments on television on C-SPAN, a historic first thanks to the internet.

Some of the comments would've been laughable had they not indeed been targeted and well reasoned. After all, the man had broken all records to date in executions as a U.S. governor, signing for some 152 people out of 153 he was presented with to be strapped to a gurney and put to death. Though not all oppose the death penalty, few realize that studies have indicated it to be somewhere in the neighborhood of 80% accurate, meaning two out of every ten executed are completely innocent of the crime they are murdered for - two out of ten. When these findings were made known shortly after Bush had begun his presidency, his administration was quick to point out that the studies also indicated that 93% were guilty of *some* crime, which is hardly a valid point considering that the new president and Vice President Dick Cheney both had prior drunk driving convictions. In fact, George W. Bush had his underage sister as a passenger when he was caught driving drunk in his earlier days. He would've done time in most states for the same crime these days. George W. Bush is known to have been arrested for real crimes at least a documented three times. Isn't that something?

The bottom line is, many saw this man as a monster. They fully well knew he stood for big business over the average Jane or Joe and that his tax cuts were primarily going to benefit the top one percent of income earners... in other words, those who had no needs whatsoever over those who do.

Bush lowered the taxes of his favorite one percent of the population from 39.6% on their uppermost superfluous of income to just 35%, though he tried to get them even lower than that. The same group was taxed 91% on their uppermost income during the Eisenhower years. Most people just don't realize that wealthy people make their money via two avenues only, Earth's resources and human labor. We're not importing either from Mars are we? So when these media pundits talk about how much in proportion the top one percent are paying in taxes, ask them to discuss just how they earned their money in the first place.

Here we are, in spite of decades of technological advancement, nowadays almost every household has two people working full time in order to make ends meet, whereas in the 1960s when I was growing up it was rare to have more than one parent working outside the home. How can it be that after 4+ decades of technological advancement, it's become more difficult for the average American to survive? Can it not be logically deduced that these tax changes have had something to do with it?

Former Apollo astronaut Dr. Edgar Mitchell discussed how his grandparents moved to Texas from the south via covered wagon in the 1870s and went on to say he walked on the moon about a hundred years later.* Once technology takes hold, it takes off, and the benefits should likewise. Instead, they've mostly gone to the wealthiest of income earners whilst most get the shaft and are more or less forced to be "*...cogs in a machine...*" as Professor Noam Chomsky has pointed out is not necessary in the least.**

* I fully realize the belief that humans have walked on the moon is sacrosanct. I would however like to question why it is that after traveling 240,000 miles away in the late 60s and early 70s, we have never admittedly gone more than 400 miles ever since? That's akin to people in France crossing the Atlantic Ocean but then never venturing past the British Isles for decades afterwards. I don't buy it. I walked around stunned for a few days after finally realizing this, but it is what it is, and their story simply isn't believable. Does it have to do with the Van Allen Belts? I'd say it's highly likely, and it's also pretty much a given that we sent something to the moon and back to pick up rocks, but as far as sending people, no, that doesn't seem believable to me. If we went to the moon in the 60s, we'd likely be having vacation trips there by now, like cruises, a cruise in space around the moon and back. Perhaps I'm wrong about that, but I can't see simply not going anymore. Then there's Dr. Mitchell, who did get awfully angry at a reporter and ordered him to leave his home when he questioned the unquestionable. I've also seen footage of Neil Armstrong refusing to swear on the Bible that he'd gone, stating he didn't think the Bible was real, and of course there's the classic footage of Buzz Aldrin punching a reporter in the face for daring to question him about his stroll on the moon.

** See, *MANUFACTURING CONSENT: NOAM CHOMSKY AND THE MEDIA*, a documentary by Mark Achbar& Peter Wintonick

Regarding what's at the core of this madness, media censorship is by no means limited to the presidential elections, since in order to gain control of the federal government one needs not only the presidency, but each state of course is represented by two U.S. senators and each congressional district a member of the House of Representatives. There are a total of 100 U.S. senators of which a mere 51% vote makes law (if split 50/50, the vice president casts the deciding vote), or 2/3 to override a presidential veto. The House, containing 435, likewise needs a 2/3 majority to override a presidential veto, otherwise they too need a majority. So, we're talking about less than 500 people, less than 400 really, who are in a position to begin to steer our nation, and thus humankind, since we clearly live in the dominant nation on Earth, in a more reasonable direction. In a more reasonable world how these people are chosen would be of paramount importance, don't you think?

Chapter 7

Media-censored U.S. Senatorial Candidate Arrested

"Both of the other two parties, both the Democrats and the Republicans are dominated by big money, by corporate money."

- Ted Glick, censored 2002 New Jersey ballot qualified candidate for U.S. Senate, (pictured below)

The following is a transcript of an interview with New Jersey Green Party 2002 U.S. Senate candidate, Ted Glick, I videoed shortly after he was released from jail after attempting to enter the television studio in order to watch a debate he should've been included in as a *bona fide* candidate on the ballot. The interview was given by someone representing a television network.

Ted Glick: We were here because we should've been inside in the debate. We were excluded from the debate. We were not approached about being in the debate. When we spoke to the general manager about it we were essentially told it was a done deal, nothing could be done about it. So we were here to say that this is supposed to be a democracy. The voters are supposed to be able to learn about all the candidates so they can make informed choices. That means candidates need to be in debates so the voters can hear what they have to say - and this is the first debate. We hope that in future debates we will be included. If not, we'll be outside of those the way we were here and we hope sooner or later reason will prevail.

Interviewer: Well, I... What is your candidacy about? (inaudible)

Ted Glick: Both of the other two parties, both the Democrats and the Republicans are dominated by big money, by corporate money. Both of these parties are overseeing a tremendous increase in the amount of money going to the Pentagon, a tremendous transfer of resources over the last 20-25 years from low income people, working-class people, middle-class people, to the top 1% of the population. We have the crisis of global warming that is not being addressed. Instead we're talking about invading Iraq, when Iraq is effectively contained while thousands of children every month are dying from the economic sanctions that are imposed upon Iraq. Innocent children are dying. The direction of the country is wrong. My candidacy is about trying to put this country back on the right course. Those views are shared by many people, and those views should be included in these debates.

Interviewer: Where do you live and what's your background?

Ted Glick: I live in Bloomfield. I have been a(n) active social trainer for 35 years. Right now I'm a coordinator of a national third party network, called the Independent Politics Network. I work with young people with leadership training. I work with community organizations. I do that right now as a volunteer. Our program is about justice. That's what we need in this country. That's what we need in this world. Unless we develop policies that are about social justice, economic justice, environmental justice - for the world's people, for our people - we are going to be in deeper trouble. We need to be moving in another direction. That's what my campaign is about. I am the coordinator of this Independent Politics Network... that's my paying work.

Interviewer: Let me ask one more question (inaudible), OK? (inaudible) When did you decide to enter the race, and why?

Ted Glick: I decided in February. One of the reasons I decided to do it was because Robert...

Interviewer: [Interrupted Mr. Glick]: Give me one second... I've got to fix my tie, and collar.

[A half dozen or so people were either watching or filming the interview up close, including a woman who was watching who later claimed she from was from the press, which will come into significance shortly.]

Interviewer: straightened his tie and collar, then continued: OK, go ahead.

Ted Glick: One of the reasons I decided to do it was in fact because Robert Torricelli was the one candidate who I knew for sure that I would be going up against and thought that Robert Torricelli continuing in office for another six years was not something I was looking forward to. I felt that he was somebody that should be opposed for any number of reasons.

I also decided to do it because I have been a member of the Green Party for any number of years and when I was asked by leadership of the Green Party to consider this, I did consider it seriously and decided that this was something I could do. Finally I did it because I felt that particularly since September 11 that the direction of the country is wrong. There's just serious, very serious, changes that are taking place, attacks on our civil liberties, our rights, the increase in our war budget, the transfer of resources from most people to the top, to the very top, that has to change. That has to change. I felt that this year, this race in New Jersey was a good race to undertake and I've been actively campaigning ever since.

Interviewer: Thanks very much.

Unidentified person: Thank you... (inaudible)

Interviewer: OK.

Dr. Ken Hildebrandt: Thanks.

Interviewer: [turning back, looking me in the eyes]: Yeah.

Did the above interview ever make it on television? I honestly can't say one way or another, though I seriously doubt it. I don't doubt that the interviewer would have liked to see it aired, however those decisions come from others who likely would not. Had it aired, just maybe there would have been some public feedback, depending upon how much it was aired and when. These are serious concerns, and the major media seem to follow the same general censoring patterns. If one corporate-owned television station went to lengths, even resorting to the use of force, to prohibit his participation so the population wouldn't see that they didn't have to pick between two sellouts for the ultra-wealthy at the expense of everyone else, but especially the poorest of the poor, another TV station would almost certainly follow suit. In a nation of over 300-million people, the richest nation ever to exist, we allow some 12-million real children to suffer from hunger every day, no kidding. Surely censorship plays a big part of this.

The only thing I recall reading in any newspaper following Mr. Glick's arrest and interviews, with both the television interviewer and another woman who claimed to be from the press, was that Ted Glick's tie was crooked. Of all the serious concerns brought up in both the above interview and the one given subsequently, a statement about candidate Glick's tie was the primary focus brought to the public's attention. Not only that, but it was the interviewer who had to fix his crooked tie, not Ted's.

Let's take a look at some of the things Glick said and did that were of importance to us as citizens choosing a U.S. Senator:

1)   He was arrested for trying to watch something he should have been a participant in as a candidate on the New Jersey ballot for U.S. Senate.

2)   *"We have the crisis of global warming that is not being addressed."* Remember, this was 2002.

3)   *"Instead we're talking about invading Iraq, when Iraq is effectively contained while thousands of children every month are dying from the economic sanctions that are imposed upon Iraq. Innocent children are dying."* The Iraqi Embargo had been killing innocent children by the thousands every month over a ten-year period. Estimates varied from 500,000* to 2-million childhood deaths during that time due to the embargo against Iraq that didn't harm Saddam Hussein in the least bit, yet did anger many a Muslim who was already mad at the United States for its policies in the Middle East. I heard one story of a small child dropping an egg he had just bought and bursting into tears. The owner of the shop gave him another egg, but this was of course before Bush's invasion in 2003. Now the streets reportedly have orphaned children wandering aimlessly, completely on their own. I was told that story by someone whose friend had just gotten back from military duty in Iraq, and for that very reason initially stated he would never return, yet he did. The threat of jail is a powerful threat, especially in our nation, which has more prisoners than any country in the world whilst all but fully allowing the worst of atrocities of violence to occur without intervention, i.e., rapes. Also, Mr. Glick was absolutely correct in stating that, *"Iraq is effectively contained."* Iraq was not even considered a threat to its contiguous neighbors following the first Gulf War.

Imagine if Glick had been given a fair shot by being included in the televised debate and ended up winning the election as a result. Then there would've been one person in the US Senate to replace Paul Wellstone who was also strongly against the invasion, and yes, one person can make a difference if her or his voice is heard. Of course the problems we face now with ISIS stem from this illegal invasion against Iraq that never should've happened. Please think about that.

* Former United States UN Ambassador Madeleine Albright was asked about the sanctions in 1996 by 60 Minutes correspondent Lesley Stahl. Their conversation is as follows:

Lesley Stahl: We have heard that half a million children have died. I mean, that is more children than died in Hiroshima. And, you know, is the price worth it?

Madeleine Albright: I think that is a very hard choice, but the price, we think, the price is worth it.

4)   *"...both the Democrats and the Republicans are dominated by big money, by corporate money. Both of these parties are overseeing a tremendous increase in the amount of money going to the Pentagon."*

5)   *"(We've seen)... a tremendous transfer of resources over the last 20-25 years from low income people, working-class people, middle-class people to the top 1% of the population."* Actually, the wealthiest of income earners were taxed at the rate of 91% on their uppermost superfluous of income when Eisenhower left office in 1961. JFK brought the rate to 70%, with Reagan first lowering them to 50%, and later to an even more astonishing 28%. Sr. Bush raised it some, and Clinton a bit more, to 39.6%, where it remained until George W. Bush lowered the rate, as stated earlier, from 39.6% to 35%. The incumbent, Senator Robert Torricelli, a Democrat, voted for those tax cuts. Why would anyone authorize giving tax cuts for those who've need of nothing whilst allowing 12-million children to feel hunger every day in the US?

By the way, for those who proclaim that there are "self-made billionaires," or even millionaires, ask yourself this: How did they make their money other than via two avenues - Earth's resources and human labor? We're not importing either from Mars. I read a mainstream article on the internet recently about a media-proclaimed, "self-made billionaire," who made his money by trading oil. Excuse me, but did he create the oil? Did he create the materials necessary to drill the oil, and did he do the work of harvesting it? If it needed to be transported (which one would assume would almost certainly be the case), did he build the ships and create the steel or whatever they were made of himself? Then please ask yourself how he's "self-made."

Summation: That's a lot to not be heard in the debates: innocent children dying *en masse* due to the U.S.-led embargo against Iraq, an impending war against Iraq, the transfer of resources from the general population to those who've need of nothing, and even more money going to the Pentagon when the U.S. at that time had already spent over three times more on defense than China, Russia, North Korea, Iran and Iraq combined. With the Cold War being over, why are we continuing to spend more and more on defense, while the average American is struggling just to make ends meet?

When I was growing up in the 1960s, I knew a man who worked in the fishing tackle department of the local hardware store. Though he and his wife had three children, his wife didn't have to work outside the home and in fact, hardly anyone I knew when I was growing up had two parents having to work outside the home. Shouldn't things have become easier after 4+ decades of technological advancement instead of worse? Why is it that when I was a child one heard of the occasional millionaire yet now we hear of billionaires, and they claim they are "self-made?"

Would the majority vote for a minority to flourish at the majority's expense if they only knew they could choose otherwise? I doubt it, yet a small number of people who are not elected prevent the masses from seeing how things could and should be. As long as people believe that the wealthy media censors are giving them the whole story, and folks don't bypass the media using technology which most here in the U.S. now have at their disposal, then most will keep voting for those whose interests do not concern the average person. In other words, they'll be voting against themselves while voting for the unnecessary horror of others, whether they know it or not.

Chapter 8

In Memory of Doug Friedline, former Minnesota Governor Jesse Ventura's campaign manager

"...we hope sooner or later reason will prevail."

- Ted Glick, 2002 U.S. Senate candidate, New Jersey

The image above on the left was taken moments after Glick's release from jail in Edison, New Jersey. I don't know the name of, nor the charge the soldier shaking Glick's hand was arrested for, but the two had apparently conversed while incarcerated and were released at or about the same time. The photo op was solely the soldier's idea once he saw me standing there with my video camera running.

Doug Friedline, Glick's campaign manager, is pictured on the right side of the next photo talking to a police officer and someone else following Glick's release from jail.

I arrived just a moment after Ted Glick began this next interview with a woman who was taking notes and claimed to be from the *Associated Press*.

Ted Glick: I was arrested.

Interviewer: Here?

Ted Glick: I was arrested inside the vestibule.

Interviewer: For what?

Ted Glick: We wanted me to be able to go into the debates and to observe it.

Interviewer: Oh, you didn't want to participate... you wanted to observe?

Ted Glick: I wanted to participate.

Interviewer: But you were going inside with the intention of observing?

Ted Glick: We told, we communicated with the New Jersey 12 management that that would be sufficient, just myself going inside to observe the debate so that then afterwards I could tell the Press or anyone else who was interested what I thought about the debate.

Interviewer: Um hmm.

Ted Glick: That is what we were trying to do. And we were able to go in the first door.

Interviewer: Um hmm.

Ted Glick: And the second door was kept locked and they told us we could not come in. We tried to engage in the negotiation process.

Interviewer: Um hmm.

Ted Glick: They were essentially unwilling to talk to us.

Interviewer: Um hmm.

Ted Glick: There was a point at which the second door was opened. I took one step forward to try to go in and my way was blocked. The police said that if I didn't move back that I would be under arrest and in about 10 seconds the handcuffs came out and I was arrested.

Interviewer: This was the police that were already here? Police were not especially called for this?

Ted Glick: They came in within a minute or two of us going inside.

Interviewer: Did they actually take you to the station and book you?

Ted Glick: Yeah, they booked me.

Interviewer: They did?

Ted Glick: Yeah, they took me and they booked me. I was handcuffed in the back of the police car.

Interviewer: Gosh.

Ted Glick: They took the handcuffs off over at the police station. Most of the time, of course I was handcuffed to a table for about 15 minutes and I was treated fine. I'm not complaining about the treatment of the police.

Interviewer: How long was whole entire process?

Ted Glick: Oh it must have been from the time I was arrested until the time I was released, about an hour and a half.

Interviewer: What time were you arrested? Do you have any idea?

Ted Glick: 7:59 (laughs)

Interviewer: So right before... Wow.

Ted Glick: When the debate was over. (laughs)

Interviewer: Wow.

Unidentified woman who was a Glick supporter: He was allowed out to come here for the end.

Interviewer: OK... um. This has, I mean you've been sort of struggling just to be included...

Ted Glick: Right.

Interviewer: ...in part of this and now you're arrested trying to be. I mean, my goodness, what do you, what can you possibly say? (laughs as if it's just outrageous) What's your reaction to all of this?

Ted Glick: Well, people have been arrested, you know, over many decades for causes that they believed in.

Interviewer: Right.

Ted Glick: That's all I was doing. I was willing to be arrested if necessary to try to underline the point that this is a democracy. We call this a democracy, and if it truly is, the voters should be able to hear from candidates who are running for office, who are qualified candidates who are on the ballot. We clearly are about winning votes. It shouldn't be just confined to two parties.

Interviewer: Um hmm.

Ted Glick: We have a democracy crisis right now and we'll be lucky if 1/3 of the voters in New Jersey come out and vote in this election. Ordinarily in an off-year election you don't get more than thirty-six percent of the voters.

Interviewer: Um hmm.

Ted Glick: And with this particular race, you know given Torricelli's negatives, and Forrester being unknown and etc., etc., I think probably getting a third of the voters would probably be doing well, but there's a solution to that and that is to open up the political process.

Interviewer: Right, right.

Ted Glick: And to allow other candidates to be given exposure and other points of view to be heard. If you want to revitalize democracy, that's one of the key ways to do it.

Interviewer: Was it Edison police?

Ted Glick: Edison police.

Interviewer: And would it be fair to say, um, you know, that these candidates have alternate viewpoints?

Ted Glick: Yes.

Interviewer: That would be fair to say?

Ted Glick: Yes.

Interviewer: OK. May I ask you how old you are?

Ted Glick: Fifty-two.

Doug Friedline: Court date's on October 1st.

Doug Friedline was Ted Glick's campaign manager. Mr. Friedline is best known for being the campaign manager of former professional wrestler Jesse "The Body" Ventura in the gubernatorial race in Minnesota. Ventura, who as an outsider to politics actually defeated the Democratic and Republican candidates, made history that's yet to be duplicated since.

Interviewer: Oh, thank you.

Doug Friedline: And let her have our website.

Interviewer: I have it already.

Doug Friedline: You have it?

Interviewer: Yes. Thank You.

Ted Glick: Yeah, thank you.

Unidentified female Glick supporter: What are you? [Notice, not "Who" but "What...."]

Interviewer: Associated Press [proudly giving the name of her employer to identify herself.]

More than one person can be heard saying the same thing: *Oooh!* [said as the as the proclaimed AP interviewer seemingly proudly walks away after giving the name of an institution to describe who she was.]

Unidentified female Glick supporter: Oh, OK.

Dr. Ken Hildebrandt: All right.

Unidentified female Glick supporter: Hey!

Doug Friedline: Excellent! Cool! Thank you.

Summation: It's too bad this interview or at least the primary concerns discussed in this interview never made it to any newspaper, to the best of my knowledge. The only thing I remember reading in any newspaper was that Mr. Glick's tie was crooked, which we've already discussed. It seemed to me that whoever interviewed him was sincere and concerned about what had happened. I suspect, perhaps incorrectly, that it was one or more of her superiors who went over her notes with her and saw the part about the interviewer from the TV station having to stop his interview to adjust his tie.

As you'll recall, the press interviewer was watching and listening to that interview before approaching Mr. Glick to do her own. No major news source I'm aware of reported things as they happened, and I was present for each of the three interactions with people representing the media who spoke with or interviewed Glick.

Regarding Doug Friedline, I was most disappointed to do a search on him and found out he had passed away in late 2006. I had been fortunate enough to have a couple of prolonged conversations with Doug, one on the phone and one in person. I can tell when someone was following what I was saying and he sure was. I believe if enough made the worst of victim's lives real, along with our situation concerning taxes (discussed throughout this book), then it wouldn't matter a hoot whether a candidate was cut off from the debates or not.

Chapter 9

The Journalist Who 'Covered' a Censored Debate

"People, it has been said, can be placed in three classes: the few who make things happen, the many who watch things happen, and the overwhelming majority who have no idea what happened."

- Nicholas Murray Butler

The following interaction was with a man claiming to be from *The Trenton Times,* who's pictured above. He had been covering the exclusionary debate inside NJ Channel 12 studios between Democratic Senator Robert Torricelli and his Republican opponent, Doug Forrester.

Reporter: Forrester said he was a liar, and you know, it was dishonorable and everything else (laughs) you want (inaudible). [looking straight into my camera smiling and laughing]

Dr. Ken Hildebrandt: Of course. (laughs) Nowweretalking.tv, let's continue the discussion here.

Ted Glick: How did Torricelli approach it?

Reporter: Well, Torricelli said he expected the negative attack because Doug Forrester doesn't have, is so out of sync with the people of New Jersey that really the only thing he can do is attack him. That's, you know, it's kind of standard. I'm not telling you anything. If you had watched it on TV you would've said the same thing.

Ted Glick: So…

Unidentified female Glick supporter [interjects]: He was busy getting arrested for trying to come into the debate.

Ted Glick: So you would say it was like no major type of… one way or another.

Reporter: Oh, you never can tell how these things… I mean, reporters cannot judge debates. They may try to but they can't, because voters do that. You guys do that. I'm sure you'll watch the replay. Is this going to be on TV someplace?

Ken: Yeah, nowweretalking.tv on the web.

Reporter: Dot tv on the web. Whatever, web site, yeah, I don't care.

Ken: Hey, that's the only way to overcome the major media, other than people communicating amongst themselves. Those are the two avenues, because the bottom line is if people...

Reporter [interjects]: You know we went through, not to criticize you at all, but we went through the whole tax payer's revolution and all these different groups who were going to third parties and they all collapsed.

Ken: Yeah, but the Green Party is actually...

Reporter [interjects]: Good luck to anybody that...

Ted Glick [interjects]: Are you talking about in the debate or just generally?

Reporter: Oh, just generally, you know, in the last 10 years they just... (inaudible).

Ken: Yeah, but when in mankind's evolution did we follow the stupidest one in the pack, like we're doing now with the president?

Reporter: I was, I mean the people on TV talk about it. I'm not covering this event. I just pulled up... (inaudible)

Unidentified female Glick supporter: What media are you in?

Reporter: *The Trenton Times*, OK, but I'm not covering the debate itself. I'm just trying to, sort of, figure out what to do about it afterwards.

Ken: See, the point is that some major issues aren't brought up, I mean.

Reporter [interjects, walking away]: Well it's... well I tell you, you couldn't get more issues brought up in 90 minutes than brought up tonight.

Ken: Yeah, but if they're on the same page regarding the issues... I mean, was the Drug War brought up? Was the Drug War, I mean, you consider it a Drug War, we have more incarcerates per capita than any civilization that's ever existed.*

* That's incorrect, though no one called me on it. Nazi Germany had more than us, both per capita and overall. So, we're second to Nazi Germany on the All-Time List, though first right here right now, even surpassing China in the number of prisoners we have, in spite of their horrible record concerning human rights and the fact that they outnumber us several times over. We don't just have more prisoners per capita, we have more period.

Reporter: Yeah. [walking away]

Ken: Well, I mean, that should've been brought up, [the reporter throws his arms out to the side] but it wasn't.

Reporter: Well. [still walking away]

Ken: Well, I mean, talk to somebody whose daddy or mommy is in jail because of the Drug War and, you know, they may want to see it brought up.

Summation: Though I don't speak Latin there's one phrase I am familiar with and I believe it's applicable here. The words in Latin are "*Res IpsaLoquitor*" which I understand roughly means, "*The thing speaks for itself,*" or "*It speaks for itself.*" Is that not applicable to the above video recorded talk with a newspaper journalist?

This reminds me of what I learned from watching *MANUFACTURING CONSENT: NOAM CHOMSKY AND THE MEDIA*, and that's if one is well informed and debates someone who does not stand for "...*Life, Liberty and the pursuit of Happiness,*" it doesn't take much time to leave one's opponent speechless. After all, how can one defend such things from a rational standpoint? They can't, but the point is, thanks to corporate media censorship, those in charge or competitive to be elected for high office don't have to.

Who can defend harming others who are less fortunate or weaker, or anyone who is innocent? Human beings unnecessarily die because of our leadership and the laws these people vote for and create, yet they're freely elected. This is not rocket science here. It's easily decipherable and sickening beyond comprehension to anyone who thinks, cares and is informed regarding same that this grand scam continues unabated, yet things will remain the same and continue to get worse and worse unless enough regular caring people don't sweat the small stuff and finally begin organizing and informing others as each sees fit to do.

Will the media be beat? Your guess is as good as mine. We know the oppressed far outnumber the oppressors and we could beat them if enough try. If it doesn't happen, then I guess it means most gave their brains to a piece of electronic equipment, their television set, even though another piece of electronic equipment, the computer, has easily discoverable evidence that the mainstream news was purposefully misleading.

Thanks to the internet facts can be verified from several sources in seconds to minutes in many cases, especially in relation to the few topics discussed in this book - amongst those, elections, the Drug War and drastic tax swings for those who've need of nothing over those who do.

In *MANUFACTURING CONSENT: NOAM CHOMSKY AND THE MEDIA*, footage is nicely flipped back and forth to scenes of Professor Chomsky's debate with the then Dutch Minister of Defense, Frits Bolkestein. The last scene spoke for itself, as the Minister looked at his watch and said: "*I'm sorry, ladies and gentleman, I must be leaving*," he then turned and exited the stage. The audience laughed as he walked off the stage. The debate moderator then stated:

"*One thing is sure, that consent has not been manufactured tonight.*"

Chapter 10

The Not-so-great Escape of Former U.S. Senator Robert (Bob) Torricelli

"The only thing necessary for the triumph of evil is for good men (and women) to do nothing..."

- Edmund Burke, 18th century British statesman

Above: U.S. Senator Robert "Bob" Torricelli, makes a getaway from questions the media censors do not ask

THE BOTTOM LINE IS, IF THE MEDIA FILTERS WEREN'T THERE people would never consent to being scammed by a government that's supposed to represent them, though it doesn't, while both scamming them financially and sending real people to live in violent human caging facilities *en masse* for non-crimes.

If there's no victim, there's no crime. The majority of the nation's estimated 2.3-million prisoners are serving time for victimless "crimes," in violent human cages away from their families and loved ones for years for nothing, nothing legitimate anyway. The Land of Liberty's prison population has gone from an estimated 500,000 prisoners in the early '80s to some 2.3-million in 2007, largely due to the War on Drugs, which has not only failed, but denies our citizens of the right to "*...Life, Liberty and the pursuit of Happiness.*"

Think about it, annual arrests for cannabis possession have been nearly three-quarters of a million in the United States now for the last several years. That means not only subjecting people who are merely possessing a plant to spend time in a human chicken coop, which is what it amounts to, only this human coop is crowded and physically dangerous, where fights and gang rapes are commonplace, but leaving society with more real criminals, i.e., those who *have* harmed others, at large as a result. That's simple deductive reasoning. If our resources are wasted elsewhere, then we'll have more pedophiles, rapists, murderers, and so forth, at large amongst the public, free to continue their crimes as a result. Please think about it. This isn't someone else's society I'm writing about here, and you're amongst the majority who are getting the shaft at the hands of a disproportionate extreme minority of greedy murderous people. Does that not upset you? We're buying the rocks for the stonings, to use a metaphor, only in our case it's to cage people, most of whom have harmed no one. If we pay taxes, we're chipping in.

Rape is one of the worst things that can happen to a human being, and in society in general it's treated as such, yet in U.S. prisons and jails it's commonplace, and not even discouraged in most areas, though as I understand things from speaking to former inmates is not tolerated in some institutions. Nevertheless, when have you ever heard of someone in jail being charged with rape? Why should we leave ourselves more at risk as a population in order to punish people who've harmed no one to be stripped of their liberty at a grand expense to all? Would not the Founding Fathers, flaws and all, be appalled by what we've allowed our nation to become?

I read an article years ago about a man who started some kind of group awareness program about this in NYC, who had himself been raped in prison as a younger man who was protesting the Vietnam War. Although his bail was set at $10 he refused to have it posted, to make his point. I'm sure he would've done differently in retrospect if he only knew what was going to happen. As he was exiting the showers, about five men suddenly attacked him at the same time, one pulling his long hair backwards as hard as he could, with each of the others grabbing an arm or a leg. He was raped by all of them. Then they suddenly released him and took off. He got up right away to confront his attackers but they were gone. He went to look for them but didn't even know who he was looking for since he hadn't seen one of them. His search proved futile so he went to a guard and told him. The guard told him to stop whining.

This story is by no means unique, nor is it confined to men alone. I have a book which was written by former President Kennedy's daughter, Caroline Kennedy, and Ellen Alderman entitled *The Right to Privacy* in which a horrible encounter is described about a female physician who ended up in jail for unpaid parking tickets. She found herself confronted by women who made her take off her clothes. She heard a larger woman coming down the hall, who she was hoping was going to save her, but instead joined in with the others. Then she was ordered to assume humiliating positions while naked. When she told them she was a doctor they started hooting and mocking her. This kind of violence in women's prisons and jails is not uncommon.

Women get beat up in prison, jaws get broken and lives destroyed. We've witnessed this being stated in a court room from a woman who had spent time in Ocean County Jail in Ocean County, New Jersey. A man no older than 18 or 19 was up next, and he too had his jaw broken in the men's part of the same jail, yet the prosecutor went after him tooth and nail, like he wasn't a real human being in considerable distress brought on by our system. So, these things happen and I'd like to add that not only do the ones sent to jail suffer, so do their families and friends.

When I was practicing chiropractic, many of my patients were treated for tense muscles either precipitated or exacerbated by stress. When one is wondering whether one's mother, father, daughter, son, wife, husband, friend, girlfriend, boyfriend, grandson, granddaughter or whoever they're close to is facing time in a violent human caging facility, people tend to get scared for the ones they care about, and it oftentimes creates physical stress which can lead to more than just muscular tightness since stress has been proven to be highly linked to illness in general. But again, this topic is rarely brought up in the wealthy-owned, wealthy-censoring media.

The Land of the Free has become the Home of the Caged, right before our very eyes, though they don't normally put these institutions in prominent locations such as off Interstates, yet I have seen them in both western New York just off I-90 and on I-81 in southern Virginia.

The Drug War affects the poor much more than the wealthy. The downside is the wealthy benefit from it by hiring people who have lost their citizen rights and therefore can be paid slave labor wages, far below minimum wage, like 17 cents an hour, 25 cents an hour, if they're lucky 50 cents an hour.

If stonings for adultery were practiced here in the United States, would you condone your tax dollars funding the bombardment of people with rocks for violations of their right to live as they choose? Our tax dollars are directly funding the terrorization and torture of our own citizens *en masse*, while keeping them away from everyone who cares about them, even though they've harmed no one. Meanwhile, arguably the most harmful drug is legal, in terms of how its ingestion can affect others, i.e., alcohol, and one of, if not "the" most addicting drug known to mankind is legal likewise, i.e., nicotine, the addiction to which accounts for some 400,000 U.S. deaths each year, and 5-million people worldwide.

It's rare for someone who smokes cannabis to smoke anywhere near as much as tobacco. Cannabis contains no compound like nicotine that fits in a lock and key fashion to its own receptor sites of the brain like opiates and tobacco that must be continuously satisfied if one is to remain free of bodily withdrawal symptoms.* If these receptor sites do not get what they're used to getting, the person will get physical symptoms which can only be satisfied by having more of the unique substance that fits in a lock and key fashion to parts of the brain. Former Surgeon General C. Everett Koop stated that nicotine was as addicting as heroin. In fact, he stated, *"Nicotine in cigarettes may be* more *addicting than other drugs, because the smoker gets so many 'hits' of nicotine each day."*

* NOTE: THC does have receptor sites in the brain, but unlike nicotine and opiates, one does not go through terrible withdrawal symptoms if these sites are not stimulated.

Surely "cannabis" AKA "marijuana" could be made to contain less THC for someone who didn't want to get high but wanted to stop smoking cigarettes. Unlike tobacco, one doesn't wake up with a strong feeling that one needs a fix. This doesn't happen to all tobacco users, of course, yet it happens to far too many, likely most. I've been around enough tobacco smokers in my life, and even been addicted to it several times myself and watched other tobacco addicts have their lives destroyed due to the prolonged use of this plant. In fact, of the five cancer patients I had to diagnose during my 13 years as a chiropractic physician, four were heavy smokers. At one time when I was looking at the MRI results of a man with cancer that had spread to his hip which it was eating away, the radiologist turned to me and asked, *"Smoker?"* Yes, he was a tobacco smoker, and he died of the disease within a few weeks. The same facility took a pelvic x-ray only weeks earlier in which the tumor was not detectable in the least, because it takes more bone loss to be detected via x-ray, unlike the more sensitive albeit expensive MRI.

Getting back to the highlight of the evening, other than a legitimate U.S. Senate candidate being arrested while an un-elected few forcibly had him handcuffed and locked in a cage during the time of the debate in which he should have been included, the following is our encounter with New Jersey U.S. Senator, Robert Torricelli, as he left the studio. A few of us were standing several cars away from the exit walkway from Channel 12 studio when Doug Friedline spotted Senator "Bob" Torricelli, walking with a woman while leaving the station.

Doug Friedline: Torricelli's over here.

Glick quickly rushed down and met Torricelli at the base of the sidewalk where it joined the parking lot. I arrived with my video camera, running, moments later. Beginning 10 feet away or so and approaching, the following conversation with former U.S. Senator Robert "Bob" Torricelli was recorded.

NJ Green Party congressional candidate, Joe Fortunato, a north Jersey attorney: Hi Bob [Torricelli], how's it going?

Ted Glick: (Inaudible, since Mr. Glick was facing away from me, and Mr. Fortunato was facing toward me as I approached.)

Senator Torricelli: I know, but that's not my call.

Ted Glick: You have a lot to do with it.

Senator Torricelli: [walking away] Well, I don't.

Ted Glick: You negotiate the rules of the debate.

Joe Fortunato: How about next time? Can we sit down and talk about it? Talk about the issues sir?

Unidentified female Glick supporter: That's what our new slogan is... *"Back Door Bob."* Like it?

Joe Fortunato: How about talk about the issues with us? Let's have a real debate.

Unidentified male: Stop ducking.

Elaine Hildebrandt: Why is it that the true people are taken away to jail while the (inaudible) people go walk on the streets telling people lies? Second Graders know that everybody should have a voice.

Joe Fortunato: Bob, how are you going to vote on the war plan?

Dr. Ken Hildebrandt: Bob! Isn't it true that you were one of the 12 dirty dozen Democrats that went along with W's tax-cutting rape for the people that benefited the one percent? Isn't that true?

Joe Fortunato: What about the war, Bob?

[Senator Torricelli and his female companion spot their limo]

Ken: How about the Drug War, Bob? You know? They're victimless criminals that are put in and have to sit their lives in cages.

Apart from a statement or two from other citizens trying to ask Senator Torricelli real questions about life and death which were difficult to hear, the above was the entire recorded interaction. Senator Torricelli had no words to even attempt to substantiate the undeniable human-induced terror and death they support while still coming across as fair and working for the best interests of the citizens of the United States. As Senator Torricelli was asked questions the mainstream media would never address fairly, if at all, he simply stopped responding.

It's tough to argue for the stress, strain and misery of many to benefit a small percentage of the population. It's also tough to argue for sending citizens *en masse* to live in violent human zoos at a rate and number greater than any nation on Earth, yet pretends to be the Land of the Free, but they just don't bring that up often on the six o'clock news, do they? We're talking about completely innocent people who are living in cages for violations of their right to "*...Life, Liberty and the pursuit of Happiness.*" Again, this has all escalated tremendously over the last few decades.

And something that one doesn't normally hear brought up is the question that since our law enforcement personnel are chasing non-criminals half the time, does that not by default leave more rapists, pedophiles, thieves and murderers at large due to the hours, days and weeks our law enforcement people are spending harming the innocent, their families and loved ones at taxpayers' expense? We've already discussed that it certainly does. It's nothing but elementary deductive reasoning. Would anyone care to argue otherwise, publicly I mean? Why not write one of the mainstream puppet commentators and ask this most basic question regarding such a profundity?

Most know that Ronald Reagan and the Bushes helped step up the Drug War. Fewer know that the prison population during the Clinton years about doubled. Even less probably know that Barack Obama's vice presidential running mate, Joe Biden, the Washington dinosaur who's been in the U.S. Senate for some three and half decades (in other words, the antithesis of "change"), pushed for mandatory minimum sentences for drug convictions in the '80s, meaning that innocent people would be taken away from their families, friends, children, and so forth to live in violent caging facilities for violations of their right to "*...Life, Liberty and the pursuit of Happiness*" for even longer periods of time. Has not Joe Biden had major complicity in harming innocent people *en masse*, and we know it?*

* See, Independent presidential candidate Ralph Nader on Barack Obama's choice of Joe Biden as his VP, at, **http://www.votenader.org/media/2008/08/23/NaderonBiden/**.

If one can't reasonably answer why one is supporting the harming of millions of our citizens, doesn't that make you sick?

People in the U.S., the most powerful and influential nation on Earth, are "*...allowing themselves to be deluded and manipulated by the system,*" to the point that they directly fund human misery and vote for those who make the laws that harm the innocent on purpose. How much sense does this make? Is this not cruel? Is this not state-sanctioned child abuse that's rationalized by the elite lawmakers and the media as being legitimate? It either is or isn't.

Remembering what Steve Biko, who was killed under the apartheid regime in South Africa, stated, "*The greatest weapon in the hands of the oppressor is the mind of the oppressed.*"

Chapter 11

Another Censored Candidate Discusses Wind, Hemp, and More

"He's (Carl Levin) reached four million (dollars) and Andrew Raczkowski, the Republican, he's raised about half a million (dollars). PAC contributions, the Republican has about $2,275. Zero percent of his money is coming from PAC. It's all individuals. The Democrat has raised $665,000, 16% of his money is coming from corporate PACs. So we have a Democrat who's actually hogged up all the corporate money."

- Eric Borregard, 2002 Michigan U.S. Senate candidate (pictured below)

AS IN 2000 WITH THE ELIMINATION OF RALPH NADER and the other legitimate candidates who were on ballots, limiting the bounds of debate by the media in the United States - by force if necessary - is their modus operandi. In 2002 our travels took us not only to events in New Jersey but we also traveled to Michigan and Minnesota in our pursuit to cover the elections.

In August we went to Michigan, where we spoke to the Green Party candidate for U.S. Senate, Eric Borregard. Eric had much to share with us, including giving us video footage of fellow Green Party candidate for Governor of Michigan, Douglas Campbell, being physically grabbed off the stage before the start of a televised debate for the office he was seeking. He reportedly had several ribs broken in the process of being ripped from his seat by two officers of some kind, who grabbed him on each side lifting him off his seat and out of the room. His would-be opponents ignored the assault that took place right next to them. One of them would be elected Governor of Michigan.

I asked Mr. Borregard a few questions, and he showed me a breakdown of how much money his opponents had raised by special interest groups, especially concentrating on the Democrat who was clearly leading the pack in money raised for the campaign. We'll begin with some questions I had for the U.S. Senate candidate, who was likewise marginalized by the media as if he didn't exist.

Dr. Ken Hildebrandt: We're here with Senate candidate Eric Borregard at his office. And tell me, Eric, you were talking to me before about wind as an alternative to nuclear power. I was wondering if you could tell me a little bit more about that.

Michigan U.S. Senate candidate, Eric Borregard: You're never going to regret wind. Nuclear power you're going to regret. There's no way to get rid of nuclear waste. And now that they're going to be shipping it to Yucca , you'll be sitting at a light and when one of these trucks comes up next to you, it'll be the equivalent of about 100 dental x-rays.

Elaine Hildebrandt: Not a train... a truck?

Eric Borregard: Just a truck, sitting there idling next to it, like a moving x-ray machine.

Ken: So how come we're not using wind? I mean, I know that but... ah...

Eric Borregard: For the same reason we haven't legalized hemp.

Ken: And that is, of course?

Eric Borregard: The alcohol lobby; the energy lobby; they're invested in coal. All those guys down in West Virginia, you know, they're strip-mining all the mountains... um, a lot of money in that, and they would lose their job(s). Engineers up here in Detroit started building large assembly lines to build the wind turbines. We can build energy we don't have to go find it.

Ken: You had heard, too, the thing that I had seen on JackHerer.com, that Henry Ford actually had an automobile that ran on hemp seed oil...

Eric Borregard: Yeah.

Ken: ...in the 1930s, and you're aware of that also?

Eric Borregard: Part of it's the economics. It was cheaper to drill for oil. That's still the case,* it's cheaper, but as time goes on it's not that much more expensive. We do have ethanol in our gasoline.

* Note: Gasoline prices in Michigan were in the low to mid $1.40 range at the time, according to, **http://www.eia.gov/dnav/pet/hist/LeafHandler.ashx?f=W&n=PET&s=EMM_EPMR_PTE_NUS_DPG**.

Ken: Right. Now you're saying it's cheaper. This guy Jack...

Eric Borregard: It's just another form of ethanol, though diesel, you can make diesel out of it, so the trucks can run on it, too. It has a lot of uses but again, also the Alcohol Lobby, they have a lot of money invested in alcohol, selling it at every local drug store and if you started selling marijuana it would probably cut twenty, thirty, maybe forty percent of their profits. (laughs)

Ken: I wonder what would happen to the violence, too.

Eric Borregard: The real thing is why should we be putting people in jail for something that is probably a lot less harmless [sic] to their bodies. Alcohol causes fetal alcohol syndrome, and (you) lose muscle control when you're driving. You know, it's a much more dangerous drug. Why should we be putting those people in jail and paying for their incarceration when our schools need money and so on, and we really don't need to be doing this at all? In fact we've created a kind of state of mind in people's, you know, that we need this kind of law enforcement. It's more of like a stigma on a particular product than any real...

Ken: And what it's doing really is enforcing that these alternative energy sources are not used. That's what it's enforcing. It's enforcing the idea that oil is going to be continued to be used. That's really what they're enforcing. It's awful.

Eric Borregard: Recently we've just reached the point, the last year or so, where all the oil there is to be used, we're at the half-way point just a few years ago.

Ken: Huh.

Eric Borregard: So, it went up like this (raising his hand up) we reached this point, it's going to get harder and harder to find the last bits, and then there's not going to be any left. So if it only takes a hundred years to go through that, probably fifty years to go through what's left. So, the next economic boom, the next big bonanza, it's green, it's going to be very green. It's going to be trains that run on electricity, wind turbines, and probably still a lot of the other electrical generation type equipment.

Ken: But not only is oil running out, the earth-raping way we have to go about getting it, plus, I mean it takes (millions of years for oil to be created). Hemp renews annually.*

* See, **http://JackHerer.com**

Eric brought us to another room to show us some printouts regarding where his Democratic and Republican opponents were getting their money.

Eric Borregard: This is Carl Levin who I'm running against, and here is the total money spent as of July 17, 2002.

Ken: Hmm.

Eric Borregard: He's reached four million (dollars) and Andrew Raczkowski, the Republican, he's raised about half a million (dollars). PAC contributions, the Republican has about $2,275. Zero percent of his money is coming from PAC. It's all individuals. The Democrat has raised $665,000, 16% of his money is coming from corporate PACs. So we have a Democrat who's actually hogged up all the corporate money.

Ken: Hmm.

Eric Borregard: ...All the insurance companies, all the oil companies, the oil industry.

Ken: Wow.

Eric Borregard: And, ah, the defense industry,* especially because he's on the Armed Services Committee and the Government Intelligence Committee. Of course, I'm on here too, zero percent. I haven't taken any donations yet. (This was toward the end of August 2002.)

Mr. Borregard then turned the page of the printout he had stapled together.

* Below from, *A World of Ideas*, with Bill Moyers, PBS (Public TV), USA, 1988:

Bill Moyers to Professor Noam Chomsky: *You have said that we live entangled in webs of endless deceit, in a highly indoctrinated society where elementary truths are easily buried. Elementary truths such as?*

Professor Noam Chomsky: *Such as... the fact that the military system is to a substantial extent, not totally, but to a substantial extent, a mechanism by which the general population is compelled to provide a subsidy to high technology industry, since they're not going to do it if you ask them to, you have to deceive them into doing it.*

Ken: These are some of those industries you were talking about.

Eric Borregard: Oh yeah, you've got to see this (pointing to a picture of Senator Levin). This is Carl Levin. I'm sure you'll all recognize him from somewhere. He's up around 5-million dollars right now actually. This is back in July but he has raised from law firms about 300,000 (dollars), pro-Israeli groups, ah... you're wondering why we're having a war in Iraq and supporting Israel. Well, he's on the committee and here's a quarter of a million reasons why he likes them. Insurance industry... you wonder why you're not getting your prescription drugs or whatever. They're going to be slowed down, he's going to take a long time to consider those. Health care professionals, you know, (he moving down the list), Medicare, yep, there's going to be problems there. Aerospace groups, defense groups, yeah...

Ken: Yeah, who was that last one?

Eric Borregard: ... (inaudible), Chrysler, oh yeah.

Ken: Oh yeah, good old MBNA, (spotting this one myself and wanting to be sure he didn't miss it since I was aware that they had also supported Bush's campaign in 2000 having done a video mentioning them specifically in this regard in February 2001.)*

* "*Among the biggest beneficiaries of the measure would be MBNA Corporation of Delaware, which describes itself as the world's biggest independent credit card company. Ranked by employee donations, MBNA was the largest corporate contributor to the Bush campaign, according to a study by the Center for Responsive Politics, an election research group.*"

- From, **http://www.nytimes.com/2001/03/13/us/hard-lobbying-on-debtor-bill-pays-dividend.html**.

Eric Borregard: I'm not qualified to be a U.S. Senator, but I think the guy down here at the Taco Bell who's folding tacos (burritos)...

Ken: Hmm.

Eric Borregard: ...is more qualified than Carl Levin...

Ken: No doubt about it.

Eric Borregard: ...because he knows enough not to stick his hands in the guacamole. (laughs)

Ken: Right. (laughs)

Before we left Eric's office he gave us a copy of a television commercial (made for a cable station, as I recall) containing footage of a brutal arrest of Michigan Green Party candidate, Douglas Campbell, who as someone on the official state ballot had sat down to participate in a televised debate with the Republican and Democratic candidates. He told us to do with it what we liked and when we misplaced the first copy he mailed us another. It was quite an arrest. Two officers, one on each side, grabbed him by one arm each and hoisted him out and behind his chair with him ending up on the floor with broken ribs.

Campbell had several ribs broken in this videotaped assault as the other members of the panel sitting to his right did not even seemingly react at all. Unlike the presented puppets, Douglas Campbell clearly stood for the common people in general over big business and other special interest groups, but Michiganders never got to see and hear him because he was yanked from the stage by people who were not elected to make such decisions.

There's yet to be a citizen vote on who is allowed in the debates and why, concerning all leading offices in this country including the presidency, yet the big business people who run the major television stations, standing up for themselves and their fellow wealthy corporation buddies, simply eliminate more reasonable fair people from even being in the contest. And the people swallow it, hook, line and sinker, time after time, election after election.

It's not a very complex scam, and with the internet, the fact that it's still working is nothing short of disgraceful, in my view. Like the well-dressed gentleman said to me in Harlem back in 2000: "*I don't want to see anything else other than his platform. I'm not interested in anything else you have. Show me his platform.*" Well, in that case it was a he, meaning Nader. But the point is, whether one likes Ralph Nader as a person or not, his platform was far more reasonable than his primary opposition, yet all he managed to do was glean some 3% of the vote, thanks to a censoring media.

George W. Bush, a man who had had more executions as governor of Texas than any governor in the history of the United States, whose signature was written on 152 of 153 death penalty cases he had been presented with during his tenure, ended up winning the presidency. The media had spoiled yet another election.

Many of those put to death at Bush's command were clearly innocent, many others likely innocent, and several drew international outrage, yet George W. Bush either ignored the facts or didn't spend the time to look into the cases before determining whether he'd have each one of them put to death. He simply relied on the court's ruling, his signature being the only thing stopping a real person from being put to death.

One of his victims, who admittedly was guilty of murder, had made it on a mainstream television program. Tucker Carlson, the generally Bush-supporting bow-tied telecaster, asked Governor George W. Bush if he had seen the broadcast. George W. reportedly then said to Mr. Carlson: *"Please don't kill me,"* with pursed lips, indicating he had likely seen the broadcast and that was his synopsis of same. Bush's actions led to a murder likewise, didn't they? George W. Bush claims to be a born-again Christian, as clearly Karla Faye Tucker had become, making them brother and sister in Christ according to their religion, yet did he remember the teaching of Jesus, whom he claims to be a follower of, proclaiming that, *"Let he who is without sin cast the first stone,"* as is recorded in, *The Gospel According to John,* (Chapter 8, Verse 7), a book he proclaims he believes is sacred?

Another of his victims was Gary Graham, AKA Shaka Sankofa. He was 17 at the time of the alleged crime to begin with, making the U.S. among just a handful of countries which would execute him even if he was guilty, though the evidence indicates he was not. He was identified by one person from 30 feet away at night as being the murderer, though six other eye witnesses claimed he was not the killer, and four others passed polygraph tests saying he was with them at the time of the murder.

There was no physical evidence linking him with the crime either. This was surely a case of questionable guilt and in reality almost certain innocence. The facts are that ten people, plus Shaka Sankofa himself, maintained that he was innocent of the crime he paid the ultimate price for committing, six eyewitnesses to the crime and four people who claimed he was with them at the time of the murder, vs. one person whose description of the killer was not near what any of the other eyewitnesses described him as being.

I remember seeing a picture in the *Daily News* of NYC of several people walking down a street, some holding signs, with the camera focused on a woman who was reportedly Mr. Graham's daughter, crying, and a man holding her as they were walking together. Bush had just ordered the killing of her father for a crime he did not commit. No, he didn't murder Shaka Sankofa (the name the former Gary Graham requested he be remembered by) himself, yet his signature was what caused this man's death. Charles Manson didn't kill anyone himself either, did he? Yet all consider him a murderer for ordering others to kill, do they not? That's what Bush's signature did for Shaka Sankofa.

This blatant disregard for accuracy regarding real human being's lives seems so foreign to me as a former healer. I remember how specific I tried to be when arriving at a diagnosis and plan of treatment for my patients, and how much I cared for each and everyone who came to my office entrusting me to a certain degree with their very health. Nearly all that was at my disposal to help was my brain and my hands, though I often relied on technology such as x-rays and MRIs to help arrive at a diagnosis.

My point is, I certainly didn't want any of them to die, though I did diagnose a handful who ended up having diseases I knew would likely take their lives and did, and had I had in my power to take their life-threatening illness away I surely would've, and I think most people think this way, whether physician or not, though clearly George W. Bush does not think this way. *"What's wrong with him?"* one might ask, and what's wrong with the people for electing such a person to have more influence over people's lives than arguably anyone alive?

George W. Bush was a person who obviously didn't mind if his actions directly caused another human to be strapped to a gurney and put to death, even though the matter could be halted by his mere say-so.
As governor he had absolute power as to whether or not he wanted to have each of the 152 of 153 people he was presented with to live or die. The decision was his. "*The buck stops here,*" stated President Harry Truman, the man responsible for the two biggest terrorist attacks of all time, by the way.

Back to Douglas Campbell: Eric Borregard had given us his telephone number encouraging us to contact him but we had already planned to travel to Minnesota before returning to New Jersey and New York, where we had a home near the beach and an apartment in the city at the time. In retrospect, I wish we had delayed our trip to Minnesota and given Douglas Campbell a call, or arranged to meet him on the way back, for his is truly representative of how far the major media will go to distort a major election. Nowhere else in our society is this kind of treatment to the innocent accepted, except in U.S. jails and prisons, of course - in both cases simply because they haven't been brought to broad public attention to reach enough people who care that their tax dollars are directly funding the catching and caging of innocent people who have not harmed or stolen from anyone, while considering of course that there are multiple scores of others who are likewise harmed when the people they know and in many cases love and live with are taken away from their homes to reside in violent human caging facilities, off limits to the general public for most intents and purposes. One mustn't forget either that by so doing we are left with more real criminals, such as murderers, pedophiles, rapists, thieves and so forth as a result of wasting our resources terrorizing innocent people for their lifestyles.

We met a young woman whose father shot and killed himself days before he was to return to a Michigan jail on possession of marijuana charges. He had already been in one of these caging facilities for a violation of his right to "*...Life, Liberty and the pursuit of Happiness,*" but not for hurting anyone or stealing anything, and rather than face going back he ended his life. It was easy to see the suffering in his teenage daughter's eyes. Her Daddy died due to our torturous prisons and our denying people by force *en masse* of their right to "*...Life, Liberty and the pursuit of Happiness.*" We're all a part of this, as Professor Chomsky has correctly stated.

Who would choose a doctor who knowingly harmed most in order to benefit a disproportionate few, simply because she or he spent more money than the other doctors advertising and so forth? How are the media able to keep such importantly impacting secrets contained within safe limits at the height of the Information Age? Here we are with nearly everyone being aware of faulty voting machines, yet long before Election Day when the public is supposed to get a clear idea of who they're voting for, a disproportionate few keeps it all a safe secret by openly leaving out qualified competition. It's hardly a complex scam.

Candidates who are on the ballots and therefore are eligible to win the seat of the race they're in are marginalized to such a point they're deemed a wasted vote, even though the public could be choosing people who far and away are more supporting of their needs and well being, yet thus far this obvious news has drawn little attention. How many other books have you read about this? Is this not easier to demonstrate and more impacting than faulty voting machines?

Chapter 12

A Corporate Country Club for Democrats

"If you tell a lie big enough and keep repeating it, people will eventually come to believe it. ... the truth is the greatest enemy of the state."

- Joseph Goebbels, Hitler's Minister of Propaganda

Above: Carl Mayer, NJ Green Party congressional candidate

UPON LEAVING U.S. SENATE CANDIDATE ERIC BORREGARD'S OFFICE, we set out for Minnesota to help the Green Party take on Paul Wellstone, who was arguably by far the most fair, reasonable, caring U.S. Senator we had at the time. Nevertheless after 9/11, like far too many others, he caved by voting in favor of mass suffering, misery and death to thousands of innocent people, i.e., war, for clearly unsound reasons. It should be noted that even if he voted against the war in Afghanistan it would've made no difference since the Senate overwhelmingly backed an invasion. If he had voted against invading Afghanistan in the aftermath of 9-11-01, many thought so doing would have ended up costing him his U.S. Senate seat in the coming year's midterm election of 2002. Tragically, Senator Wellstone died in a plane crash on October 25, 2002, just prior to the election. Ironically, we heard the news on television upon returning to our motel room after meeting Professor Noam Chomsky for the first time. One of the last things we told Noam before leaving was that we planned on heading back to Minnesota, this time to help with Senator Wellstone's campaign, since the Greens at that point obviously had no chance, and he was in danger of losing his seat.

As it turned out, back in August when we got to Minnesota we found out that it hadn't yet been decided who among two were going to run on the state's Green Party ticket for U.S. Senate, either Ed McGaa or Ray Tricomo. So we went back to New Jersey in plenty of time for the first scheduled televised debate among the U.S. Senate candidates, only to witness the arrest of the Green Party candidate, Ted Glick, which we discussed earlier.

Weeks before his arrest, we met U.S. Senate candidate Ted Glick in person for the first time outside a private club in the outskirts of Princeton, New Jersey, a club that had annual dues of some 60 to 65 thousand dollars, on a large estate just a matter of minutes away from some of the poorest inner city streets I've ever seen in Trenton, New Jersey. Reportedly, five U.S. Senators were in attendance at the estate on the day we met him, all were Democrats. One was Jon Corzine, 2006-2010 governor of New Jersey, who was then a U.S. Senator. A permit for a gathering to draw attention to what was happening inside was obtained, and reportedly some Libertarians were in attendance too, at some point, in addition to mostly members of the Green Party.

As soon as we arrived and parked a short way down the street at the end of the other vehicles, I walked toward the small gathering of a dozen or so people with my camera in my hand. I ended up interviewing U.S. Senate candidate Ted Glick, Joe Fortunato, a Green Party candidate then running for congress in the 8th District of New Jersey, and Carl Mayer, who was likewise running as a Green for congress in a different district than Mr. Fortunato.

After interviewing both Ted Glick and Joe Fortunato, we ended up turning around and going back in order to interview the last candidate, Carl Mayer, after hearing him on WBAI radio as we started making our way home, in an apparent taped discussion since there was no one from any radio or television stations at the event while we were there.

We'll begin with Carl Mayer, followed by Joe Fortunato, since you've yet, at least in this manuscript, read anything about them. Then we'll return to Ted Glick.

Dr. Ken Hildebrandt: Carl, I had to turn back. You were on the radio on my way home on (W)BAI (a listener-supported radio station out of New York City).

Carl Mayer: Oh, was I?

Ken: ...and you gave a great rant.

Carl Mayer: Oh, was I (inaudible)?

Ken: So, this is Carl Mayer. Did I pronounce that right?

Carl Mayer: Yeah, Mayer.

Ken: All right, now what's going on here today, Carl? The part I got before the radio station went out was about Al Gore's *New York Times* editorial last week and you had some interesting comments to make regarding that editorial.

Carl Mayer: Last week in the *New York Times*, Al Gore wrote an editorial in which he said the historic mission of the Democratic Party is to fight for the people, not the powerful. Not one week after his editorial, the leading Democratic Senators are partying at one of the most exclusive clubs in the country, the former mansion of Seward Johnson, the founder of Johnson & Johnson. It costs $65,000 to enter those gates, just to get in, $65,000.

Ken: What is the acreage I heard you say on...?

Carl Mayer: Two hundred and thirty acres.

Ken: Wow. (Remember, this isn't rural Virginia where my wife Elaine and I live now, this is in central western New Jersey where real estate prices are among the highest in the country.)

Carl Mayer: Sixty-five thousand dollars to get in.

Ken: Hmm.

Carl Mayer: A lot of people live in homes in this country that are less than $65,000. It's just to get into the club. There are all sorts of corporate sponsors of this fundraiser, and there are corporate members of this club like Arthur Anderson is, a convicted corporate criminal. They're convicted of obstructing justice, for shredding documents in the Enron case. They're a member of this club and yet Corzine and four other Democratic Senators...

Ken: Yeah, who are the other four Democratic Senators, that was the other...

Carl Mayer: Tom Harkin, Jean Carnahan, Tim Johnson from South Dakota, and Max Cleland from Georgia.

Ken: Wow.

Carl Mayer: Max Cleland of Georgia, and they're all going, as Bruce Afran here pointed out (Bruce Afran was a Green Party New Jersey U.S. Senate candidate in 2000), it's like going to John Gotti's social club. It's like the police commissioner going to a party at John Gotti's social club, the same thing as Jon Corzine having a party at Arthur Anderson's social club. They're both criminals, the only difference is Arthur Anderson stole a lot more than John Gotti ever did.

Ken: I think it's indicative that we don't have a Democratic Party that's called the Democratic Party, that we have one that's Green.

Carl Mayer: Yep.

Ken: All right.

Carl Mayer: Rush Holt, who is marinated with corporate PAC money. Rush Holt is, he is nothing but a corporation in disguise running as a person. He has taken money from WorldCom, from Deloitte and Tush, from Ernst and Young, Price Waterhouse, all the accounting firms that were responsible for the various frauds like Tico and Enron. Here, you can see right here (pointing to a placard someone else was holding), 1-800-BUY-HOLT.

Ken: Now, there's somebody else running against him (too)?

Carl Mayer: Buster Soaries, yeah, he's the Republican nominee. He's actually an interesting nominee. He's an African-American minister* and he's done a lot of work in the community, and ah, his campaign is not funded like Rush Holt's. Rush Holt would make (Croatias?) look poor, he has so much money. He spent 4.9-million dollars in his last few campaigns.

* Technically all Americans, if one traces one's lineage far enough back, are African-American. After all, we do have a common ancestor (along with everyone else in the world) who was from Africa. Yes, we're all, "families apart," as the late great musician and visionary Jimi Hendrix wrote shortly before he passed away in 1970. We're all related, everyone on earth, yet few realize this undeniable reality. The false barriers keep us divided amongst ourselves.

Ken: Yeah.

Carl Mayer: He takes money from these accounting firms and then he voted against a bill that would've made the accountants more accountable to the people, that would have reduced and eliminated accountant's conflict of interest. It was proposed by a member of his own party, Dennis Kucinich, and um, he voted against it because he's in the hands of the accountants.

Ken: Hmm.

Carl Mayer: He hasn't... there isn't, there isn't (hardly) a PAC he hasn't taken money from. He's taken from defense contractors. He's taken from the nuclear power industry.

Ken: Hmm.

Carl Mayer: He's taken from Wall Street firms and securities industry while the securities industry is defrauding America. He's taken from the, ah, the med or the drug companies. He's taken more money from the drug companies than any other member of Congress, on the Democratic side, and he voted against a bill to put a cap on prescription drug prices for seniors because he votes with the drug companies, not the... not the, ah, people.

Ken: Ah, incidentally, as do almost always, all the Republicans, right?

Carl Mayer: Well, that's true.

Ken: That's, well, I mean, we gotta give it to your opponent too.

I was referring to his other opponent's membership party, the Republican Party, of which I doubt his opponent would've been nominated as a candidate, had he been openly opposed to their platform. If he had been in accord with most of the Republican Party's platform, then even if he had done helpful things for the community and was a likeable guy and so forth, whether he knew it or not he was supporting unnecessary pain and suffering, same as if he had been a Democrat. Both parties' platforms support the War on Drugs which is really an inhumane war against our own citizen's right to "...*Life, Liberty and the pursuit of Happiness,*" and has resulted in millions of casualties, some sent to violent cages, some with loved ones, parents, spouses, etc., when other much more harmful and addicting substances are perfectly legal.

Nicotine addiction accounts for some 400,000 U.S. deaths each year, since that's the addictive substance contained in tobacco. Tobacco addicts have specific receptor sites in their brains which the drug nicotine fits into in a lock and key fashion, same as opiate addicts have receptor sites for opium, as has been discussed. Of course, alcohol ingestion has a direct relationship with physical violence and automobile accidents, yet it remains legal likewise. I don't know of any other drug, whether injected, digested, or inhaled, that can actually make people completely forget hours of their time when under its influence other than anesthesia. So, considering the loss of muscle and motor control, as was brought up by U.S. Senate candidate Eric Borregard earlier, and that people can actually forget time and do things that they don't even remember doing, like driving and ending up killing innocent people, sometimes killing themselves along with them, sometimes not, how can anything else be deemed illegal from a rational standpoint?

Remember, we're supposed to have the right to "...*Life, Liberty and the pursuit of Happiness.*" Taking people from their homes and making them live in cages, oftentimes for years, ought to be for something other than what the person decides to put into her or his body. This is a violation of their liberty, and it comes at an expense to all, as has been explained. If we spend our money chasing innocent people, that leaves more real criminals at large as a result. This is basic deductive reasoning.

Ken: (in conclusion): So, here we are. Here's the facilities folks (as I pointed my video camera toward the outer wall and gates), for the so-called Democratic Party (or at least, some of its leading U.S. Senate members), and, a mere sixty-five grand to get you through those gates.

Chapter 13

More Candidate Censorship Compliments of The Corporate Media

"The corporate media won't cover us unless we force them to, and we have to seek other outlets and I'm very glad you're here doing this."

- Joe Fortunato, NJ Green Party US congressional candidate (Pictured below)

Dr. Ken Hildebrandt: We're outside of our little fundraiser, or rather the Democratic Party's fundraiser* for the upcoming election, in Elitesville, that is, between Princeton and Lawrenceville, New Jersey. What a contrast to five miles ago. So, what do you think of the upcoming election? We've got Joe Fortunato (here) and you're in what congressional district?

* Not to say this was a Democratic Party officially-sanctioned event, just that key members of its party were in attendance.

Joe Fortunato: I'm in the 8th congressional district, which is Passaic County and Essex County.

Ken: What is your message to the voters in your area? I mean, who are your opponents?

Joe Fortunato: Well, the Democrat incumbent is William Pascrowl, a middle of the road centrist Democrat, and the Republican is named, Jarad, or Jared Silverman, who's never, to my knowledge, run on a Federal level for office before, and I'm a Green Party candidate, (on the ballot running for the same office). Essentially the message is that we need an alternative to the two-party system. Democrats and Republicans are bought and paid for by major corporations such as Enron and WorldCom. We're here today, as you mentioned, outside a Democratic fundraiser where the elite and the millionaires are backing Democratic Party candidates such as Corzine and Torricelli, and we're here with a different kind of message.

Ken: You have an upcoming debate, I understand, between these two. Well, hopefully so.

Joe Fortunato: There will be a candidate's forum in October, with the AARP, and we take a very different position on issues of our elders, as well as on health care. We support universal health care for everyone. Neither the Democrats nor Republicans will do that. They fight each other's proposals for limited prescription drugs in the Senate. The Greens call for universal health care for all. That's one difference. Another difference is on campaign finance reform.* There are many differences. It's a fundamentally different way of looking at things. We are running a campaign which says give democracy back to the people and away from the major corporations and their bought and paid for political parties.

* In the fall of 2009, I was lucky enough to make contact with Doris Haddock, AKA "Granny D," who walked

across the country between the ages of 88 and 90 for campaign finance reform. After exchanging e-mails, we ended up conversing several times via telephone, and had planned on meeting in person in the spring of 2010. Unfortunately Doris passed away on March 09, 2010, at age 100. In one of our lengthier conversations, she told me that her real motivation for walking across the country was for "publicly `funded elections," but if she had had a sign stating that on her cross-country walk, she felt few would've understood her message. In other words, it required more of an explanation than what could be placed on a simple placard. Publicly funded elections were a high priority for Doris, and she worked hard for them right up to the end, in spite of her decades long battle with emphysema. She informed me that there was pending legislation for same in some 27 states, and that Maine and Arizona already had laws in place. I had known about Maine, but not Arizona. I asked her about eventually seeing this reach a Federal level, and she agreed that was her ultimate goal. What an amazing woman. If enough others put forth a fraction of the effort she did, we'd steer this nation and world toward a more sane direction in a short time.

Ken: Now, the district's representative (in congress) this time, I guess he voted with Bush's tax-cut plan for the elites, both of them. Are you aware (of that)? As far as the first tax cut...

Joe Fortunato: Did, in my... ah...?

Ken: Well, as far as the original tax cut, which basically took the highest tax bracket... they were taxed at the rate of 39.6 %, and they took it all the way down to 35%.

Joe Fortunato: Right.

Ken: I mean, the great benefactors...

Joe Fortunato: Right.

Ken: ...of the first tax plan.

Joe Fortunato: Right.

Ken: You know, and everyone else gets shafted as a result. Almost all the House, I'm sure all the House Republicans voted for it.

Joe Fortunato: Well, that's right, my opponent's a Democrat and he makes progressive-sounding noises from time to time, on taxes, on education, but, um, essentially has voted with the administration right down the line on our, where our, most of our tax dollars go, which is to the military.

Ken: Yeah, no doubt.

Joe Fortunato: ...For these bloated military budgets.

Ken: Over 50%. There comes a high cost of oppressing the rest of the world, I guess.

Joe Fortunato: Well that's for sure, you know. For instance, two years ago we voted 1.3-billion, with a 'b,' *billion* dollars, ah... for the Columbian military to fight a phony Drug War in Columbia.

Ken: Unbelievable.

Joe Fortunato: And, theah...

Ken: I don't think what people understand, too, is that this Drug War, if they continue to attack these people, there's going to be that many more murderers, and there's going to be that many more rapists, and there's going to be that many more pedophiles on the street as a result.

Joe Fortunato: Well, absolutely.

Ken: It's insane.

Joe Fortunato: We should've learned something from Prohibition. It looks like we haven't.

Ken: But, I mean, as a consequence, if the police are occupying themselves with these activities, that's that much time taken away from seeking murderers and whatnot. I brought this up in one of my earlier films, that I saw on the History Channel (that) there were two serial killers. They had hundreds of kills before the authorities were even alerted that anything was wrong.

Joe Fortunato: Right.

Ken: You would think that if they weren't busy chasing people for what they were doing on their own property, you know, (as I turned my camera toward the mansion's gates) I mean, they can be having meetings here on how to screw the people (sarcastic laughs), you know. That's legal. But these other things are not. Doesn't make any sense to me, but anyway, I didn't mean to get sidetracked there but...

Joe Fortunato: Well.

Ken: Well, good luck in your, in your campaign.

Joe Fortunato: Thank you. Thank you for covering us. You know, that's a big part of the battle. The corporate media won't cover us unless we force them to and we have to seek other outlets and I'm very glad you're here doing this.

Ken: Well, what I'm saying, too, is that if the people spread the word, then we can make this... All you have to do is communicate. (If) Paul Revere could spread a message over two hundred years ago, you could spread a message that's about seven pages long (an approximation, perhaps way off, of the party's platform if printed out). You do have the Green Party platform on your site, do you not?

Joe Fortunato: Absolutely.

Ken: Well, all they need to do is look at that, and look at the Democratic platform, and then look at the Republican (platform) and go make their choice.

Joe Fortunato: Go to www.gpnj.org.

Ken: All right, thank you very much.

Joe Fortunato: Thank you.

Remember what the man in Harlem said about platforms: That was the only thing he was interested in of all the literature we had on the table. It doesn't matter if the candidate is male or female, somber or silly, what matters is what the candidate's platform is, or at least that's what matters most. Mainstream candidates may reach out and pull a branch here and there, but there are people running against them who are going for the roots of several major problems, none of which should exist.

If enough people checked out the candidate's platforms, with those possessing voting rights voting along the lines of common sense and decency, while those not possessing voting rights (along with everyone else who cares a hoot about their world) encouraging others to do this simple research for themselves, each doing what he or she could to pass the material the major media were hiding from them to as many people as they could, using both the internet and talking to others, the minority who own and operate the candidate-censoring media could be defeated or at least significantly weakened in a single election.

No election was ever won by a single vote. Our votes are next to meaningless. Where the power to fight the media lies is in informing others about what they are hiding. So, if you're under 18 or have lost your voting rights, don't think you can't have a say. We're all in this together. There are people trying to overcome their oppressors, whom they outnumber several times over. There are those who aren't doing a thing to change the fact that a disproportionate few are ruining their lives, their loved one's lives, their descendants' lives, along with everyone else they know, merely because said disproportionate few have taken hold of the media outlets though same can now be easily overcome with an organized, even half-organized, effort.

It's not just theory that this is happening, that we living in the most dominant society on Earth are collectively allowing ourselves "*...to be deluded and manipulated by the system*," as Noam Chomsky has stated. You, me, and everyone else, is either fighting this pervasive ignorance at the height of the Information Age or not. The decision is up to you. You're either on your own side, or you're not; on your children's side, or you're not. We have an unnecessarily more dangerous world than need be, due to greed, deception (primarily via the media), apathy, and thoughtlessness. If you allow this kind of deception to continue unimpeded, then you're allowing a disproportionate few to guide a completely inefficient horrible world on a sure dead-end path without protest. That's up to you, as it's up to me. But we should all remember we're in the same boat and not let petty concerns get in the way of our organizing and passing basic information on via a tool the general people have never had before, i.e., the internet. Like it or not we're in the same sinking ship, but make no mistake about it we're all in the same situation, whether facing same or not. Hopefully there's enough time to stop it from sinking.

If we don't act, we know where we're headed. After a while of cooperative effort, we may just get to appreciate one another, and overlook one another's flaws, and gain control of our mutual situation. Hopefully this manuscript will reach enough people in time.

Had I not seen *MANUFACTURING CONSENT: NOAM CHOMSKY AND THE MEDIA*, broadcast in the wee hours of the morning on PBS, (not being aired in the daytime reportedly due to the lobbying of people such as Pat Robertson, it was only aired late night, early morning*), as I sat with my terminally ill mother at the hospital, you would've never seen this book. Were it not for Noam Chomsky, as well as Mark Achbar and Peter Wintonick who made this documentary explaining the murderous methods of the media, or some of the methods anyway, you wouldn't be reading this book. Numerous others have helped give me the vision I have, which I hope you get to see likewise and share with others best you can. The belief in human hierarchy is nonsense. We're all but a breath away from checking out of here. All are vulnerable. All are in this together. All are related. A cooperative effort makes so much more sense, and is so much more gratifying, isn't it?

* Admittedly from my imperfect memory, though according to the ending of this piece by Achbar and Wintonick it seems quite plausible. - **http://flag.blackened.net/liberty/manconsent.txt**

Who would choose a known lousy doctor, who it could be proven unnecessarily had mass complicity in real human suffering and misery, just because he or she advertised more? Then why do we do this in relation to our elected officials whose policies guide our very lives in the interests of a disproportionate few over most? Cannot we spread this basic message to others?

Chapter 14

Corporate Power

"What you do makes a difference and you have to decide what kind of difference you want to make."

- Jane Goodall

U.S. Senate candidate for the Green Party in 2002, Ted Glick, (above), was, as stated earlier, the first one I interviewed that day in August outside the club where some U.S. Democratic senators were getting their earfuls from corporate sponsors.

Dr. Ken Hildebrandt: Hey, Ted, congratulations on being the first candidate to ever be endorsed by nowweretalking.tv (I had this site for over a decade but finally let it go) …

US Senate candidate, Ted Glick: OK.

Ken: …4thepeople.org, [I no longer have that site name] and ppbnj.com (refreshing him about who I was since I had spoken with him on the phone some days beforehand).

Ted Glick: OK.

Ken: I was just saying as I was walking down here, I ended up in inner-city Trenton. I made the same mistake I made last time (going to an indoor track to work out years before), taking the first turn at the end of I-195 here, and what a contrast. Five miles. What a difference between these estates and a real inner-city. So, tell me, Ted, what's going on here today?

Ted Glick: Well, the Democratic Party, Democratic senators, are feeding at the trough, at the corporate trough. (inaudible) $60,000 to be a member of this club and those are the people who are inside, are doing their networking…

Ken: Ah hah.

Ted Glick: …are Democratic Party elected senators and representatives. And we're here to say that for both Democrats and Republicans that's not acceptable anymore. We need to move away from this type of a system, where big money dominates how who gets elected and we need to move to a system that is democratic with a small "d"…

Ken: Ah hah.

Ted Glick: ...where anybody can run for office, where you don't have to be a millionaire, or connected to millionaires, in order to campaign. We're here to point out that even though there's been some legislation passed following this corporate fraud and corporate crime scandal, following WorldCom and Enron, Adelphia and Global Crossing and the rest of them, that there's still a great deal of cleaning up that has to be done and the Green Party is going to be continuing to lead that effort. Our candidate Ralph Nader in 1996, he knew the problems that were coming. He didn't know specifically what was going to happen. He was very aware that corporate, corporations, corporate power, was too influential.

Ken: Do you have any idea what the voting population is in New Jersey? I don't mean to put you on the spot...

Ted Glick: In terms of how many people actually vote?

Ken: Well, how many are registered voters?

Ted Glick: I think it's probably in the neighborhood of, maybe 70, 75 percent I'd say of the eligible electorate. I don't know the exact number but I think it's in that neighborhood.

Ken: Right, but I mean what is the (actual) number?

Ted Glick: Numerically?

Ken: Yeah.

Ted Glick: Well, the number of people who voted in the 2000 election...

Ken: Right.

Ted Glick: ...was about, I believe, about 2.7-million.

Ken: OK

Ted Glick: 2.7-million actual voters.

Ken: So then all we need to do is get the word to over 50%, or maybe not even that many, really, of those...

Ted Glick: Right, right.

Ken: ... people in New Jersey, which is not all that great a distance in square miles and I think it can be done, Ted, personally, and I really think it's inexcusable if it doesn't get done.

Ted Glick: (inaudible)

Ken: I want to see you get in there. But everybody needs to do some effort, not just you and not just, you know, a few of us.

Ted Glick: Well, this is a grassroots campaign and in a grassroots campaign, word of mouth is absolutely essential. People need to talk to other people about the fact that there is an alternative. People need to call in to radio talk shows and say: *"Hey...*

Ken: That's a good way.

Ted Glick: *...do you know about Ted Glick?"* People need to send, write letters to the editor...

Ken: Right.*

* Actually, I don't know why I agreed with him about writing to the editors, since expecting the media to use its resources against itself would be self-destructive for them, so unless it's a small paper or an independent newspaper, you won't see much about how more rational candidates are censored undemocratically from our debates. It's likely a waste of time to ask the enemy to reveal their own scam. Take a look and see who your local paper is owned by, and whether or not it's owned by a corporate conglomerate.

Ted Glick: People need to raise with organizations that they're part of, churches, unions, community groups, whatever they may be, um, raise the fact that there's an alternative... (inaudible).

Ken: Now, you have your platform on the site, too?

Ted Glick: Yeah, our website.

Ken: That's what I tell people. I say: *"Listen, go look at the platform of the Green Party candidate. Look at the platform of the Democratic candidate, and look at his history too in this case, and then do the same thing with the Republican and then make your choice."**

Ted Glick: Right.

Ken: That's my call.

* I think people should investigate all the candidates running by looking at their platforms at least, and if a presidential race, then one should likely also consider how many state ballots the candidate is on. For example, in the 2008 election, Ralph Nader, the Independent, made it on 45 state ballots and was an official write-in for four other states, whereas Cynthia McKinney, the Green Party candidate (whom I've spoken with on the phone, met in person once and have corresponded with via e-mail) was on but 32 state ballots, and as a write-in for 18 others. I like Cynthia, yet the numbers in 2008 clearly stood in favor of Ralph.

Chapter 15

Media-censored Presidential Elections Metastasizes to the Republican & Democratic Parties

"Think of the press as the great keyboard on which the government can play."

- Joseph Goebbels, Hitler's Minister of Propaganda

Above: Former U.S. Senator Mike Gravel at the "Alternate Debate" he and members of his campaign presented in Philadelphia on October 30, 2007, after being excluded from the televised MSNBC Democratic debate.

[After finally starting this book, writing and transcribing our findings from the years, I ended up putting my project aside from late October of 2007, until the beginning of March 2008, with good reason.]

THE METASTASIS SPREAD TO THE MAINSTREAM PARTIES, at first the Democratic Party undemocratically eliminating Mike Gravel, the former U.S. Senator from Alaska who released the *Pentagon Papers* in the early 1970s, revealing the lies of three different presidential administrations to involve our nation in an unnecessary war, costing the lives of some 3-million Southeast Asians and 58-thousand Americans, in addition to those disabled and those orphaned. Imagine all that suffering, misery and death for nothing but to line the pockets of a disproportionate few. That's what happened as can be seen from what Gravel revealed in the early 70s.

Isn't this the kind of person we needed in the debates, with the U.S. finding itself involved in not one, but two highly questionable wars? In the immediate aftermath of 9-11, we had most of the world on our side, but that has changed. Even in the U.S., it's common knowledge that the war in Iraq was based on completely bogus claims about weapons of mass destruction, and it's also widely known that we turned our backs on Saddam Hussein's most hideous crimes when he committed them. What about the infamous picture of Donald Rumsfeld shaking hands with Saddam after he gassed the Kurds? And as far as Afghanistan, we hold a lot of the blame there likewise, by helping build up the Taliban in their resistance of the former Soviet Union, but none of this was discussed, because the media, with the blessing of the leading Democrats, eliminated the man who read *The Pentagon Papers* in front of the U.S. Senate, so their contents were a matter of public record.

Former Senator Gravel opted to have his own alternate debate in Philadelphia a block or two away from MSNBC studios that night, and I felt that with writing this book I had to be there. Little did I know that two weeks later I'd be driving from southern Virginia to Las Vegas, Nevada, to cover Senator Gravel's alternate debate there, since the other networks followed the lead of MSNBC... this time CNN.

Eventually Dennis Kucinich was likewise eliminated from the Democratic Party's debates, though they hardly included him when he had been present, with an open slant right from the get-go toward Hillary Clinton and Barack Obama receiving the most attention, followed by a distant John Edwards, with the remaining media rejects getting a moment here and there.

The Republicans followed suit shortly thereafter by eliminating Dr. Ron Paul, a longtime congressman who set an all-time record for the most amount of money raised in a single day, primarily via individual contributions. Who are these un-elected people who undemocratically removed such a candidate from a televised debate without valid reason?

Much to my pleasant surprise, in spite of Rudy Giuliani not being marginalized in the least and being respected by the moderators, the Media's Mayor dropped out of the race altogether in January, quickly giving his support over to John McCain, perhaps with the long-shot hope of being chosen as McCain's running mate, potentially leaving him but a breath away from the presidency.

With Rudy out, thus went any "spoiler issue" for this election in many ways. In my opinion at that time, only he matched Bush's arrogance and seemingly complete disregard of other's concerns.

With no major "spoiler issue," I thought it was going to be an interesting campaign, but things changed. It was quite a disappointing time to be sure, and still is. I wonder what I could've done differently. Since no one has a time machine, all we can do is move forward from this point onward.

The only way I see a third party win happening is if there's a strategic effort to inform the public regarding a very limited number of life and death issues, the point being made that the media withhold such information, and the people beat the liars with what we have on hand at the height of the Information Age. The right concise pointed video could change the course of humankind, there's little doubt of that. Where there's doubt is, will such a video be made and will enough put forth the effort to bring it to others? Both remain to be seen.

Likely best to both plan for the next election while bringing media-buried truths to enough others so that the media, and our leaders, will no longer be able to ignore these hidden issues of life and death. It's also likely many of them are duped themselves. I wonder how many members of Congress even know that the U.S. overthrew the Iranian government in 1953, bringing their oil back under Western control, and reinstating a known tyrant?

If the odds for success may seem slim, that's mere illusion. For the Scottish philosopher David Hume (1711-1776), who is regarded as, "*The most important philosopher ever to write in English*," according to *Stanford Encyclopedia of Philosophy*, located at, **http://plato.stanford.edu/entries/hume/** was surely correct in asserting:

"*Nothing appears more surprising to those who consider human affairs with a philosophical eye, than the easiness with which the many are governed by the few.*"

- David Hume

I didn't open the e-mail from the Gravel campaign until around midnight on October 30, 2007, indicating that A) he had been eliminated from the MSNBC Democratic Presidential Debate scheduled later that evening and that, B) he would be holding an alternate debate at around 9:00 P.M. at a venue his campaign quickly rented a block or two away from the televised puppet show. Gravel stated that if things were "sliced and diced" nicely, recalling that videos on the internet are not scheduled for one particular time only, it could be passed on for months perhaps, eventually equaling or even surpassing the coverage of the other candidates. I liked the way he appeared to be thinking at the time, since I had been trying to get a similar message through to third party candidates who were marginalized by the media for years, stating that since the differences between them and the mainstream puppets was nothing less than life and liberty over misery, oppression and mass murder, it was hardly a tough decision for one presented with some evidence.

So, in spite of planning on writing the night through, and having slept during the day so I'd be able to do just that, it was going to be quite a challenge to make it from southern Virginia to Philadelphia by 9:00 PM that night. As it turns out I got there about a half hour late or so, mainly because there was no westbound entrance for the street I was to get off at to make it to the venue. Thus I had to go ahead and backtrack through neighborhoods until I got back to the short highway leading into the heart of Philadelphia where hopefully I'd find out where I was supposed to be. As I got closer to the puppet show, helicopters could be heard overhead and police cars seemed to be everywhere, yet I somehow managed to find a place to park that was in easy walking distance to Mike Gravel's event, though it was quite close to the media's circus event of unqualified sellouts discussing mostly non-issues.

Gravel, on the other hand, was a breath of fresh air, it seemed. I felt it had been well worth the struggle to get there and not having as much sleep as I had wanted. Two weeks later, I would end up driving from our home in Southside, Virginia all the way to Las Vegas to cover yet another alternate debate Mike Gravel was having, this time being censored by CNN. At that time I was able to speak to one of his assistants about scheduling an interview with the former U.S. Senator who had released the *Pentagon Papers* in the early 1970s, at his office back in Arlington, Virginia, about a four hour ride from our home. I ended up having my sit-down, jacket-and-tie interview with this American and International hero at his office on December 19, 2007, having written up the questions I wanted to ask shortly after returning from Vegas. By early February I had a two-part interview posted at, http://youtube.com, which I felt could very well change the outcome of the upcoming election if only enough people saw them, thought things through, and did what they could to bring this information to others.

That didn't happen. Gravel ended up joining the Libertarian Party but didn't end up getting their nomination, so he was out of the race.

This book brings several people's testimonies together to demonstrate how the media are giving us the shaft. It's not just Ken's opinion, it's what is, and one can research enough of this for her or himself to verify that my assertion - that the media are deliberately censoring our major elections and that stated censoring directly results in our ignorant funding of mass human suffering and misery with our tax dollars - is absolutely true. It's not just an opinion, it's a fact. This is what they do. Think back to the presidential debates... were all six candidates who made it on enough ballots to win allowed to participate? Is this democracy? Who eliminated the other candidates?

Since trying daily to get people to wake up about their media-misguided elections since 2000, my most valuable skill is likely in effectively communicating the hidden status quo, in regard to less than two handful's of profound concerns affecting everyone's lives that a disproportionate few who own and operate the mainstream media have been purposefully distorting and/or omitting entirely, thus painting an entirely different view of reality than what is. How could they do that, one might ask? A lot of it has to do with too many people "allowing" others to do their thinking for them.

Chapter 16

The Military-Industrial-Media Complex

"In the councils of government, we must guard against the acquisition of unwarranted influence, whether sought or unsought, by the military-industrial complex."

- President Dwight D. Eisenhower, January 1961

Above: Former U.S. Senator & 2007-2008 Democratic presidential candidate, Mike Gravel

Mike Gravel Interview – December 19, 2007:

Dr. Ken Hildebrandt: Hi, I'm Dr. Ken Hildebrandt from MajorMediaBypass.com. We're here today with Senator Mike Gravel, who's a presidential candidate who's been greatly marginalized by the mainstream media, and I'd like to ask Senator Gravel a few questions.

The world's most quoted living author, your friend Professor Noam Chomsky of MIT, has stated that we live in a highly indoctrinated society where elementary truths are easily buried. He has also stated that *"Education is a system of imposed ignorance."* That being said, can you please give those who either read or watch this interview a truncated synopsis of what you're likely most famous and respected for, that being for releasing the *Pentagon Papers* in the early 1970s during the Vietnam war when you were a U.S. Senator?

Senator Gravel: It certainly would be that, because what was involved was so fundamental to a democracy. In a democracy the people must know what is going on in government, otherwise they can't respond to what the government is doing.

When I released the *Pentagon Papers*, I really thought I had a good chance of going to prison. And so I was frightened. But I felt it was so, so vital to the... to our society for the people to be informed. And, I had been... when I was 23 years old I was a Top Secret Control Officer. I had been in Intelligence, and so I knew how ridiculous it was to... to classify these documents, which are nothing but documents about the history of how we got involved, how three successive presidential administrations had lied to the American people to get us involved in the swamp of Vietnam that cost 3-million Southeast Asian lives, that cost 58-thousand American lives - all of these lies in a Democracy. That had to be overcome and I was prepared to put my career on the line to try to overcome that. I did it, I survived. And of course, as Chomsky has pointed out, that is one of the most significant things of my career.

Ken: As I understand it, others were asked to do the same thing but only you had the courage to take on this task, is that correct?

Senator Gravel: Yes it is. The papers were offered to George McGovern, Gaylord Nelson, Pete McClousky, Bill Fulbright, and for various and sundry reasons, reasons that they chose not to accept the papers or to release them.

Ken: You were a Senator, U.S. Senator, between what years?

Senator Gravel: 1969 and '81. I served when Richard Nixon was elected. I served with Gerald Ford and with Jimmy Carter.

Ken: Senator Gravel, you've stated that General Electric kept you out of the MSNBC debates, sponsored Democratic debates, held in Philadelphia on October 30. How did you come about knowing these were the people censoring you and not MSNBC?

Senator Gravel: First off, because I had been repeatedly talking about the military-industrial complex, and of course they are one of the largest military contractors in the United States. And had been talking about the whole nuclear issue and they're the proliferators of the world.

...they gave away their role by the simple fact that I first pointed out to Hillary that I was ashamed of her because of the way she voted on the Iran resolution, Lieberman II resolution, and it was shortly after that, that they cut me out. Now, CNN had tried to cut me out earlier and did not succeed. And so it was as a result of what I attribute... Howard Dean (see hilarious photo below of the infamous "Dean Scream," one of the few pictures in this book that is not mine, and one that still makes me crack up every time I see it to this day) and the Democratic Party in cahoots with NBC and GE, where they made a decision that they had had enough, that they've really got to silence me.

A friend of mine in India wrote an e-mail to GE complaining about the fact that I was cut out. They responded to him saying, and this was the PR person for GE. What they should have done, is they should have referred him to NBC or MSNBC, but no, the PR person from GE responded to his e-mail saying that *I did not qualify by their criteria*... That was the final nail in their coffin with respect to their getting involved in censoring a presidential candidate.

So here you have a defense contractor, a private corporation, making a decision as to who is going to... whose voice is going to be heard in the course of a presidential campaign. And of course they own... not only do they own NBC and MSNBC and Tele Mundo and several other communications companies, because they own these, so they can control the information and so they're one of... one of the five major corporations that control the communications, the information that Americans receive about how their society, how their government is working in, quote, "a free society."

Ken: The United States now houses a quarter of the world's prisoners, more than China, more than Russia, Iran, Syria and so forth. Our prison population has gone from an estimated 500,000 inmates when you left office as a U.S. Senator in 1981 to over 2.3-million people today. Most of these prisoners have harmed no one, yet their incarceration not only harms them, but also their families and loved ones. Plus, by default, if our law enforcement officers are busy chasing and apprehending non-criminals a great deal of that time, by simple deductive reasoning we are assured that this waste of resources is leaving that many more real criminals, such as murderers, child abusers, rapists and thieves and so forth at large. What is your position on this undeclared yet very real civil Drug War that has brought forth unspeakable suffering to millions, including children, while leaving the general population more susceptible to real criminals as a result?

Senator Gravel: What you've just recited, these statistics are appalling and shameful and it's shameful for the United States of America to be in this position. To my knowledge I'm the only presidential candidate that has stepped forward and said that we have to end the "War on Drugs." The war itself, not the addiction problem... that's a public health problem.

The war itself has ravaged our inner cities and I've taken the position that if I become President of The United States I will seek legislation to be able to pardon everybody - everybody - who's been convicted of a crime involving marijuana. Marijuana is not a gateway drug. Marijuana is not addictive. Marijuana should not be... have a legal problem. You should be able to buy marijuana at the liquor store just like you buy alcohol. It's not nearly as addictive as alcohol is. And so anybody that's been convicted of a marijuana infraction in the law should be pardoned immediately and gotten out of jail. That would go a long way, a long way, to addressing this problem of incarceration that we have. And it's bankrupting the nation, morally, spiritually... ripping our families apart. You can't believe the damage we're doing to individuals who come out as felons, and have their civil rights impaired, have their whole lives ruined as a result of this.

Ken: We had Thanksgiving with a family... it was the guy's, the son, it was his first Thanksgiving in six years that he's had with his family, and he told me unspeakable horrors of hearing young 18, 19 year old kids screaming as they were being raped, you know the new initiates, and really horrible things and he had to fight for his... you know, to defend himself. It was really horrible conditions.

Senator Gravel: (shaking his head and shrugging his shoulders in astonishment and disgust)

Whew... it's a training-ground for felons, making felons. They weren't felons when they went in but they were made into felons.

Ken: Alright, last question. Do you believe that you can win the presidency if A) enough caring people give what they can give and B) if enough put forth the effort to inform others by using the internet to spread information about your campaign in spite of the elite-owned-and-operated main stream media censoring you?

Senator Gravel: One of the things that I don't understand, and I don't think anybody else does, is what is really going on in this election.

First off, we don't know the impact of these unbelievable sums of money that Obama and Hillary are raising. You know, we all know that money is the corrupting agent of politics and yet mainstream media has anointed those who should be president because they've raised the most money. Well, that must mean that they're the most corrupt, because they've raised the most money.

Will I get elected? All I know is that on the internet I'm very, very highly thought of. Will the American people be able to push aside the control of the media to make a decision on a person who's not known, who calculatingly the American media shuns aside? I don't know. All I know is that in the two or three blind polls that have been taken, I come out way, way ahead of everybody else. What it means is that if my particular positions are identical to what the American people want to see enacted into law... Now, if my positions are what the American people want, then obviously there's a dislocation between what the people know of my positions and me. And so, if that can be overcome, I'd become President of the United States.

Can that be overcome? I don't know. All I know is that there's a year between now and the election and will that be overcome during that period of time? I don't know. I think the media's gone crazy over what's happening in Iowa and New Hampshire and all the others and all the money being spent and all the charges. This is all going to settle down and then the American people are going to begin to focus on what's been happening. And we may be headed for a perfect storm, a war, the economy in the tubes and the people totally dissatisfied with the Democratic Party which now controls the Congress, total dissatisfaction with the Republican Party... All of this is coming to bear on a decision by the American people in '08.

'08 may be the tipping-point for the future of this country. I think it will be. And will the American people step forward and choose a person who is "not politics as usual," who is a person who wants to empower you, *you* to be able to make laws and decide the policy and decisions? That's the position I have and will that permit me to become President of the United States? I want to be not your Commander in Chief, not your President. I want to be your legislative leader. You're the ones that are going to be able to enact the laws that are going to affect your future.

Ken: Do you want to explain a little about your National Initiative, just because I didn't cover that?

Senator Gravel: Well, what... What I'm talking about when I talk about the lawmaking... I drafted legislation called the National Initiative. It sets up the procedures. It's a Constitutional Amendment, and it has procedures that the American people can vote for. It'll take 60-million Americans to enact it into law. It goes entirely around the government, and so when roughly around 60-million Americans have voted for this, it becomes the law of the land and that means that Americans will be able to enact and vote on laws in every government jurisdiction in the United States.

This is very significant. This is changing the paradigm of human governance. We do that here in the United States, it will go around the world like wildfire. And it will mean... because I have unreserved faith in the majority of the people to make a better decision than their elected leaders who are a very distinct minority. We are ruled by a minority in our society and that's what has to change, and what can change it is going to be the National Initiative for Democracy.

Ken: Great. Thank you very much, Senator.

Senator Gravel: Thank you for having me. OK!

Ken: All right.

After our interview was over, Senator Gravel, who had been suffering with a cold and thus had already left as I was packing up my camera equipment and so forth, one of his campaign workers brought my attention to a video then posted at, **http://youtube.com**, in which someone had run into Howard Dean as he was headed toward the Democratic debate and was able to video his question to Dr. Dean about Mike Gravel's exclusion from the night's event. As I recall, Dr. Dean indicated that although others had eliminated Gravel from the debate, he and others within the Democratic Party supported them in regard to their censorship of Gravel.

I was later told by someone else involved with the campaign that the video had been later taken down because it had been entered in a contest. I'm wondering what contest was more important than arguably the very fate of our world. These elections result in life and death for many, and major influence over everyone's lives. Dr. Dean, as a physician, is certainly aware all options need to be on the table before making life and death decisions, not just on an individual basis but likewise for the masses. Though Stalin stated *"A single death is a tragedy, a million deaths is a statistic,"* that's only because of far too many people not taking life seriously at the grandest of levels. Surely we cannot evolve as a species with such primitive behavior as the norm, as it is.

Below is an official statement that Professor Noam Chomsky e-mailed me regarding Mike Gravel's campaign on January 05, 2008:

"Alone among members of Congress, Senator Mike Gravel had the courage to take a stand that not only helped bring the atrocious Indochina wars to an end, but also made a great contribution to breaking the wall of secrecy that governments erect to protect themselves from their own citizens. I am of course referring to his release of the Pentagon Papers, properly called 'the Gravel edition,' which provided the public with a unique opportunity to become educated about affairs of state.

In the years since, Gravel has continued to show the same moral integrity and courage, particularly with regard to war and aggression, the severe threat of nuclear war, the destructive impact of the military-industrial complex on American democracy, and the programs of aggressive militarism that have led even Europeans to rank the U.S. as the greatest threat to world peace, far above Russia, China, Iran, North Korea, or other states assigned this role in the U.S. doctrinal system. It may be that these consistent and honorable commitments are responsible for his being largely excluded from the media, even from presidential debates. And the same integrity and courage should be an inspiration for people who care about their country, the fate of its people, and its role in the world."

– Noam Chomsky

Chapter 17

On the Eve of the 2008 New Hampshire Primary with Professor Noam Chomsky

"However the media, if they were serving a public function, would not choose to reflect such, to adopt such criterion, no, they would give fair opening to anyone who's running in the race."

- Noam Chomsky

Above: Professor Noam Chomsky at the conclusion of his one-question interview with Dr. Ken Hildebrandt, this time representing, **http://overcomethemedia.com** (I must've had 100 different websites since 2001, always in pursuit of the perfect name. This was one of the ones I no longer use but put a bit of energy into at one time....)

 January 08, 2008, the eve of the New Hampshire Democratic and Republican Primaries.

SINCE I WAS IN THE AREA FOR THE NEW HAMPSHIRE PRIMARY, Noam Chomsky's assistant, Bev Stohl, was kind enough to squeeze me in to see Noam for 15 minutes between his appointments on January 08, 2008. I took but a few moments to video but one question of Noam as per below:

Dr. Ken Hildebrandt: Hi, I'm Dr. Ken Hildebrandt of OvercomeTheMedia.com, [I had just purchased that web site name two or three days before, though my wife Elaine found an e-mail in which Professor Chomsky gave me the thumbs-up for the name back in 2005. For whatever reason, I never bought it until 2008.] We're here with Professor Noam Chomsky of MIT, the world's most quoted living author, and I'd like to ask Noam a question. Here we are on the day of the New Hampshire primary and once again more reasonable candidates, arguably more reasonable candidates, such as Mike Gravel, Ron Paul and Dennis Kucinich, have been greatly marginalized by the major media, even to a point of eliminating them from public debates. Have you any thoughts regarding this?

Professor Noam Chomsky: What the media are doing is, they have a criterion, like it or not. The criterion is polling data which in turn reflects mostly the amount of money you've picked up, which means usually the level of corporate support, and somebody like Mike Gravel is not going to accumulate that kind of financing. However the media, if they were serving a public function would not choose to reflect such, to adopt such criterion, no, they would give fair opening to anyone who's running in the race.

Ken: Very good. Thanks.

Professor Noam Chomsky: OK

Chapter 18

2010 Skype interview with California Governor Candidate, Laura Wells

"They started it in 1919 when the farmers got mad in North Dakota. They got mad at the outside bankers. They, the farmers, were doing all the work and the outside bankers were making all the money which is just what's happening right now. And so now, years and years later North Dakota has a budget surplus and every other state has a budget deficit."

- Laura Wells

Video of the following transcript is available at Ken's YouTube site. It's entitled "Party on the Titanic" and is at
https://www.youtube.com/watch?v=elNdX5t5Ri8

Ken: Greetings. I'm Dr. Ken Hildebrandt. We're here with 2010 California governor candidate Laura Wells who was actually arrested for simply trying to sit in and watch a debate that she should have been a part of. And, let's not forget that we've had two presidents in recent history, Reagan and Bush, Bush II, who were governors before they ended up being President of the United States so how democracy unfolds in the state of California could arguably end up having an impact on our world and certainly our nation.

So tell us Laura, what happened on October 12, 2010.

Laura Wells: Well, October 12 there was a gubernatorial race in… and it was a debate in San Rafel which is just north of San Francisco. And so the two, the only two candidates out of the six candidates that were invited to the debate were the Democrats and the Republicans which I started to call the Titanics because they're big they seem unsinkable but boy, we better hope for the rest of us that they are sinkable and, I know they are. So, as a Green Party candidate I of course was not to be included in the debate but we were there, outside and, if you're an individual in the US, what passes for free speech is a barricaded zone, that's where you can be. Corporations can give all the money they want to elections but they're, you know, they're corporate persons. Real persons don't have the same where-with-all.

So, I was there and some reporters were talking to me and somebody came up and said, "You know you should be in the room at least and I have an extra ticket. As a matter of fact I have two extra tickets. You and your friend can go in." So, the two of us had our tickets, the guard passed us through, we were standing on the staircase, the stairway outside the building where the debate was to be held when suddenly security guards came up and surrounded me, not my friend, they left her completely alone and said, "You don't belong here. That's not your ticket. You're not supposed to be here." And I just thought, you know what, I am supposed to be here. There is no, they said, "You aren't supposed to be here, you aren't supposed to be here." That was just dead wrong. And so I stayed and they ended up doing a citizen's arrest of me, took me to the

San Rafel police, put me in metal handcuffs in the back of the squad car. The whole thing about dipping the head and everything to get this dangerous person outside of being in the audience of the debate. So that's what happened. Then they wrote up the citation, which is perfect, trespassing at a private party. Yes, the party on the Titanic. And set, coincidentally, the court date for November 2nd, Election Day.

So, that was the story.

Ken: Unbelievable! Tell us a couple things, or a few things, that weren't heard because you weren't in there. I'd like to start off tying two subjects together because they are kind of intertwined and that's cannabis and hemp.

Hemp seed oil, or hemp, was actually described in a February 1938 issue of *Popular Mechanics* as a billion dollar crop. They usually didn't talk billions back in those days. And it's also only recently been stated that it can supply nearly all of our energy needs. And yet it's illegal. And then we look at cannabis, which accounts for some 800,000 arrests every year in the United States, which coincidentally is the same, or near the same number of kids who go missing.* So obviously if our resources are being tied up in one area, then those kids aren't being found. And I mean our priorities are totally messed up. But anyway, what is your take on both cannabis and hemp?

* http://www.missingkids.com/KeyFacts - CORRECTION: Over 400,000 children go missing, not over 800,000

Laura Wells: Well there was a proposition on the ballot in California in November and so it's making headway and sooner or later, it will be, it was about the legalization of marijuana and, so what, sooner or later it will get legalized. Now what would be the benefits of that, and I had a BFO, a Blinding Flash of the Obvious a few years back where I realized that the powers that be had to come down that strong on marijuana because you could grow it in your backyard and it could be entirely outside of the consumer/capitalists kind of thing and, industrial hemp would be a source of energy... I mean basically, it grows like a weed. And, it could take the pressure off our forests, you could make so many things out of industrialized hemp, industrial hemp. It's ridiculous and you know, a sign of the priorities as you were saying that it's not legal. But I think its day is coming.

Ken: Well, I think if the Green Party candidates get in there hopefully it will happen that much sooner because I mean even with this last proposition in California how many people said, "Look, you know we're having x amount of kids who are going missing who we're not finding because we're going after this other..." You know they just don't seem to make it real enough and give it that punch. You know, that's the way I see it anyway.

Laura Wells: ...Yeah...

Ken: Moving right along, what about the other big issue that you brought up was that North Dakota has its own bank, its own state bank and they're the only state who's not in the red right now. Can you tell us more about that whole issue?

Laura Wells: Right. They started it in 1919 when the farmers got mad in North Dakota. They got mad at the outside bankers. They, the farmers, were doing all the work and the outside bankers were making all the money which is just what's happening right now. And so now, years and years later North Dakota has a budget surplus and every other state has a budget deficit.

So, what would happen..., and one of the good things about individual, one of the Green Party principals is that the global work and the personal work, work together. And people are individually taking their money out of those huge banks and putting them into credit unions and private banks. And that, if we had a state bank in California, would be what the state bank would partner with, the local banks, the credit unions, you know the small, when I said the private banks, I mean the local private banks and, make better loans, with lower interest to homeowners as well as small business owners as well as students and what interest was charged would come back, fold back into investing in California, not Wall Street or Federal Reserve and all of that. We would be, being the eighth largest economy in the world, California, bigger than most other countries, we would have like the equivalent of a central bank. That's what you have. You take control of your own money supply.

Ken: Wow, that's something, the eighth largest economy in the world. I don't think very many people know that either. You know that's a very important point. And as Chomsky has brought out that we live entangled in webs of endless deceit in a highly indoctrinated society where elementary truths are easily buried. I hope that at the height of the Information Age we can start bringing the truths about our elections out to the people, to enough people, where we bypass the media and start voting for more reasonable candidates.

Ken: Thank you Laura for being here with us.

Laura Wells: Thank you Ken.

Ken: …and good luck in the future for all of us.

Chapter 19

2012 Interview with Highly Censored Presidential Candidate, Jill Stein, M.D.

"But for me, as a medical doctor, the most compelling reason to legalize marijuana is a health reason. And that is because marijuana is a dangerous drug because it's illegal. It's not illegal because it's dangerous. And there's enormous danger and hazard that attaches to it because it is illegal."

- Presidential candidate Dr. Jill Stein

Video of transcription below available at Ken's YouTube site,
http://youtube.com/drkenhildebrandt - **https://www.youtube.com/watch?v=Gm7SUERLKk0**

Ken: Today we're here with Dr. Jill Stein, who is a presidential candidate who has made it on the ballot on how many states so far for the Green Party?

Dr. Jill Stein: 21 and counting.

Ken: Right.

Jill Stein: Hopefully up to 42, 46 maybe even 48.

Ken: Now you've won every primary so far, right?

Jill Stein: Exactly, by landslide margins I'm glad to say.

Ken: I'd like to talk to you about a few issues. I've been basically researching this since 2000, but not only presidential elections, but congressional elections and senatorial elections and gubernatorial elections, and I've seen candidate exclusion that's really ah, I've found quite disheartening even at sometimes by arrest if necessary... So, how many state ballots are you shooting for and do you think you have a chance to get into those debates, I mean would you like to push for?

Jill Stein: Yeah, so in terms of state ballot lines, we're shooting for as many as we can get, we hope we'll get 42 maybe 46 or maybe even 48. And, you know it is I think the strength of the Green Party and a real tribute to the party that we have organizations all over the country that are invested in our democracy and are determined that ordinary people will have a voice in this election. That's what it comes down to because the other candidates on the ballot are all going to be corporate powered and Wall Street powered and it means more of the same. So, you know the Green Party is the one survivor that has survived this incredible era of political repression where in so many ways the powers that be suppress the voice, not just of candidates but of ordinary members of society, ordinary Americans who need health care as a human right, who need education as a human right, who need their housing, who, you know, who need a job with decent wages, you know. This is why we fight these battles and that's what the Green Party's about. I'm glad to say we have in just about all states, we now have ballot drives going on so I'm very hopeful that we will get on the ballot in most states.

Ken: Last time around Ralph Nader, only Oklahomans didn't, they were the only ones who didn't have the choice of voting for him as write-in or somehow so let's hope you get on enough. Basically, like I've said, I've seen this kind of censorship over the years so I just want to quickly, I know you're in a hurry, so let's touch on three issues. One of which came up today actually and that was about reverting the tax rate from 35% for the top 1% of income earners on their highest income to 39.6%, which it was before Bush had lowered them. Now, that rate was 91% in the year 1960. What is your position on this?

Jill Stein: We need to do the numbers. That alone is not going to do it. I mean that's a step in the right direction but look, the top 1% is making out like bandits here. You know they tripled over the last couple decades, they actually tripled their share of income that went from like 9% up till like 24% of income all going to just the top 1% and that's just income. Cause if you look at income over time that becomes wealth. The top 1% has the wealth of 90% of the population. One has what 90 have!

That's just not fair and that's not sustainable and that's the direction we're proceeding in whole hog. So, a number of steps need to be taken to give ordinary working people a fair shake. Why should there be this, this massive gushing upward, it's not a trickle down of wealth it's a massive gushing upwards of wealth taking from ordinary working people who are basically subsidizing the very very rich to get very very richer.

So, we need to connect it. I'd like to see what the numbers are going to 39% from 35. That's great but we need to tax those at the top more. We need to have a truly progressive income tax so that millionaires are paying more than quarter millionaires and billionaires are paying more than millionaires. And besides, I should make one other point. The real income at the top is coming from capital gains. It's not coming from wages. So there's no way that we're going to fix this without addressing the need to treat capital gains like income. Once you start doing that, cause right now capital gains has been whittled and whittled away. It used to be 40%, it's now down to what, 15%. So, that needs to be brought up at least to the level of wages. And that's, you know that's a start.

We need a Wall Street transaction tax so that we don't have this reckless waste, fraud and abuse on Wall Street and that will go a long way to put money back into the pockets of ordinary people.

Ken: That rate had been as high as 94% under Eisenhower and Kennedy hacked it to 70 and then Reagan took it to 28 and then finally they realized they had, actually it was senior Bush who upped it back to 39.6*, and it's really incredible that they get away with this. OK. So, two more quickly; cannabis, I remember asking Ralph Nader about this in 2004. I mean it's you know, arguably, it could actually decrease a lot of our reliance on foreign fuel, if not all. I mean some people have said all. Those, I guess there's probably further studies that need to be done. But even Ralph had admitted to me that it would, you know, give us billions and billions of dollars of increased income which would be a nice shot in the arm for all the other uses it has also. So, what's your position on hemp?

* Correction: Sr. Bush raised it to 31% from Reagan's 28. Clinton raised it to 39.6%.

Jill Stein: I agree with all of what you've said, that there's enormous potential in hemp for a number of industries. It really is a jobs growth industry in many ways, food particularly, there's (sic) some very important nutrients in hemp. Food, fiber and potentially bio-fuels although there are some issues there about food supplies and so on. So, but the potential is there.

Ken: But less from what I understand because it's so much more efficient as far as the bio-mass.

Jill Stein: That may be, you may be absolutely right, and it is something that we should, you know that should be a priority to be looking, you know to be exploring right now and to be doing research on that. But for me, as a medical doctor, the most compelling reason to legalize marijuana is a health reason. And that is because marijuana is a dangerous drug because it's illegal. It's not illegal because it's dangerous. And there's enormous danger and hazard that attaches to it because it is illegal. Like the incredible culture of violence that surrounded alcohol when alcohol was under prohibition and it was illegal.

Ken: And the prison-industrial complex.

Jill Stein: Oh yes.

Ken: I mean people are subjected to horrors.

Jill: Exactly.

Ken: Actually former Senator Mike Gravel said about this is that go in you know not really criminals but they come out hardened criminals. They have to fight to survive. It's awful. You know Senator Webb is on his exit now but even he said, he went to Japan and there wasn't the violence between the prisoners, nor between the prisoners and the guards like we see here. And yet you know rapes are joked about on situation comedies and so forth. It's not funny I mean there's [sic] over 800,000 arrests each year for cannabis, and that's roughly the same amount of kids that go missing each year (CORRECTION: half that number of children go missing each year). I'd say that by simple deductive reasoning you'd be finding more of these kids who are (missing).

Jill Stein: Yeah, absolutely.

Ken: It's really inefficient. I was a chiropractic physician. I just know from a physician's standpoint this is just insanity.

Jill Stein: It absolutely is and it's extremely, you know, not only the violence surrounding the criminal drug culture and you actually pull the rug out from under that by legalizing marijuana because marijuana is the work horse of the whole drug industry so just by legalizing that one drug you basically take the revenues out of the entire criminal drug culture. Not entirely but in large measure enough to really, you know, help slow it down in a big way. But in addition to the violence there's a whole additional issue of effectively the racist criminal justice system. I should say the criminal injustice system and the way that this war is used to fill our jails with African-Americans, Latinos and people of color* in general.

* I don't understand this "people of color" thing. I thought we got away from "colored people" on purpose for obvious reasons. I've yet to meet a colorless person in my life. Have you? It's a scientific fact that we all have a common ancestor out of Africa who was dark skinned, therefore we're all related and are thus "families apart" as Jimi Hendrix sang in *Machine Gun* in the late 60s and early 70s. He even sang it on *The Dick Cavett Show* and sat next to none other than *Father Knows Best*'s Robert Young at the height of the Vietnam War. Can you picture that today? I just can't see someone getting up and singing an anti-war song, two actually, on any major program today, with someone akin to Robert Young politely listening and then sitting next to the artist who sang it. Can you?

This is just, this is devastating on a human rights basis, it's devastating to communities of color, where, you know, just an outrageous number, I think it's one out of every three African-American men is either in jail, on probation or on parole. So, this has been absolutely devastating to an entire community. And the entire war on drugs has been used in a very racist manner and for that reason as well needs to be ended by legalizing, regulating and taxing marijuana. Nobody out on the street is checking the ID of your kid to make sure that they are old enough to be purchasing marijuana on the street. However in a legalized, through legalized and regulated use, you know, uses by minors will be a thing of the past.* So, there are many, you know, there are just many things to be gained by legalizing and regulating marijuana. Thank you. I'm going to have to run. Thank you so much.

* I disagree, not that it matters as much as those who want it illegal claim, for it certainly won't harm people anywhere near as much as violent incarcerations.

Ken was recruited by Carey Campbell of the Independent Green Party of Virginia (below) to run for congress himself immediately following the previous interview with Dr. Stein.

Conclusion of Part I, pretty much as it appeared just prior to Election 2008, yet still very much applicable today as it was then

Bringing Information to Others

"*Pass it on, Pass it on to the young and old.*"

- Jimi Hendrix

THINK ABOUT IT: We're having a civil and international war of no practical value other than serving the ultra-wealthy; thus tax-paying citizens of the United States of America are funding actual mass human suffering and misery, especially of children, imposed upon innocent people both within and beyond our borders, yet this reality is distorted by the media as being something that's actually esteemed as being legitimate and in the public's best interests. I am of course referring to the Drug War also known as, the War on Drugs which is really a "*War against innocent people's right to '...Life, Liberty and the pursuit of Happiness,' as well as the loved one's of same, and everyone else by default, by deflecting our law enforcement personnel against real criminals, leaving more at large amongst us.*" Plus, we're getting royally scammed in regard to the paying of taxes, subsidizing those who've need of nothing, while royally shafting those who do.

"*The most important thing for me and for you is to think about the consequences of **your** actions. What can **you** effect? These are the things to keep in mind. These are not just academic exercises. We're not analyzing the media on Mars or in the eighteenth century or something like that. We're dealing with real human beings who are suffering and dying and being tortured and starving because of policies that we are involved in.*"

- Noam Chomsky

If we were to have stonings, would people object to purchasing the stones? If people had a neighborhood meeting, would most object to far less than one percent hogging the pie? Are we not all funding the caging of our own away from their families, oftentimes under extremely violent and torturous conditions *en masse* for no legitimate reason or not? Are these real people or not? Do our tax dollars directly fund this horror or not?

None of this is rocket science. How can we justify putting someone in a cage for what they choose to do with their life when we're supposed to live in the Land of the Free, especially when substances like alcohol, which make one suffer losses of inhibitions and muscle control, and nicotine, which is arguably one of, if not the most addicting substance known to humankind, are perfectly legal and their consumption is even encouraged, especially in relation to alcohol? These substances together account for hundreds of thousands of horrible U.S. deaths per year, yet instead of trying to lessen these numbers we instead spend billions inflicting pain on innocent people.

Is this not shameful beyond words? Is this not the height of the Information Age, when we can get any information we want practically in seconds, including information about presidential, senatorial, congressional and gubernatorial candidates? So then why do we continue to vote for people whose policies are endangering all humankind just to benefit a disproportionate minority of inhumane compassionless people who've need of nothing and want of much?

They didn't have the internet and free elections in Hume's day.* We do. What's our excuse for losing to a disproportionate minority of horrible people at such a grand expense to all? Isn't that something to think about? Is it not time we take control of our situation?

"Nothing appears more surprising to those who consider human affairs with a philosophical eye, than the easiness with which the many are governed by the few."

- David Hume

Ignorance is our block. Knowledge is our answer. Please tell others about what's going on. We're all in this together. If enough try to lift the log that needs lifting we'll do it, thereby taking a major step toward the preservation and advancement of humankind, or humans will be no longer, in a very short time. That's what the evidence clearly shows. It's up to us to inform or die as a species, whilst torturing our own along the way, too, of course. Will a disproportionate few continue to misguide most at the likely expense of survival as we know it, or not?

"Surely we have a responsibility to leave for future generations a planet that is healthy (and) inhabitable by all species."

- David Attenborough

"We gotta stand side by side. We gotta stand together and organize."

- Jimi Hendrix

"But real success can only come if there's a change in our societies, in our economics, and in our politics."

- David Attenborough

A disproportionate few are misguiding most at the very risk of the continued survival of our species within this century. That's been established. Is it not time to "*...bring it to others?*" Cannot the people examine the candidates' platforms and tell others about how insane it is to vote according to murderous elite's fictionalized reality? Expecting the media, i.e., the enemy, to do this for us is the height of folly, is it not? Are they not the very censors whose censorship knowingly results in mass suffering, misery and death, and that's the very reason they censor the more reasonable candidates? Do murderers rehabilitate on their own? Why would you trust a proven mass murderer, or sponsor of same? Can you not examine the candidates' platforms and see for yourself where they stand, whether for more murderers, pedophiles, rapists and thieves or not, torturing innocent people or not, and then vote your conscience?

The oppressed outnumber the oppressors by far, as brought up by Hume centuries ago, and your sharing with others some basics the media hide might be the key to success in a bout we don't know which way is going to go. You can tell as many people as you want what's going on and request they do likewise, and you could very well be the determining key as to whether human beings make it on this planet or not. Can either of us truthfully claim otherwise? Is it any exaggeration the very survival of humankind is at stake?*

* Please recall the study submitted to the U.N. in 2002 cited in the Introduction and in several other places in this manuscript, *Planet's Future At Stake, U.N. Report Says,* as reported in the *Toronto Star,* though originating from London and available now at, **http://www.roadtopeace.org/research.php?itemid=437,** a little more than halfway down the page.

"I think one should be very optimistic... The large majority of the population already agrees with the things activists are committed to. All we have to do is organize people who are convinced."

- Professor Noam Chomsky

"What can be done? Here are a few thoughts. The time has come to stop locking up people for mere possession and use of marijuana."

- US Senator Jim Webb from, *A TIME TO FIGHT,* Chapter 13: *A CRIMINAL INJUSTICE,* page 229

(Note: If Barack Obama really wanted national change wouldn't he have picked someone more like Webb over someone responsible for helping to establish national minimum sentencing guidelines who'd been in DC for decades?)

WE'RE ALL IN THIS TOGETHER, and the only way things will get better is if we bring to others some of what the media hide, and vote accordingly. The media sure won't do it for us. I'd rather vote for someone with a more reasonable platform than an outwardly seemingly reasonable person who supports mass suffering, misery, death and inefficiency, who advertised more, and I wouldn't take any of the enemy's polls seriously either. Either we'll be casting our votes for more of the same, as per the normal self-destructive way, or we'll finally vote in favor of ourselves and others. I'd rather try than not try, and fight than not fight, and work than not work. If enough others make an attempt we'll all reach our goal; otherwise we won't. How can anyone just take it without a struggle once they know?

Will we remain entangled in webs of "endless deceit," or will enough tell others how the media have been fictionalizing reality at the expense of humankind?

Should we not at least try to overcome the media who are destroying all of us? That's for each to decide for oneself, taking into account that this simplistic scam comes at children's expense primarily. What will you say to them if given the chance down the road when asked if you'd been informed? What if we only missed by a little?

I don't know which way the scale is going to tip. No one does. All I know is that if I try, it'll give us that much more of a chance, the same as if you try it'll likewise give us that much more of a chance. We are all in this together, and only with a cooperative effort will any of us get anywhere.

Apollo astronaut Dr. Edgar Mitchell (pictured below) summed up where we humans stand on April 19, 2008. *"We're at a tipping point..., and it's not clear which way it's going to go, but **WE** are the ones that are going to determine which way it's going to go, and it's up to us."*

"When the honestly deceived learn the truth, they either quit being deceived or quit being honest."

– Unknown

Part II –
Down the Rabbit Hole

Introduction

"When you're studying any matter, or considering any philosophy, ask yourself only, 'What are the facts and what is the truth that the facts bear out?' Never let yourself be diverted by either what you wish to believe or what you think would have beneficial social effects if it were believed. Look only and solely at 'What are the facts?'"

- Bertrand Russell, pictured below to the left of Professor Chomsky in this 2009 photo, a cropped version of which made it into MAD magazine's historic 500th issue as a celebrity snapshot

Part of what's here will be from the 2012 - 2016 elections, the latter of which is well underway as I write this introduction to Part II of II. Race, Israel/Palestine, and some key excerpts of a historic event held at the National Press Club in 2013 called *The Citizen Hearing* are also discussed. We will be opening up a few entirely new domains, domains that are related to concerns discussed in Part I, but buried a bit deeper in the mainstream media. I thought long and hard as to whether or not to include these domains, but since they are important aspects of reality I thought they ought to be known. Were I to die tomorrow, and none of us knows how much time she or he has, if I sustained any kind of consciousness afterwards I'd truly regret not bringing these matters to light, so here they are. They are important and no one else I know has linked these domains as has been done in this manuscript.

Remember that discussing things that don't "mimic conventional pieties," as Chomsky has brought out, leaves one open to seeming like one is from Neptune if stuck with concision without the time to enter the details as will be presented in forthcoming chapters. That stated they are 1) the "Secret Government" discussed by the well-respected journalist Bill Moyers in a documentary entitled *The Secret Government: The Constitution in Crisis,* first broadcast over a quarter of a century ago regarding The National Security Act of 1947, yet unknown by most today; 2) the intentional human manipulation of weather which has been well documented to have been going on for over half a century; and 3) the ongoing intelligent interactions with Earth human beings from either mechanical or biological systems from outside our planet since at least 1947. By the way I AM from Neptune. I was born at the former Fitkin Hospital in Neptune, New Jersey.

Chapter 1

Guns and children

"Our lack of vision is in the context of a media system that mostly keeps us in the dark."

- Norman Solomon

The following is from the 2014 Charlottesville, Virginia US Congressional Candidate forum posted at, **https://www.youtube.com/watch?v=Yh-yNdiS_7U&feature=youtu.be** at Ken's YouYube channel **http://youtube.com/drkenhildebrandt**

Moderator Sue Friedman: Candidate Hildebrandt.

Ken: OK, regarding guns, I feel there should be no restrictions and I think that the media, once again are taking something, I'm not saying it's not a problem but consider this. In the hour we've been sitting here a thousand children have died of neglect, just (gestures with hand as if sweeping them off a cliff as per the photo above) for what a fraction of the Pentagon budget could cover.*

Now do you think these people really care if they don't care about them?

That's a holocaust of children every 250 days because our priorities lie elsewhere. They're real. How would we explain this to a superior intelligence?

* See *Bad News When Madmen Lead The Blind* by Norman Solomon at **http://fair.org/media-beat-column/bad-news-when-madmen-lead-the-blind/**

NOTE: It's now about 700 children per hour who die of neglect, or around 17,000 per day.

Chapter 2

The Absurdity of Racism –From the Charlottesville, Virginia candidate forum

"*Evil men make me kill you. Evil men make you kill me. Evil men make me kill you even though we're only families apart.*"

- Jimi Hendrix, from his song *Machine Gun*

Above: Back, left to right: Sue Friedman, Lawrence Gaughan, Ken Hildebrandt, Paul Jones
Front, left to right, Dena Imlay, Susan Roberts

From the 2014 Charlottesville, Virginia US Congressional Candidate forum posted at Ken's YouYube channel specifically here **https://www.youtube.com/watch?v=sCbJghVFS9c&feature=youtu.be**

Moderator Sue Friedman: ...if you'd like a response about voter process and voter registration.

Ken: Well, I can just keep saying the same thing. Well, I do thank Lawrence Gaughan for being here, because last time the Democrat wouldn't face me and that's not right. We all need to be here. And I think that debate inclusion again, no matter what you do, no matter what you say, no matter how much you spend, all this, if you don't show up at the debates, debates mean everything. That's where you talk to the public and you get you get to banter the issues back and forth and you really get to look at things.

I do want to address the issue of change. I don't mean to belittle anyone but I think Obama gave it a bad name. He was in with the mainstream. There was only so far he could take things.

And it's not a race issue. We're all the same race, the human race. We all have a common ancestor who was dark skinned out of Africa. So, racism is just complete absurdity. OK. So, to like a person for race or not to like them for race is crazy.

But the change thing, I think Obama did damage to that and I'm sorry to see that he did because people say, 'Oh, well others have said this before.' No, he was always backed by the others and he never gave real reasons for change. I don't like the word belief.*

I once interviewed Hans Holzer who said, *"There are three dirty words in my vocabulary, belief, disbelief and supernatural."* I agree. I steer clear of discussing beliefs and things I don't understand. I discuss easily discovered reality that's hidden.

Chapter 3

Achieving Peace in Israel/Palestine

"And what we hear is what you said, 'Palestinians had this generous offer and they refused it.' No, it's the opposite."

– Noam Chomsky

Ken's interview with Professor Noam Chomsky on the day Obama was first inaugurated on January 20, 2009

Ken: Greetings. We're here with Professor Noam Chomsky of MIT, the most quoted livingauthor,andI'd like to ask Noam a couple questions about Gaza... Here we are, it's Inauguration Day, we have a new president in office and can you tell us about the chances for a reasonable settlement?

Noam: I mean it's pretty straight forward actually. For thirty years there's been an extremely broad international consensus on the shape of a peaceful settlement, a little variation here and there but the basic idea is, there is an international border called the Green Line pre-June '67 border. There should be a settlement on the international boarder with, the US formulation was minor and mutual modifications, so you straighten out some curved lines and that sort of thing, maybe a little exchange of territory, but that's the basis for the settlement. And it should be a peaceful settlement which recognizes the rights of all states in the region to live in peace and security within recognized borders it's the wording of the main UN resolution. Other things about it, you know, just, how do you work out Jerusalem, you know, ways about refugees and there's another range of things. OK, that's the international consensus.

It was brought to the UN Security Council in 1976 by the Arab states with the support of the PLO. The US vetoed it. They vetoed it again in 1980. I won't run through the whole record but it's a record of US international isolation to keep from implementing the international consensus. Now, the votes, the Security Council and the US just vetoes it. In the General Assembly the votes are you know like a hundred and fifty one to three. the United States, Israel and Marshal Islands or something like that. And it runs right up til today.

Ken: The Clinton offer, some people say, 'Well, the Palestinians should have just taken that.' Could you comment briefly on...

Noam: It's propaganda. Clinton, you see there were two Clinton offers. People only talk about the first one. The first one was at Camp David in 2000 when the US and Israel did, Israel never made an offer, but Clinton sort of made a vague offer. The Palestinians didn't accept it which is true. And Clinton recognized shortly after, that the offer was completely unacceptable to any Palestinians and he then proposed what are called his parameters, that's in December 2000. He said, 'OK, here are the parameters of a solution, a little vague, but more forthcoming than the Camp David offer which he knew that nobody could possibly accept. Well, he then made a speech in which he said both sides have accepted the parameters, both sides have reservations.

They met in Egypt, in Taba, in January of 2001, Clinton's last month and the two sides negotiated and they went way beyond the Camp David agreement. They came very close to a resolution and in their last press conference they said, 'If we had a few more days we could probably resolve everything roughly in terms of international consensus.' Well, Israel terminated the negotiations prematurely. That was the end of that. That's what actually happened. But that story is, and it's not, it's not really debated. I mean the facts are very clear. They're not challenged. But it just doesn't fit the party lines so it's suppressed. And what we hear is what you said, 'Palestinians had this generous offer and they refused it.' No, it's the opposite.

Ken: "Should've taken it." (I've heard countless times)

Noam: And, you know, you just can't talk about that. I mean it's like the references to Hamas. Every statement about Hamas in the press, you know, it's 'Iranian backed Hamas which is intent on destroying Israel.' Try to find a statement that says, 'Democratically elected Hamas which is calling, which has joined the international consensus on a two state settlement which the US and Israel are blocking.' You can't find that statement.

Ken's 2008 brief YouTube video regarding Israel/Palestine

Concerning the latest aggression of Israel into Gaza in which hundreds have been killed and thousands maimed, one should recall the words of the founder of Israel himself, David Ben-Gurion, who stated, "The has been anti-Semitism, the Nazis, Hitler, Auschwitz, but was that they're fault? They only see one thing; we have come here and stolen their country. Why should they accept that?"

Remember, these people moved in, in 1948 and went to Palestinian homes and said, 'You don't live here anymore.' It happened to a former roommate of mine's stepfather's family. Imagine owning your home and being told to move out, that you didn't live there anymore.

And the United States is funding no small part of the weaponry that they use against these innocent people and a peaceful settlement could easily be attained.*

*See previous video transcript of Ken's talk with Noam Chomsky from January 20, 2009

Chapter 4

Historic Mainstream Coverage of the Virginia, US Congress District 5, 2012 Election

"Like here, for example, is a collection of stuff from a friend of mine in Los Angeles, who does careful monitoring of the whole press in Los Angeles and a lot of the British press, which he reads, and does selections, so I don't have to read the movie reviews and the local gossip and all this kind of stuff, but I get the occasional nugget that sneaks through and that you find if you're carefully reviewing a wide range of press. Well, there are a fair number of us who do this and we exchange information."

- Noam Chomsky

In 2012 I was happy to receive what I considered fair coverage by WDBJ7's Chris Hurst and Joe Dashiell. At one time it had been picked up by the *Los Angeles Times* and posted on their website clear across the country. So, it's good they made it available for as long as they did at WDBJ7. The screen shot above was taken from their program and is being used with their permission. The station also kindly let me reproduce what amounts to a transcript of nearly their entire broadcast below. There are a lot of nuggets in this piece.

One must understand that this is regional media, not national. I don't think the powers that be would ever allow all that was revealed in this broadcast to be seen nationwide, not even once.

WDBJ7 Roanoke's Susan Bahorich: This morning we meet the third and final candidate running for Congress in Virginia's 5th District. WDBJ7's Chris Hurst sat down with Green Party candidate, Ken Hildebrandt.

Chris Hurst: Good morning I'm Chris Hurst and this morning we interview our third and final candidate running for Congress in Virginia's 5th District. The 5th is in the central part of the state stretching vertically across the commonwealth and includes Bedford, Franklin, Henry and Pittsylvania counties in our viewing area and runs all the way to Fauquier County. Dr. Ken Hildebrandt is the Independent Greens of Virginia candidate for Congress in the 5th District. He was a chiropractor from 1987 to 2000 in New Jersey. In 2000 Dr. Hildebrandt began working as an independent web journalist and in 2006 he and his wife Elaine relocated to Nathalie, Virginia in Halifax County. Thank you for being with us this morning Dr. Hildebrandt.

Ken: Thank you for having me.

Chris Hurst: It's good to see you. The first question is, why did you run for congress? You say that you've talked with your wife and you decided that you had to run. Why do you have to run?

Ken: Well, I've been doing this for twelve years. I've been covering elections since 2000 and we half moved

here in 2004. We were split between here and New York City but I've been down here since 2006. We've documented elections all across the country and that's what I've been doing and I was usually, even though I saw t that some third party and independent candidates were marginalized I thought that they could make it more real than they were making things.

So, what happened was Carey Campbell of the Independent Greens watched me interview Jill Stein, Dr. Jill Stein, who's running for president for the Green Party. He watched me do this interview in DC. At the conclusion of the interview he asked me where I was from. I told him Southside. He said, "Do you want to run?" I said, "No" and he said, "Do you have anyone else in mind?" I said, "No." (chuckles)

And then he said, "Do you know if this opportunity will even be there in the future?" He didn't mean just for me, or at least that's not how I took it.

Chris Hurst: Um hum.

Ken: I said no and upon the third no, I said I would check it out with my wife…

Chris Hurst: Yeah…

Ken: And by the end of the day I said I was running.

Chris Hurst: The opportunity to have a three party race instead of the normal two party race?

Ken: Well, it's not going well. I mean our rights are eroding and people aren't even aware of how they're eroding.

Chris Hurst: What do you mean by that then?

Ken: Well the Patriot Act and then also the NDAA, the National Defense Authorization Act which basically said that they can take you at any time, for any reason and hold you indefinitely without charge. And, 'Mr. Change,' president 'Change,' sorry… signed on the dotted line and now it's law.

Chris Hurst: So these are kind of unreasonable certain procedures and types of violations that you think are going on?

Ken: Well, yeah. I mean I'm worried that even be at a point of having elections before too long.

Chris Hurst: Um hum… What's the party's stance, in the Green party on fiscal issues, when we talk about budget we talk about trillions of dollars in deficit. What is the Green Party's stance, what would you do in congress?

Ken: What would I do in congress? Well, first off the biggest issue I'm bringing to the table as far as the economy is that of industrial hemp, which was called a "NEW BILLION-DOLLAR CROP" in the February 1938 issue of Popular Mechanics.

Chris Hurst: Right.

Ken: It's now been estimated it could be as much as a trillion dollars.

Chris Hurst: We'll talk a little more about.

Ken: So that's one way of bringing it down, I'm sorry (for interrupting him)

Chris Hurst: No, go for it. We'll have plenty of opportunity to talk about industrial hemp a little bit more. What else though in terms of any types of taxes or departmental cuts or any of that?

Ken: Lot's. There's (sic) a lot of easy things that we could do. We have answers right in front of our faces and we're just not using them.

Chris Hurst: Um, hmm.

Ken: OK, for example the wars. We need to get out of the wars (Iraq and Afghanistan, remember, this was 2012). We're spending an awful lot of money on these wars.

Chris Hurst: K

Ken: And really you know and how could you go ahead and attack a whole country based on a few renegades? It just doesn't seem right. These are the longest two wars in the history of the nation by the way and the second one, we got into it illegally.

Chris Hurst: Social issues we'll talk it more but do you have types of social issues that you do have a platform for?

Ken: Sure. Absolutely. What I'd like to see… The US since Reagan got into office has gone from, we were similar to other industrialized countries in the amount of prisoners per capita, and now we're far and beyond (everyone else). We have more prisoners in general than anyone, even China!

Chris Hurst: Um, hmm.

Ken: We have a quarter of the world's incarcerates. This has been due to the Drug War. So, what I would like to see is the legalization of cannabis immediately and let all so-called offenders that have been arrested for marijuana be released immediately. It's based on 1930s propaganda…

Chris Hurst: Um, hmm.

Ken: …that's well known. (It) doesn't make people go crazy. It's not a smart thing to do.* It's probably bad for you,** but so is fattening food. And what happens is it's a waste of our resources, because every year we arrest some ¾ of a million people for possession of a plant and meanwhile over 700,000 people go missing. We'd be finding more of those people if we weren't wasting resources elsewhere.

* I now disagree with that statement.
** As above.

Chris Hurst: Is there any way to put people back to work on that issue?

Ken: Hemp, yeah? Hemp would draw in tons of jobs right like that (snaps fingers).

Chris Hurst: And that would be a Southside way to bring.

Ken: Not only Southside. It would particularly be a Southside issue because it's big, as in one of my YouTube videos that I have up, as far as I show all the closed factories and everything and said, 'This doesn't need to be.' Because we got involved in NAFTA and the World Trade Organization we lost a whole bunch of jobs and what this would do, would help make up for that.

Chris Hurst: Can Southside still be a manufacturing and agriculturally based economy?

Ken: I think so, yeah. I mean you've got those factories that are just closed down. They're just sitting there in Danville and elsewhere and even in Halifax County.

Chris Hurst: And again we'll talk about industrial hemp a little bit more a little bit later. We're also giving our viewers the opportunity to ask the candidates a question. Tim Martin of Collinsville, Virginia e-mailed us this question.

"Social Security and Medicare are benefits all working U.S. citizens pay in out of their wages for retirement and should always be there. What do you propose to do to save them to ensure they will always be there for us?"

Chris Hurst: What do you say on Social Security?

Ken: Do away with the cap.

Chris Hurst: The tax max?

Ken: Yep.

Chris Hurst: Yeah. How high can it go?

Ken: As high as it goes.

Chris Hurst: Because it's at like $109,000 right now. It should be higher than that?

Ken: Well, when you think about it people make their money from two sources only that I'm aware of and that's Earth's resources and human labor. We're not importing either from Mars.

Chris Hurst: Um, hmm.

Ken: So, yeah, they should be paying into it. They should be paying their fair share.

Chris Hurst: What percentage of someone's income should go towards Social Security?

Ken: Same as everybody else, 15.

Chris Hurst: No matter how much you?

Ken: Why not?

Chris Hurst: OK. We also have another question too for you and that is, with the president, you say 'President Change.' You don't have a high opinion?

Ken: Not at all.

Chris Hurst: What about ObamaCare? What's wrong with that? You're wholeheartedly against it?

Ken: It's horrible. It's a marriage between corporations and America. Now we literally become Corporate America.

Chris Hurst: What can we do to ensure health care for our citizens?

Ken: Public option, and it was kept off the table.

Chris Hurst: You know that's a pretty radical notion?

Ken: Not really.

Chris Hurst: No?

Ken: No.

Chris Hurst: Not for America?

Ken: No.

Chris Hurst: Why not?

Ken: It might be considered radical by the mainstream media but it's not considered radical by the people you talk with.

Chris Hurst: Um, hmm.

Ken: And it's not considered radical by practitioners. I mean when I first went into practice Medicare was one of the worst insurances. When I left it was one of the best and it wasn't because it improved all that much it's because all the others got worse.

Chris Hurst: Hmm.

Ken: They're in it for profit. You're eliminating the middle man. How could that be radical? You're eliminating the middleman. These people are profiteers and they're making money and not all Americans will be insured under his plan. There will be millions left out. The other way you have everybody included and it's less money. How is that radical? If it's radical, I mean, OK, it's also rational.

Chris Hurst: Heather Marin has a question for you she's from Lynchburg and it's about healthcare and it's concerning this topic. I want to see what you think after you listen to the question.

Heather Marin: Do you guys support insurance companies covering preexisting conditions?

Chris: That was something in the President's health care plan that you would cover people with preexisting conditions is that something that should be guaranteed for all?

Ken: Well, I would think so.

Chris Hurst: Yeah? Did you see any cases as a chiropractor where that was not the case?

Ken: Preexisting conditions. You always ran into that.

Chris Hurst: And was it frustrating for you. Did you ever have to deny coverage for them?

Ken: I didn't deny it, they did.

Chris Hurst: Um, hmm. And so what was frustrating then about that?

Ken: Well, because then the people are stuck with their having to foot the bill instead of the insurance company that they think they have.

Chris Hurst: Um, hmm. What were some of the reasons you might have gotten out of practicing medicine.

Ken: Basically because of what I saw that I learned over many years how to become a better doctor, a better healer. At the end, or well, for quite a few years, when people came into me and if they had pain unless it was bone cancer they were going to walk out of that office feeling better than they came in and nothing but my hands and my head did it.

Chris Hurst: Um, hmm.

Ken: That was a gratifying feeling and it took me years to learn how, taking seminars throughout the country and also applying myself, you know, reading whatever I could to become a better physician.

Chris Hurst: Um, hmm.

Ken: And then when I saw how much pain was being produced en masse via Washington just because it was basically they're selling out due to, for profit, it was profit over people. And to me there's just no excuse for that.

Chris Hurst: And you change that in Washington if elected?

Ken: Well, I would get on the floor and I'd be one voice out of 435 who'd tell it like it is and point to the people and say 'Do you have any idea what you're doing?'

Chris Hurst: Hmm.

Ken: You're responsible for the predictable consequences of your actions, as Chomsky has said, and look at what you're doing, you're compromising, compromising, compromising, all the time, in order for the profiteers to get more of what they don't need and for the people not to get what they do need.

Chris Hurst: Referring to Noam Chomsky up at MIT?

Ken: Well, that's (sic) my words, that's (sic) not his (meaning the rest of my statement above).

Chris Hurst: But you did reference him earlier, I just want to, for clarification.

Ken: He's a friend of mine.

Chris Hurst: He's a friend of yours. All right.

Ken: If it wasn't for him I wouldn't be here doing this now.

Chris Hurst: He inspires you?

Ken: Well, I saw a program on him called MANUFACTURING CONSENT: NOAM CHOMSKY AND THE MEDIA and it was aired in 1995 in the middle of the night, because, as I understand it the likes, well, many people lobbied against its being aired in the daytime.

Chris Hurst: Um, hmm.

Ken: And this was on PBS incidentally.

Chris Hurst: Right.

Ken: So I watched this and I saw, my gosh, this guy is rational. He's dealing with politics from a scientific standpoint and then I realized it didn't have to be all this speculative way that we were looking at things, that we could actually deal with politics scientifically.

Chris Hurst: You talked about industrial hemp. We had a chance to catch up with you on the campaign trail. Our visit with Ken took WDBJ7's Joe Dashiell to the southern end of the fifth district.

Joe Dashiell: Ken Hildebrandt wasn't looking for the thrill of a carnival ride when he and his wife Elaine hit the midway at the Danville/Pittsylvania County Fair. He was searching for votes and one issue was at the top of his list.

Ken: One of the biggest things is industrial hemp. That could revive this area like it needs to be revived.

Joe Dashiell: Hildebrandt made his pitch to members of a rescue squad and introduced himself to others as he walked through the fairgrounds. He carried a vintage magazine to make his case.

Ken: I've got this *Popular Mechanics* magazine from February 1938 right.

Man Ken was showing it to: OK

Ken: And back then they called it a "NEW BILLION-DOLLAR CROP." You could imagine what it would be worth today.

Joe Dashiell: More evidence he argued that legalizing industrial hemp, a cousin of the marijuana plant, could revive southern Virginia's economy and help solve national problems such as America's dependence on foreign oil.

Ken: Well, that's what we're trying to do because it's the shot in the arm this district and the nation really needs now.

Joe Dashiell: Do you worry at all as being seen as a one issue, or very narrow…

Ken: No, not at all that's what I'm hooking people in with but it's such a big issue that touches our economy, you know it touches our foreign policy in that we wouldn't have to import as much oil, some have suggested maybe even none, OK, with 6% of the land mass used. Now that's something that has to be investigated further but at the very least it could minimize that (our dependence on foreign oil) so it's an issue that touches many areas.

Joe Dashiell: Hildebrandt isn't asking for contributions. He admits he can't afford the campaign tactics of well financed opponents, but he believes the power of the internet and social networking will help spread his message to thousands of 5th District voters.

Ken: I wish we had more backup and more help but we've been making it happen.

Joe Dashiell: Hildebrandt says he was a reluctant candidate recruited by a leader of the Green Party. He ultimately decided it was his responsibility to run.

Ken: The founding fathers were more spunky and we need more spunk in our politics and what I'm saying is I have things to be spunky about.

Joe Dashiell: And Hildebrandt says he's in it to win.

Joe Dashiell: Some might view this as a symbolic candidacy?

Ken: No, no, not at all. I wouldn't have done this. I used to be a Track runner I was one of the best milers in the northeast and I had some guts, beat a lot of people who were more talented than me but when I hit that line I was finished. And I plan on giving it 100%. I wouldn't be in the race if I wasn't.

Chris Hurst: Industrial hemp, how do you convince the masses that it is a viable option?

Ken: Well, I think what I pointed out there with the 1938 Popular Mechanics, when they call it a billion dollars and they see that that was in February 1938, that makes them think. That's why I carry that, I already got it used and it was already a little bit weathered, but now it's a lot more weathered. I've used that throughout my campaign trail.

Chris Hurst: It would make sense in order to be able to use industrial hemp as an agricultural product you would have to make cannabis also legal, and can that happen? Can you get that off Schedule 1 of the DEA classification cause?

Ken: It should be.

Chris Hurst: A lot of people say that it's, just bureaucracy, whatever it may be, it would never be able to be taken off as a Schedule 1 controlled substance.

Ken: Well, I often say people know, should be able to know what happened and what's happening, but not what's going to happen. So when they start making predictions like that, look, none of us has a crystal ball. OK, we can look into the past and find out that it was founded on propaganda, primarily by Harry Anslinger.

Chris Hurst: Um, hmm.

Ken: He was a former prohibitionist. He took it state by state. He got it illegal state by state and then when he was done with all the states he went to the UN.

Chris Hurst: There are people who think it was in order to support the Bureau of Alcohol, you know, to continue to support that after prohibition had ended. Is that part of what you think is a rational for cannabis?

Ken: Who knows? (I wish I knew why I said that because he hit the nail on the head.) There seems to be a lot of evidence that it was based on prejudice against Mexicans and African-Americans, against poorer class people.

Chris Hurst: You don't believe that smoking marijuana, marijuana in any form is dangerous to a human body.

Ken: I'm saying it's probably not good for you* but it's certainly not like alcohol or cigarettes. I mean alcohol causes, I mean somebody goes and beats up their wife, their family, their friends, whatever and nicotine you'll see somebody taking a break at a supermarket or something and they're out there quick getting that fix and cannabis doesn't have that either.

* I no longer think that.

Chris Hurst: Um, hmm.

Ken: There have actually been studies. There was a British study done where people were shown to drive even better under its influence. You're not going to find that with alcohol. So, it's a far more. I mean people you'll ask which would you rather have, somebody smoking a joint behind you or somebody having a six pack? I mean they're totally different. To keep it illegal, and what do they do I mean if you're going to have any drug really, what they should have is rehab. If somebody feels like they have a problem with this, and I don't really think there's (sic) many people with marijuana that have a problem but people could have a problem with anything.

Chris Hurst: OK

Ken: Even food.

Chris Hurst: They should have rehabilitation?

Ken: Yeah, rehabilitation.

Chris Hurst: More so than they have now?

Ken: Yeah, well I mean throwing someone in a violent prison. Down here we don't have as much of the violence.

Chris Hurst: Um, hmm.

Ken: As the rest of the country.

Chris Hurst: Right.

Ken: But I mean for somebody to get thrown into a cage and get raped, that's crazy. When I was interviewing Senator Gravel back in 2008, or 2007 rather, he was saying they come out criminals. They didn't go in being criminals. And when I interviewed Dr. Jill Stein she said the worst thing about cannabis from a physician's standpoint is its illegality.

Chris Hurst: It goes toward that whole overpopulation of prisons then?

Ken: Well yeah, I mean we hold 25, the Land of the Free now holds a quarter of the world's prisoners.

Chris Hurst: Let me ask you this because on your YouTube channel you talk about chemtrails. Let's play this clip.

Ken: Laughs.

Clip: While filming a craft that was leaving an expanding trail Ken says, "That's obviously pumping out chemicals and it's not a contrail. That's a chemtrail. Wow."

Chris Hurst: Do you believe in chemtrails?

Ken: Laughs - All I know is that I've been around walking this planet for over fifty years and I never saw proliferating trails until rather recently.

Chris Hurst: Uh, huh.

Ken: And you can even smell them in valleys. Now I'm not into any big conspiracy or anything else, I'm just saying that it's going on. What's to get? You can smell it if you go into a valley and you're a non-smoker.

Chris Hurst: What does it smell like?

Ken: Hard to explain. It doesn't smell natural in a forest though, I'll tell you that much.

Chris Hurst: What do you think it is?

Ken: Well, I've heard barium and I've heard aluminum.

Chris Hurst: And what do you, but what do you think?

Ken: Well, what I think, you see somebody e-mailed me and said, 'There's this special on TV, Ken, that you might want to see.' We don't even have television and so we went to the local pizzeria and watched it. It was *Chemical Contrails* on the Discovery Channel. And they were saying there that there were increased levels of barium and aluminum in the soil afterwards.

Chris Hurst: The government won't acknowledge it. Do you think they should?

Ken: Yeah I think they should. Representative Kucinich put it In the Space Preservation Act of 2001 but the term was stricken in 2002, why?

Chris Hurst: It's true it didn't make it out of committee (That doesn't answer why the term was stricken from its update, but time was running short.) but I do want to say in 30 seconds tell us why voters in the 5th district should vote for you.

Ken: Why should they vote for me? Because I stand for you not for corporations. I don't stand for profit over people I stand for a more rational, reasonable world....

Chris Hurst: All right.

Ken: Where everybody has a voice.

Chris Hurst: Dr., we appreciate it. Thank you for visiting with us and giving our viewers the opportunity to know you a little bit more.

Ken: Thanks for having me.

Chapter 5

Elaine and Ken's "spotlight videos" for the 2014 Election

"The February 1938 issue of Popular Mechanics referred to hemp as the "NEW BILLION-DOLLAR CROP." It's now been estimated to be over a trillion dollar crop, which can be used to make over 25,000 products including fuel, food, fabric and medicine, yet it's illegal. It's the economic shot in the arm our nation and Virginia's 6th district needs now."

- Elaine Hildebrandt

In 2014, Elaine Hildebrandt ran for US congress in Virginia's 6th District, whilst Ken ran for the 5th. Though Elaine had no signs, no advertising, and little time at all for the campaign and there were no candidate debates, she received an astonishing 12% of the vote in the 3 way race. The transcript of her 3 minute "spotlight feature" is below. Elaine's video is entitled *Elaine Hildebrandt spotlight feature regarding Congressional Campaign* is posted at Ken's YouTube channel **http://youtube.com/drkenhildebrandt** specifically at **https://www.youtube.com/watch?v=gY6rVTv1B4w&feature=youtu.be.**

Hi, I'm Elaine Hildebrandt and I'm running for US congress in Virginia's 6th district. I'm a former elementary school teacher who mostly worked in Manhattan before joining my husband Ken as independent journalists primarily focused on elections in the United States. Ken did most of the reporting. I did a lot of the background research, and still do, as does Ken.

The primary issue we're trying to get out there is that of industrial hemp. The February 1938 issue of Popular Mechanics referred to hemp as the "NEW BILLION-DOLLAR CROP." It's now been estimated to be over a trillion dollar crop, which can be used to make over 25,000 products including fuel, food, fabric and medicine, yet it's illegal. It's the economic shot in the arm our nation and Virginia's 6th district needs now.

When Ken asked presidential candidate Ralph Nader about this in Iowa in October 2004, Mr. Nader referred to industrial hemp as a crop "that would advance our national security, by decreasing our reliance on foreign oil."

And what about hemp's cousin marijuana? We are hopeful people soon grasp the reality that when law enforcement are busy chasing over ¾ of a million people for plant possession each year that means more real criminals will be at large as a result, which is simple deductive reasoning. And statistics back this reasoning. In 1970 the US had some 300,000 prisoners and 90% of homicides were solved. Now we have at least 2 million additional human beings living in cages than we did in 1970 yet now only between 61-65% of homicides are solved. In other words it used to be that 1 out of 10 got away with murder but now it's 1 out of 3.

We're not asking for any money whatsoever for our campaigns. We ARE asking you to try to help us help everyone by sharing this vital information with others, enough others so that we poll high enough to be included in the televised debates, which we have been told is 10%. Though it should go without saying, it can't be, our names MUST be included in the polling.

There are other simple yet profound solutions in addition to what's stated in this brief introduction and those issues are addressed on our campaign sites.

If you're tired of the way things are going in Washington, here's your chance to do something about it, whether you have the right to vote or even live in the United States, by sharing the vital information available via our websites, **electken.com** and **electelaine.com** with as many as you can. It's not about me, nor about Ken, but rather about all of us, who ought to be living in a far more reasonable world. Many thanks to the Independent Green Party of Virginia for asking us both to run for US House of Representatives at this most critical time of state, national and global history.

Below is the transcript of my unscripted, unrehearsed spotlight video which Noam Chomsky stated in an e-mail was "First Rate!" and said I could quote him. In all my years of writing him he never used an exclamation point (called "screamers" by many academics) until writing me about this which is posted at **https://www.youtube.com/watch?v=XZrnodh35FU&feature=youtu.be.**

My getting that response from him really made my day.

Hi. I'm Dr. Ken Hildebrandt. I'm running for congress in Virginia's Fifth District.

The reason why I'm running, I used to be a chiropractor in New Jersey for 13 years. And, over those 13 years, I realized more and more that my patients' stress was coming from Washington. It was actually human created stress. More and more I saw that people were behind the eight-ball financially. And yet, I remember that as a kid in the '60s, I knew somebody who worked at a local hardware store in the fishing tackle department and he raised his whole family and his wife didn't have to work outside the home. And I wonder, 'Well, why is that?' Well, let me tell you that part of the reason why it is, and that's that in the 1960s, or early 1960s when Eisenhower left office, the wealthiest were taxed 90% on their highest income. Now that figure is down to 39.6%. So you can see that the reason why when I was a kid we heard of millionaires but you never heard of billionaires. Now you hear of billionaires and most other people who are pretty much behind the eight-ball.

The other stresses were the Drug War. If you take a look at the Drug War, especially, take a look at cannabis, marijuana. It's a plant! How can a plant be illegal? I would see people who were stressed out themselves, or their mother was getting arrested, or their father or their son or their daughter or friends. And they were extremely stressed because they were going to be sent to live in a violent cage for possessing a plant. Now that didn't make much sense to me either. And as it turns out, as I researched matters even more, I found out that there's a cousin plant to cannabis, hemp, and hemp has over 25,000 different uses that we could be using right now. And it would actually reduce our reliance on foreign oil as was brought up when I brought this question to Ralph Nader back in 2004.

So here we can reduce our reliance on foreign oil by growing it here and we're not because it's illegal? Now how much sense does that make? It doesn't make any sense at all. And the bottom line is that in Washington, the way things are being run right now, it doesn't make any sense.

From a medical standpoint, I took everybody's life seriously. I took seminars across the country to learn to become a better healer. And I only had my hands and my head to do it. And then I saw how careless they were in Washington. I mean how did the Land of the Free go to the Land of the Caged? We have more prisoners in the United States thanks to this Drug War than any other nation on Earth, including China even though they outnumber us by far. Now that's ridiculous. And by simple deductive reasoning you can see that if they're chasing people for possession of a plant, then that means they're not chasing people who are you know, pedophiles, rapists and murderers, missing children won't be found. And those are backed up, that's not simple, just simple deductive reasoning, but it's also backed by statistics. In the 1960s 90% of homicides were solved. Nowadays it's only like 63%. So remember that this Drug War comes at a real high price. It comes at a price of leaving more pedophiles, rapists, murderers at large, more missing children. And, what are we doing sending people to live in cages? How will future historians look back at this time? I mean, seriously. So, over the years things have gone... back in 2000 people thought, well some outsider, they're a spoiler. Well that myth has gone out the window. And it's been replaced by another myth, that is, why even try? Well, let me tell you something. In Congress right now there are no Independents at all who weren't once part of the game themselves, one of the two parties. And they're all, basically they still have the same puppeteers, the same big corporate interests and other special interests fund their campaigns and therefore we live in a very irrational world. So, a better world is possible.

Please check out **electken.com** and give us a chance. Help spread the word, put effort in to overcome their big bucks and we'll win. I'll only be one voice in Washington, but I'll be one voice in Washington who's telling it like it is and that's more than we have now.

Thank you.

Chapter 6

Introduction of the US Congressional candidate forum sponsored by the League of Women Voters in Charlottesville, on October 30, 2014

"So, if we straighten out the tax structure and legalize industrial hemp, those two things will help us tackle that 18 trillion dollar debt we have."

- Ken Hildebrandt

Left to right, Sue Friedman, Dena Imlay, Lawrence Gaughan, Ken

Many new doors were opened at the candidate forum in Charlottesville, Virginia on October 29, 2014. The first one is a brief overview of some focal issues of Part I. It's titled *Dr. Ken Hildebrandt's opening statement at Charlottesville candidate forum* and is posted at **http://youtube.com/drkenhildebrandt** at **https://www.youtube.com/watch?v=fksPwohgx9s&feature=youtu.be**.

Moderator Sue Friedman: ...I do ask each candidate to be respectful of the agreed upon time lines. Now, for our opening statements with an order determined by a drawing held earlier this evening we will ask first, candidate Hildebrandt.

Ken: Thank you. I thought we were going to get three minutes but two minutes, that's OK. There's a lot of problems in Washington and there's (sic) a lot of solutions that aren't being used. Number one, industrial hemp. We can be growing our own energy right now. Why are we digging for it? Why are we mining for it? Why are we having disasters like Fukishima and the Gulf? Because of the illegality of a plant, industrial hemp, which has some 25,000 different uses. It's the economic shot in the arm our district and nation needs now. It used to be illegal in the state of Virginia not to grow Hemp. OK, so it's based on silly propaganda and we need to end that.

We need to end all plant illegalities. It's really crazy too for law enforcement to be chasing people for plant possession, plants that were given to us on this Earth. And, even poppies, yes that's right. Look at the ahh... In early 2001 the Taliban had eradicated poppy production in Afghanistan, OK, and now we have our soldiers over there patrolling their fields and Obama saying well ahh, you know it's their old culture. Wait a minute. Colin Powell went over there with 120 million dollar check for them to give them for eradicating the poppies. We can't do what they did? That's nonsense. So we have our government working for poppy production and then over here arresting people.

Last thing, tax structure - We need to revert it back to what it was like in the 60's or 70's. In fact it was the top 1% were taxed 70% on their highest income all the way up until Reagan got into office. What I'm suggesting is that we break down the top 1% category because times have changed and um, you know it's not the same as, 250K as a billionaire but we need to even that out. So, if we straighten out the tax structure and legalize industrial hemp, those two things will help us tackle that 18 trillion dollar debt we have. We need to stop electing puppets and have people in office. Thank you.

Chapter 7

The Secret Government is not a conspiracy theory, nor is weather modification

"There's been a coup, have you heard? It's the CIA coup. The CIA runs everything. They run the military. They're the ones who are over there lobbing missiles and bombs on these countries. It's not even the military that does that. The CIA run this and of course the CIA is every bit as secret as the federal reserve and yet, think of the harm that they've done since they were established since World War II. They are a government until themselves. They're in business. They're in drug business and they take on dictators. We need to take on the CIA."

- *Ron Paul*

"Mark Twain, years ago, said that 'everybody talks about the weather, but nobody does anything about it.' The remark was not original with him, but no matter. If Twain were here today, I'm sure he would change his mind. Man is doing something about the weather, for good and for ill."

- Walter Orr Roberts, National Geographic, April 1972, conclusion of feature article entitled, *WE'RE DOING SOMETHING ABOUT THE WEATHER!*

Above: Lines in the sky in NYC

Above: August 2014 still shot from a video taken by Elaine as the helicopter circled our home. We try to capture these private free air shows on video when they happen where we live here in what's basically a forest mixed with farmland in what's called Southside, Virginia.

This is titled *The National Security Act of 1947 created a "Secret Government"* is also from the Charlottesville US Congressional Debate Forum and is available at Ken's YouTube site at **https://www.youtube.com/watch?v=GCLJfZS9tAc&feature=youtu.be**.

Moderator Sue Friedman: Candidate Hildebrandt.

Ken: OK. There's (sic) many things that we need to do legislatively, immediately. We need to legalize Industrial Hemp. We need to put in legislation also about the tax structure. Legalize all plants. They gave me this the last time, I said, well you have one thing, well here I'm giving three.

OK, so legalize all plants. Alright, that covers that. That covers the marijuana, that covers the Drug War, well most of the Drug War, and legalize Industrial Hemp and revert the tax structure back to what it was like in the 60s.

OK. Now we get into the fun stuff. This is the reason why I'm running up here and I think I'm the best candidate. Things go much deeper than what you're seeing. Professor Noam Chomsky has said that "We live entangled in webs of endless deceit, in a highly indoctrinated society where elementary truths are easily buried."

Why is all this money going to the military-industrial complex? Well let me tell you something. There was an act in 1947, the National Security Act. That created a secret government. It exists, it's not a conspiracy theory, you can look up Bill Moyers' special on it. And, they act outside of the constitution. Senator Inouye said they have their own air force, their own navy and their own fund raising mechanism. Now they're not having bake sales are they folks? So, they have been tied to the Drug War and that's probably why we really invaded Afghanistan.

So we need somebody who's going to know a little bit about the secret government and will really dive in there and tackle some of those issues and not be scared to. And, I'm one of those people because that secret government has gotten totally out of hand. They're even involved in weather manipulation. You can look up Senate Bill 517 and House Bill 2995, weather manipulation without public oversight.

Moderator Sue Friedman: Thank you.

The Space Preservation Act & Chemtrails is also from the 2014 Charlottesville US Congressional Debate Forum and is posted at **https://www.youtube.com/watch?v=NPdazAnB8Bk&feature=youtu.be**

Moderator Sue Friedman: And now an opportunity for a response and our candidate Hildebrandt.

Ken: OK, great. Again, industrial hemp. I mean that's the thing that… What you do is… sure it has to combust but you eat up more CO2 in the process of photosynthesis. So that's your answer. We should be growing our own oil. Why aren't we doing that? That's complete insanity that we're not doing this.

You know… and I remember I asked Ralph Nader this back in 2004 and he said, "It would be nice if the two candidates talked about the multi-billion dollar crop that would advance our national security by reducing our reliance on foreign oil. Thank you." Well make it a little more real Ralph, OK! That's big! Reducing your reliance on foreign oil? That is so huge!

And also, as my wife Elaine has discovered in research that, remember she's running in the sixth, ElectElaine.com, that you can even make the panels of the cars out of hemp and it will help eat up CO2. Come on! We have problems!

But we also need to investigate what is this huge aerial operation going on over our heads, that we can't even ask about because Kucinich put it in the National Security Act (I meant to say "The Space Preservation Act") of 2001 and then he took it off an update of the bill in 2002 and then he was going to meet up with me and presumably that's why he backed out, because someone cried, 'National Security.' That's the only thing I know that can trump free speech.

Moderator Sue Friedman: Thank you.

The Laugh's on US! - Weather Manipulation isn't Sci-Fi is likewise from the 2014 Charlottesville US Congressional Debate Forum and is posted at Ken's YouTube site at **https://www.youtube.com/watch?v=XHCWslaVjXE&feature=youtu.be.**

Moderator Sue Friedman: Candidate Hildebrandt

Ken: Great question. Over…well, ten, twelve years ago this was a big issue for me. I could see things were heating up. This is a question that's not put in, that's not factored in.

Earlier I talked about weather modification. See those lines that planes leave now. You don't see those prior to 1995. You might be able to show me some old World War II black and white footage. OK, so they left some things occasionally but look, this is not jet fuel exhaust. Jet fuel… when you see a vapor trail, that vapor trail leaves right after the plane. Every one of these planes that you see that leaves a line all the way across the sky, you look on your little ID'er, it's gonna say that they don't know who it is.

There's a big program. This is probably being done to block the sun's rays and it's not being factored into the equation because it's not being talked about, which is crazy because it's happening. Chemtrails are real.

You will not see crisscross lines (earlier than the mid 90s or so). You can look up, you can Google some pictures. I said 'Some 'cloud formations' that you may not have seen.' I have "X" clouds, star clouds, asterisk clouds, all kinds of things that you never saw before and that don't exist in nature. That's because they're tinkering with our atmosphere. And they've been doing it for a long time.

When I first met Noam I said, "Look it Noam. Look at what, look at what W said, he said we haven't figured out how to control the weather yet," and we both had a big chuckle. Well the laugh was on us. Because I found a 1972 issue of *National Geographic* entitled, "*We're Doing Something about the Weather.*" And that's the first time I saw one of those trails. And in that article they admitted that they can seed in the eye of a hurricane and it would slow its winds by 30%. Now how come that wasn't done with Katrina? And how come that wasn't done with Sandy?

Moderator Sue Friedman: Thank you.

Chapter 8

Downed Extraterrestrial Craft near Nuclear Base

"We must guard against the acquisition of power whether sought or unsought by the military- industrial complex."

- President Dwight D. Eisenhower

Above left to right, moderator Sue Friedman, part of audience clapping at end

Overwhelming Evidence of Downed Extraterrestrial Craft Near Nuclear Base in 1947 from the 2014 Charlottesville US Congressional Debate Forum and posted at Ken's YouTube site at **https://www.youtube.com/watch?v=dhuqoql1q_0&feature=youtu.be**.

Moderator Sue Friedman: Candidate Hildebrandt

Ken: OK. The military-industrial complex… Eisenhower warned, he said, "We must guard against the acquisition of power whether sought or unsought by the military-industrial complex." He was well aware of the UFO issue and he knew how things with the military-industrial complex were getting out of hand.

Let me explain how some of this relates. There have been reports of downed craft. You can hear the ABC Roswell broadcast. And by the way, Roswell was the base for the 509th. They're the ones who bombed Hiroshima and Nagasaki so don't think these things… they have a lot of interest in nukes, these lights, like in shutting them down* and this and that. *See Chapter 10

… Colonel Philip Corso who used to be head of foreign technology at the Pentagon. He said he got the Roswell file and they had a lot of stuff in there on things that we were working on. And he said that he took that information and freely gave it to industry, for them to make a profit, back to us… He didn't realize that but I mean he was like oh good, you know they're giving it back to the population. Well again, because of that secret government thing we don't hear about that technology or anything like that.

So again… and also I want to bring up about this military spending is that like when we give aid, this is before Egypt was overthrown, when we gave aid to them it was contingent that they buy 3 billion dollars' worth of our hardware from us. That's usually… this whole notion of us giving all this money away is a bunch of malarkey. You know all the countries agreed to give I think it was .7 of their gross domestic product to foreign aid, this is like in the 70s. I don't think anybody met it. So, we're not giving it away it's going to the military-industrial complex, the profiteers. It's got to stop. It's out of hand.

Conclusion of the 2014 Charlottesville US Congressional Debate Forum entitled *Dr. Steven Greer's testimonies from Astronauts & Pilots* regarding UFOs and available at Ken's YouTube site at **https://www.youtube.com/watch?v=m9HSMh8xWl8&feature=youtu.be.**

Ken: (Note, camera A had its battery run out so it took a few seconds to get camera B up and rolling) In essence I said, 'Dr. Steven Greer said he might...' and then the camera picks up with - be able to make it with his wife Emily tonight. Hi Steve if you're watching this. He lives right here in Albermarle County. He has taken the testimonies of astronauts, pilots, military personnel and so forth over twenty years about this whole ET thing. I mean the wealth of information... and if you think the government investigated something for twenty years that was just a figment of the peoples' imagination... I mean please. So again, those issues are true.

They're actually modifying our weather. I had somebody killed (close to us. I interviewed a neighbor of hers who lost his entire trailer but managed to save himself and his family) in a tornado when they were modifying... Elaine saw them spraying between clouds. I was walking the dogs and a tornado took her. They can't be tinkering with our weather like this.

So, what we need to do again, back to the basics. Plant illegalities, get rid of them. End the Drug War. OK? We have two million three hundred thousand prisoners, more than anyone in the world. We need to revert the tax structure back to what it was like in the 60s, pay off our national debt. OK?

And, we need to have a more fair egalitarian society and I really hope that you vote for me to represent you. Thank you.

Moderator Sue Friedman: Thank you so much. Let's give all of our candidates a hand.

[applause]

Moderator Sue Friedman: I'd like to thank the audience for joining us both here in person and viewing at home. And I also want to thank the League of Woman Voters again in the Charlottesville area for hosting this candidates' forum, the city of Charlottesville and of course Channel 10. And, remember, vote on November 4th. Thank you so much.

Ken: Thank you!

[applause]

Chapter 9

The UFO issue expanded markedly during WWII with what were called "foo fighters." By 1947 UFOs were acknowledged as real, though they were called "flying saucers" until the early 1950s.

"The phenomenon reported is something real and not visionary or fictitious... The reported operating characteristics such as extreme rates of climb, maneuverability, and actions which must be considered evasive when sighted or contacted by friendly aircraft and radar, lend belief to the possibility that some of the objects are controlled manually, automatically, or remotely."

- Lt. General Nathan Twining, September 23, 1947

Critics of UFOs reject them for the simple reason that distances between other possibly intelligent beings from other solar systems would prohibit their coming here, but what about androids? Has our primitive society in its infancy of technological advancement already sent probes out of our solar system? How much more advanced do you suppose a civilization a thousand years ahead of us would be, or a million years? To the best of my knowledge, no one knows the source of these foo fighters, but they sure did seem to be under intelligent control, following bombers usually off their wingtips yet never interfering in any way. They were encountered in both theaters of war and both sides thought they were some kind of secret weapon of their opponent.

These foo fighters weren't very big, certainly nothing like what people think of as flying saucers, but rather balls of light, not unlike what I was lucky enough to video myself thanks to the coaxing of my wife Elaine on July 01, 2003 on the beach in Mantoloking, New Jersey and posted at **https://www.youtube.com/watch?v=iLgiihLsV5c**, something we both thought was an approaching helicopter traveling along the shore's edge from north to south.

When it got a bit closer and I tried to zoom in on it, it halted its southern direction, did a 360 degree circle before whisking out of sight heading up and to the north. You can hear the waves crashing on the beach, but there was no sound from whatever this was and I had absolutely nothing to say. My brain had not yet fully comprehended what my eye had witnessed through the camera's viewfinder. In about a minute or so the three of us who were there, Elaine and a neighbor, all realized it was a UFO.

We rushed home to view the footage and I posted it that evening, years before YouTube was around. I was lucky enough to have figured out how to have a video website since early 2001. So, the number of people who've seen our video is a lot more than 20,000, still disgraceful I think no matter the number is, because no one can explain this in any conventional way.

Chapter 10

Key testimony regarding a UFO interfering with nuclear weapons from the Citizen Hearing on UFO Disclosure held between April 29 and May 03, 2013, at the National Press Club in Washington, DC

"Everyone had been silenced... I never spoke a word about my incident for almost 40 years and my wife never knew."

- David D. Schindele, Captain, US Air Force, Retired

The transcript of this incredible video along with his reference to a mainstream publication, *The Saturday Evening Post*, validating parts of his testimony and referencing the long term government employed UFO researcher, Dr. J. Allen Hynek, is truly what I refer to what Noam Chomsky calls, "the occasional nugget." One has to hold onto those nuggets, especially when dealing with this topic, or one will stand the chance of sounding like one is "from Neptune" as Chomsky has asserted. I'm not contradicting the chapter's title. The article in *The Saturday Evening Post* did not cover the events regarding the nukes being knocked off line, because all that was kept secret reportedly at the direction of the OSI.

Transcript of Captain Schindele's testimony below from Episode 7, Nuclear Tampering Part I at
https://vimeo.com/ondemand/chd courtesy of **http://citizenhearing.org**, beginning at 19:15

Captain David D. Schindele: My name is David D. Schindele, Captain, US Air Force, Retired. In 1966, I was involved in an incident while stationed at Minot Air Force Base, North Dakota. I was told to never speak of the incident again, and also told that as far I was concerned, it never happened. Because of that, I'm before you today with a bit of trepidation, I must say a lot of trepidation, as I have never before shown my face in person on this matter.

I was a Minuteman ICBM launch control officer, First Lieutenant, and a deputy missile combat troop commander in a two man launch control crew with my crew commander who held the rank of Major. I was attached to the Strategic Air Command, and part of the 742nd Strategic Missile Squadron, one of three squadrons of the 455th Strategic Missile Wing based at Minot. I held a top secret clearance, which was required for my job.

It all began one morning when I was watching TV while having breakfast and I heard the local news announcer mention that some residents in the town of Mohall, North Dakota, had seen strange lights overnight to which they attributed to a UFO. This got my attention because I was scheduled for duty that morning at a launch control facility called November Flight, about three miles west of Mohall about thirty-seven miles north of Minot Air Force Base. I lived in the town of Mohall at that time, and I drove to the air base to attend the morning pre-departure briefing at wing headquarters, where all fifteen missile crews would normally meet each day prior to pulling alert duty at their respective launch control facilities.

During that pre-departure crew briefing it was mentioned that some missiles at November Flight had gone off alert, but there's no further information provided. I immediately connected this to the news item that I heard earlier in the morning regarding a possible UFO sighting near the town of Mohawk. When the briefing was over several of the launch crews seated near me commented about the news item, which they had also heard that morning, and there was speculation about a possible connection with November Flight. My troop commander had also heard the news item and we were both anxious and quite curious about what we might find, as we drove out to the launch control facility…

This is the November launch control facility from air view from Google Earth… There's an access road, to the right, to the facility, from the north coming down to the flight facility where there's a main gate and perimeter fence. The perimeter fence goes around the launch control facility building top side, and there's a garage to the right of the main gate.

The usual procedure upon arrival is to inspect the grounds and building, but this time my commander immediately went into a security section of the building to debrief security personnel guards. This was, this security center was the top most north side of the building near the main gate. I entered the facility from the back door at the end of the facility and then encountered the site manager, a tech sergeant, who immediately took me into the day room and asked if I had briefed on the previous night's events. I said I had.

We then proceeded toward the windows on the west side of the day room where he described to me a large object with flashing lights had been hovering just outside the fence that night and he spread his arms out in front of him to indicate its size, the size of the object. Based on his description I estimated the object may have been eighty to a hundred feet wide and approximately a hundred feet from the building, maybe a bit closer. I immediately asked if it had been a helicopter and he said that it just hovered without a noise being heard, quite unlike the usual noisy helicopters heard from within the building. I also asked him what the flashing lights were like, but he could not answer. They were unlike any he had ever seen. They were not like the usual blinking lights on planes, but something like a pulsating glow. He then said the object while hovering close to the ground had glided to the right toward the north end of the building and out of sight.

The object then came into view from the security section of the building and hovered just behind and slightly to the right of (the) main gate, concealed partly by the large garage located within the fenced area to the right of the gate, as you can see here (referring to slide of Google Map image) the garage is…, the second position of the object.

This location put the object almost directly above the heart of the launch control capsule located sixty feet below ground. All our ten missiles are located four to fourteen miles away from the launch control facility. This capsule was located approximately underneath the garage. This was the launch crew quarters and the launch control center for all ten interconnected nuclear tipped missiles that were located away from the launch facility.

Security personnel confirmed everything that the site manager had related to me. My commander and I then proceeded to take the elevator down to the launch control center, the capsule to relieve the two men officer crew below. After entering the capsule our eyes were immediately transfixed on the launch control console which showed that all missiles were off alert and unlaunchable. We had never seen such a thing before.

The outgoing crew briefed us on the wild events that had transpired overnight and indicated that the missiles malfunctioned at the time the object was hovering directly above the capsule and next to the main gate.

We speculated about the possibility of the EMF pulse that might have created the situation. We had no doubt however that the ten outlying nuclear tipped missiles of November Flight had been compromised, tampered with, and put out of commission by the object that had paid a visit.

Normally it's quite unusual to even have one missile down except for maintenance, and wing headquarters was very proud of having more than 95% up time for all 150 missiles…

The following morning after we had were relieved by a follow on crew we arrived topside and I attempted to further query the flight security controller who had been on duty at the time of the situation but he interrupted me and he said that he had been instructed not to discuss the incident.

That is why my commander then told me that he had received a call while I was on a scheduled rest break down below and he told me, and he was told that we were never to discuss the incident. When I asked where the directive came from he said the OSI. He evidently received a call from the OSI.

With no discussion allowed on the subject between him or me together or with anybody else, my troop commander and I were left in limbo and left on our own to conjure, in our own minds, how other simulations, situations might unfold and be handled. Normally the air force will train us on all procedures. We were in a simulator constantly, training. This serious (lack) of follow through by the air force is more than bewildering and served to keep this situation on our minds. Together there were a dozen of us involved in this incident. My commander and I were not there during the encounter, but we had to deal with the ramifications of the incident, and I'll never forget that frightening emotion on the faces of topside airmen who were gathered with me when I was briefed by the site manager.

Because those of us at the launch control facility, besides those of us at the launch control facility there had to be many more people involved with this including maintenance people who had to re-target and realign missiles. Also official security personnel to guard and protect missile launch facilities and who knows how many others on base, were concerned?

Everyone had been silenced. The incident was never discussed and I never heard a word of any evidence from anyone I associated with. I never spoke a word about my incident for almost 40 years and my wife never knew.

Ken: Wow

Captain Schindele: After several years of searching the internet in hopes of finding someone who could give me a clue about my incident.

Committee Chair Interrupts granting Captain Schindele an additional two minutes to his allotted ten.

Captain Schindele: I then found what was described by Captain Robert Salas and I felt immediate joyous freedom from the haunting memory. I then informed my wife.

Since then I have run across several missileers who were there with me in the wing and two of them have gone public with their own experiences. Two others have described to me their unique experiences but they have pleaded that I not divulge their names. They fear of losing their air force pension, or losing their personal integrity in keeping secrets or being ridiculed.

I also know of two other officers involved in incidents, but they will not admit to their secrets probably for the same reasons.

And then there's the later Captain Val Smith, of my squadron, who is mentioned in official documents released via file. He was interviewed by the late Dr. J. Allen Hynek of Blue Book fame, who wrote an article in the *Saturday Evening Post* published on 17 December 1966 (holds up magazine), which described the incident which Smith was involved with in 25th August 1966.

Hynek stated in the article, 'This incident was not picked up by the press, was not picked up by the press. This is typical of puzzling cases that I've studied during the eighteen years I've served as the air force's scientific consultant on the problem of ufos.'

Display the third slide please.

Just prior to the release of this *Post* article, the *Minot Daily News* got wind of it and it published on 6 December 1966 a front page news item, with a major bold headline that read 'Minot Launch Control Center Saucer Cited as one case of Outer Space Visitors,' the front page.

I remember this article and thinking, oh, maybe I can start talking. In 1966 when I was at Mayna?, the evidence was everywhere that something quite unique was happening, but I was embedded in a shell of silence. The air force knew the truth. The air force knew that I knew the truth and that is the only reason they warned and instructed me that it never happened.

Applause

Chapter 11

UFOs and nukes go way back, to July 1947, outside Roswell, New Mexico, home of the 509th, the ones who bombed Hiroshima and Nagasaki

"The Army Air Forces has announced that a flying disk has been found and is now in the possession of the Army."

- Taylor Grant, ABC radio, July 08, 1947

Above: A clearly embarrassed Major Jesse Marcel is pictured with scraps from a weather balloon which we we're supposed to believe he and others in charge of nuclear weapons had mistaken for being something out of this world. The officers were reportedly sent a "blistering rebuke" from Washington for their mistake that went around the world, yet were left in charge of nuclear weapons. Oh sure, that sounds like a believable story - Face-Palm.

Additionally, Marcel came forward later in life and told the real story that this pile of scrap replaced the real debris minutes before the press conference and that he had been familiar with everything that flew and this was unlike anything he'd seen or heard about at that time and ever since.

Indeed there were incidents prior to 1947 involving unidentified flying objects but the topic truly surfaced when a "so-called flying saucer" crashed at a ranch outside Roswell, New Mexico according to this ABC news radio broadcast, which can be found easily on the internet, even in audio at YouTube and likely other places, as well as here, **http://roswellproof.homestead.com/abc_news_july8.html.** The transcript is below.

Taylor Grant: Headline Edition, July 8th, 1947. The Army Air Forces has announced that a flying disk has been found and is now in the possession of the Army. Army officers say the missile, found sometime last week, has been inspected at Roswell, New Mexico, and sent to Wright Field, Ohio, for further inspection...

[The American Broadcasting Company and affiliated stations presents Headline Edition with Taylor Grant... Today's edition presents a roundup of the latest developments in the finding of a flying disk... To stay in step with history in the making, stay tuned to Headline Edition. And now here's Taylor Grant.]

Taylor Grant: Late this afternoon a bulletin from New Mexico suggested that the widely publicized mystery of the flying saucers may soon be solved. Army Air Force officers reported that one of the strange disks had been found and inspected sometime last week. Our correspondents in Los Angeles and Chicago have been in contact with army officials endeavoring to obtain all possible late information. Joe Wilson reports to us now from Chicago.

Joe Wilson: The Army may be getting to the bottom of all this talk about the so-called flying saucer. As a matter of fact, the five hundred and ninth atomic bomb group headquarters at Roswell, New Mexico, reports that it has received one of the disks, which landed on a ranch outside Roswell. The disk landed at a ranch at Corona, New Mexico, and the rancher turned it over to the Air Force. Rancher W. W. Brizelle [sic] was the man who discovered the saucer. Colonel William Blanchard of the Roswell air base refuses to give details of what the flying disk looks like.

In Fort Worth, Texas, where the object was first sent, Brigadier General Roger Ramey says that it is being shipped by air to the AAF research center at Wright Field, Ohio.

A few moments ago, I talked to officials at Wright Field, and they declared that they expect the so-called flying saucer to be delivered there, but that it hasn't arrived as yet.

In the meantime, General Ramey described the object as being of flimsy construction, almost like a box kite. He says that it was so battered that he was unable to determine whether it had a disk form, and he does not indicate its size. Ramey says that so far as can be determined, no one saw the object in the air, and he describes it as being made of some sort of tinfoil. Other army officials say that further information indicates that the object had a diameter of about twenty to twenty-five feet, and nothing in the apparent construction indicated any capacity for speed, and there was no evidence of a power plant. The disk also appeared too flimsy to carry a man. Now back to Taylor Grant in New York.

Did history just make a major shift then or what? Let's take a deeper look.

Chapter 12

Nuclear Physicist/UFO Researcher Stanton Friedman gives testimony at the Citizen Hearing on Disclosure, regarding Roswell and more

"Out of the blue he said, the guy you really ought to talk to is Jesse Marcel. He handled the wreckage from one of those saucers when he was in the military. I practically dropped my teeth."

- Stanton Friedman

"By July 1947 it was clear to any aliens in the neighborhood that we have a primitive society whose major activity is tribal warfare and that soon, less than a hundred years, which is nothing on a cosmic time scale, we would be able to visit aliens out there, taking our brand of friendship, everybody else calls it hostility."

– Stanton Friedman

Transcript of Stanton Friedman's testimony below from Episode 11, Roswell Part I at
https://vimeo.com/ondemand/chd courtesy of **http://citizenhearing.org**, beginning at 10:55

Panelist Senator Mike Gravel: Mr. Friedman, you're an old witness here, so you know the rules.

Laughs

Stanton Friedman: I am the oldest witness.

More laughs

Senator Gravel: (inaudible) close to us.

Stanton Friedman: I'd like to show the opticals, the visuals that I supplied - just to go through them quickly, very quickly. (The) biggest study done (in) the United States Air Force, Project Blue Book (inaudible).It's 3200 sightings never referred to by the debunkers.

The next one please (meaning the slide). Symposium on Unidentified Flying Objects. Those are the hearings of July 29th, 1968. I was the youngest then, laughs, of the contributors to that. 254 pages well worth looking at.

The next one please. Dr. J. Allen Hynek's book, he was only the Air Force Project Blue Book (scientific) consultant for twenty years and chairman of the Department of Astronomy at Northwestern. You'd think when astronomers take whacks at UFOs they would at least look at Allen's book, but they don't.

The next one, there's the University of Colorado study, 965 pages, $539,000 dollars it cost us. The press gave us the vision that this proved there was nothing to flying saucers. A more careful look at the report shows that 30% of 117 cases studied in detail could not be identified. You didn't hear that when the report came out.

So, let's get those out of the way and then we'll go on to my prepared testimony.

People have often asked me, 'Why would aliens want to visit Earth?' I've noted many reasons, graduate students doing their thesis on a primitive society, mining of dense metals as we have the densest planet in the solar system, etc. Most important to me, is that I consider that all civilizations would be concerned about their own survival and security. That means keeping tabs on those primitive societies in the neighborhood that show signs of being able to bother them.

By July 1947 it was clear to any aliens in the neighborhood that we have a primitive society whose major activity is tribal warfare and that soon, less than a hundred years, which is nothing on a cosmic time scale, we would be able to visit aliens out there, taking our brand of friendship, everybody else calls it hostility.

The facts that demonstrate that are nuclear weapons, powerful rockets and radar, the beginning of advanced electronics. Isn't it amazing that the only place in the world at that time where you could study all three of these was southeastern New Mexico?

Our first nuclear weapon was detonated at Trinity Site, White Sands Missile Range, July 16, 1945. White Sands is where we were testing captured German V2 rockets, and some of our own. And that where we had our best detractor rockets, sometimes they went south instead of north. And as it turns out there were at least 3 flying saucer crashes in New Mexico.

In early July 1947 there was a crash in the small town of Corona, less than 80 miles from Roswell Army Air Field in nearby Roswell. A hundred miles west there was an unpublicized crash in about the same time, the plains of San Augustin, there's a book coming out this year by Arthur Campbell.

And there was a crash retrieval operation in Aztec, New Mexico, the four corners area, March 1948. New book is available.

I was the first to hear about the Corona crash, as discussed in my book Crash at Corona, with Don Berliner.

Simple story - I began lecturing about flying saucers in 1967 while working as a nuclear physicist in industry… such companies as GE, Westinghouse, etc. In 1978 I was in Baton Rouge, Louisiana to speak at Louisiana State University. I was at a TV station to do three interviews to promote my lecture that evening at LSU. I'd done two of the interviews and the third reporter was nowhere to be found. The station manager knew I had other things to do. He was giving me coffee, looking at his watch. He was embarrassed but he wanted to keep me there for that third interview.

Out of the blue he said, the guy you really ought to talk to is Jesse Marcel. He handled the wreckage from one of those saucers when he was in the military. I practically dropped my teeth. What do you know about him? He lives in Houma. That didn't tell me anything because I didn't know where Houma was. It was a big city in Louisiana. And I did visit there later to speak to Jesse. We are ham radio buddies, he told me, the station manager. You should talk to him. OK, the third reporter I'd heard lots of stories and you sort of put it in your gray basket – We'll see what we can do.

It was a great crowd the next day, that night, and the next day I was at the airport early, called Information and got a number for Jesse Marcel and called him. He told me his story.

I found out later he couldn't deny his involvement as his name was in papers across the country. I didn't know it when I called him. People say why did he talk to you? Well, he didn't have a choice he had to talk to somebody because he couldn't sit and lie about it, but it was public record. Soon thereafter I heard about the Plain in San Augustin crash after a lecture in Bemidji, Minnesota.

I shared both stories with an old colleague Bill Moore who lived in Minnesota. He had a third story from the *Flying Saucer Review* of the UK which is still being published which is pretty amazing that it's gone on this long. An English actor named Huey Green had noted that he heard about a crashed saucer in New Mexico when driving from Los Angeles to Philadelphia, the date was recalled as early July 1947. That was not a trip that you made very often back then. You can imagine what roads were like back in that time. Bill went to the University of Minnesota Library newspaper department (and) found the story verifying what I'd been told, giving us new names. (In) the next year and a half we found 62 people in conjunction with that case. That went up to 92 a few years later, and these guys have added, I don't know, hundreds since then.

Remember, we're talking about the most elite military group in the world. I got lucky. I called the *Roswell Daily Record* which I hadn't known existed before then, looked at editor and publisher. I mentioned that I had some articles noting the crash of a saucer as reported by Walter Haut, Hawt, it's spelled four different ways and I was shocked to be told before I could even finish a sentence, 'Oh, his wife works here.' Boy, talk about serendipity how lucky can you get? I talked to the wife. I talked to Walter. He was a big help to all of us in our research on Roswell, well thought of throughout the Roswell community.

I found the son of the rancher. Telephone operators were nice then. I said I'd like to find anyone named Brazel. 'What city?' I don't know, southeastern New Mexico. She said 'Oh I've got William Brazel in Carrizozo' Is that southeastern New Mexico? 'Yes.' OK, let's take it. He had just gotten his phone two weeks before. How lucky can you get?

Now one I planned. One of the people that shows up in the key picture that got worldwide distribution at that time was Colonel Thomas Jefferson DuBose, chief of staff to General Roger Ramey head of the 8th Air Force which is where the 509th was. This is in Fort Worth, Texas.

I checked with West Point (and) sun of a gun he was still alive. He was in his 80s and he was very forthcoming when I went to visit him. And Don and I went down and we have it on tape, a DVD out there, with General, Retired General DuBose. You don't often get a chance to talk to the general about something this important.

Several of us here will be speaking at the Roswell Festival, which is early July. Much of the early Roswell research I better stress was done before the internet. It was hard finding people. You called Information and hoped they knew something and so forth. And you're very lucky that today a key witness is right here, Colonel Jesse A Marcel, Jr., a medical doctor called back in the Army at age 68 to fight Iraq, flew over 200 combat hours as a flight surgeon in helicopters. His father was Major Jesse Marcel and he also handled wreckage in 1947. There are many Roswell debunkers who do their research by proclamation, not investigation. Their motto is 'Don't bother me with the facts my mind is made up.' 'What the public doesn't know I won't tell them.' We've all found these people. As a physicist I want facts not fantasy, so I'm most grateful for this opportunity to be here.

Senator Gravel: Thank you very much.

Applause.

Chapter 13

Roswell witness Colonel Jesse Marcel, Jr., MD gives testimony at the Citizen Hearing on Disclosure

"I was eleven years old at the time, however, and he brought us into the kitchen and saw a scattering of this strange debris on the kitchen floor which he had pre-positioned. He said look at this. I think this is what you call a flying saucer or remains thereof."

- Colonel Jesse Marcel, Jr, MD

I have a recording of an interaction of my asking Dr. Marcel a question at a Paradigm Research Group conference about whether he'd seen any of the debris which if it was twisted out of shape would bounce back to its original form afterwards. He replied that he didn't see any of that metal himself but his father told him he had, as above.

Transcript of Dr. Jesse Marcel's testimony below from Episode 11, Roswell Part I at **https://vimeo.com/ondemand/chd** courtesy of **http://citizenhearing.org**, beginning at 35:20

Senator Mike Gravel: ....Colonel, please proceed.

Dr. Jesse Marcel, Jr.: I am the son of Major Jesse Marcel. who was the intelligence officer for the 509th Composite Bomb Group based out Roswell Army Air Field in 1947. The 509th as you may recall was the squadron who ended the war with the atomic bombing of Hiroshima and Nagasaki. My dad's credentials obviously were very impressive. In the course of his career in that he not only was one of the few officers selected for the 509th but he also went to radar school and also was a staff member of the Air Force Intelligence school. The radar school is important because in that he'd been very familiar with all kinds of weather balloons and (inaudible) targets and paraphernalia associated with this kind of device, weather balloon or Mogul balloon. Mogul balloon is a still a balloon with off the shelf material.

I myself followed a career in medicine graduating from the LSU Medical School in 1961 and I joined the military shortly after my graduation and internship. My first (inaudible) in the military was being stationed aboard the USS Renville, which is a troop transport ship destined for Cuba, which spent several weeks spinning around in circles south of Cuba in preparation for the invasion which fortunately never happened or else I wouldn't be here.

I ended my career an Army colonel in Dec. of 2005 after a 13 month deployment to Iraq as a flight surgeon. And I ended my career as an Army colonel in December 2005 after a 13 month tour in Iraq where I gained 200 hours of combat flying, just things like that, just having fun like that really. I did not come home entirely unscathed. Now I got severe PTSD, from all of the, rigmarole and also developed a weakness in my legs that they think is related to some sort of toxic contamination that I became exposed to in Iraq, but that's neither here nor there.

Actually my story with the Roswell part began in the wee hours in the morning of July 1947 when I was awakened by my dad who was returning from an assignment to collect debris from an unknown origin at a ranch out of Roswell. this was the Foster Ranch, and this was the debris that Mac Brazel had run across. Apparently, the rancher by the name of Mac Brazel, notified the local sheriff of Chavez County of the downing of some sort of aircraft on his land, he was not quite sure what the nature of this was. He had seen weather balloons go down there before, so he was not sure if it was that either, but it was something very different.

The sheriff in Chavez County contacted Col. Blanchard who was the commander of the air force base in Roswell, now Col. Blanchard new my dad was the intelligence officer, so he dispatched my dad and a CIC agent, Sheridan Cavitt to investigate what this was, whether this was one our planes or an unknown crash site so it was their job to ascertain what was out there and to bring representative portions of this back to the base so they could study it to make a final determination of this.

As it turns out our house happened to be on the way to the Roswell base, and this was in the wee hours of the morning, so my dad knowing that he had seen something very special wanted my mother and myself to look at this also because as he said you'll never see this again. So, what he did he dropped off at the house awakened my mother and myself and, again in the wee hours of the morning. This was summertime I had been playing all day with my bicycle and things like that. I was eleven years old at the time, however, and he brought us into the kitchen and saw a scattering of this strange debris on the kitchen floor which he had pre-positioned. He said look at this. I think this is what you call a flying saucer or remains thereof.

I was not sure what a flying saucer was at that time. You know I was more interested in bicycling, using my 22 caliber rifle for practice. At any rate the first thing he wanted us to do was to check the debris out, make sure there was no electronic components in it. We were looking for vacuum tubes, resistors, condensers and things like that. But there wasn't any. And he already knew that but he wanted me to satisfy my own curiosity. The debris itself consisted of three components, three types. There was a foil, a very tough metallic foil of some nature that I can't really describe. I have to add that I did not see the bending of it but my dad witnessed it he said you'd fold it over and it would unfold to its original form. In addition there was black plastic debris, like a broken photograph. The strange thing that I saw that's being passed around now (to the committee) this is a replica, of one of the I beams I saw in the wreckage in that you will note there are some symbols written along the inside surface of this, they were a purplish-violet hue, semi reflective of light. But this is basically what this was.

Senator Mike Gravel: This is a replica?

Dr. Jesse Marcel, Jr.: Yes sir it's a replica. If it was original, I wouldn't have it.

Laughs.....

Senator Mike Gravel: You never know.

Dr. Jesse Marcel, Jr.: But at any rate my dad drove the debris to the base that night, I think that night or early the next morning where he was assigned by Colonel Blanchard to fly the material to General Ramey's office in Fort Worth. This was flown in the belly of a B-29 and an armed guard. This old picture of my dad taken in General Ramey's office holding what was obviously a radar target. They had already switched the debris. The look on his face is quite telling, 'You gotta be kidding me! This is not what I saw,' and it's not what I saw either. At any rate that's when the cover began in General Ramey's office. So, my dad got home and sat my mother and myself down and said in no uncertain terms, you will never talk about this. This is a non-event, and yes sir, I was an army brat, so I was following orders, I never discussed any of this with any of my friends or anyone else until after Stanton Friedman interviewed my dad in 1978.

Senator Mike Gravel: Thank you. Thank you very much.

Chapter 14

Denice Marcel, granddaughter of Jesse Marcel and daughter of Col. Jesse Marcel, Jr., MD gives testimony at the Citizen Hearing on Disclosure

"It was not anything from this Earth. That I am quite sure of."

- Major Jesse Marcel, Sr.

Transcript of Denice Marcel's testimony below from Episode 11, Roswell Part I at
https://vimeo.com/ondemand/chd courtesy of **http://citizenhearing.org**, beginning at 34:40 with Senator Gravel's introduction and Denice's testimony at 48:00

Senator Mike Gravel: I want to clear up something, because we've got three Marcel's here. We're talking about your father who was a major, intelligence officer, is that correct?

Dr. Jesse Marcel, Jr.: Yes sir.

Senator Mike Gravel: OK, then you're a colonel, and a medical doctor in addition to that, and then you've got your son. You'd be Marcel number 2, he's Marcel number 3... and then we've got Denice who I presume is your....

Jesse Marcel III: Sister.

Denice Marcel: Sister. I'm a daughter also.

Senator Mike Gravel: We got the whole family here and we're going to get testimony from all of you....

Moving ahead to Denice Marcel's testimony.

Denice Marcel: Well first of all I also want to thank the committee for taking the time to listen to our family's history. My name is Denice Marcel, I am the granddaughter of Jesse Marcel, Sr., and the daughter of retired Colonel Doctor Jesse Marcel, Jr. My grandfather was the first military officer at the UFO crash site in Roswell, New Mexico. While there he collected some of the crash site debris.

He was so amazed with the characteristics of the debris he decided he had to show my father and grandmother. And whatever it was that they had seen it has had a great impact on our family. When we moved to Clancy, Montana in the early 70s my father built a telescope in our back yard. Now this wasn't your average ordinary telescopes. To start he dug a hole in our back yard the size of a small room. For months I remember my mother and us kids helping him polish this very large mirror. From there he began constructing the telescope including building a rotating dome. This was the telescope that was later loaned to the Helena Astronomy Association, and he had built this from top to bottom.

My dad was a man who had witnessed something. This was a man who was driven. That telescope opened up a whole new world for our family. It was around the age of nine that I first became aware of UFOs, not only because of the telescope but also because there were times that my father and us kids would camp out at night specifically looking for movement in the skies hoping to catch a glimpse of a UFO.

One has to remember, we didn't have the internet then. UFOs were not discussed like they are today. I do not think that my parents would lead us to believe at such a young age that UFOs existed if my father and grandfather had not witnessed something extraordinary. In January of 1997 I accompanied my father and Ken Jeffries to Washington, DC for a hypnosis session that Dr. Neil Hibler would conduct over the course of three days. Dr. Hibler was one of the world's leading experts. He used hypnotic regressions for forensic purposes.

I had been very fortunate to be able to participate because I had just been certified as a hypnotherapist. The sessions were successful. While under hypnosis my father said he couldn't believe how vivid he'd seen his dad. I saw the emotion in his face and how it touched his heart seeing his father so clearly that day. During the sessions my father recalled being woken up by my grandfather telling him to come and look at a piece of a flying saucer, a term which most people, including himself, were not familiar with.

When asked about the materials my father's descriptions do not waver from what he had been describing throughout the years. One of the more interesting facets of the debris descriptions are the symbols or hieroglyphics that my father had seen on the I-beam. While under hypnosis the facts remained the same. Just like when he was a child he motioned grabbing the I-beam and holding it above his head to get a better look at the purple reflecting symbols.

The military claimed these symbols were merely Christmas wrap tape, but it's very unlikely and does not seem possible that three people did not recognize simple holiday decorations on some Scotch tape.

Another interesting fact my father recalled was that soon after the incident his father told the family never to talk about it again, that it was a non-event.

Now why would they have to remain silent about a weather balloon? It just doesn't make any sense to me.

It has been said that since my father did not remember anything new from those sessions, and did not remember seeing any exotic debris, electronic components or anything that resembled motors, which they were specifically looking for, this material could not have been from a UFO, that the material was just too mundane.

I believe this argument works against itself, because if it had been some radar device there should have been some very basic electronic components and it would have been mundane therefore my grandfather would never have brought it home to show his family. The only explanation that he brought this home was because he was very excited about what he had found.

My grandfather and father were very dedicated military men and always followed through with their orders. They both remained silent to the public about the incident until my grandfather had been approached by Stanton Friedman nearly 30 years after the event.

During interviews my grandfather was asked about the materials and he would say, "It was not anything from this Earth. That I am quite sure of." These words would change the course of the Marcel family.

The reason he was ordered to go to the site was because he was an intelligence officer familiar with most all of the materials used in aircraft (and?) travel. He was very qualified to make an assessment of the crash site debris. And for the record, my grandfather had nothing to gain when he spoke to Stanton Friedman. He just felt the same way that I do, that the world should know the truth. It has affected my family's life in so many good ways and some bad, but because of this I was given the greatest gift of all and that is to have an open mind.

I feel that sometimes agendas are put in front of our rights of being citizens and not everything that the government has told us is the truth because when it comes to the Roswell incident I believe my grandfather and my father.

Last and certainly not least it is my hope that for my father, my grandfather and all of the other wonderful people who have found the courage to step up and tell the truth this week will be given the respect and recognition that they deserve. Thank you.

Applause

Chapter 15

Jesse Marcel III, grandson of Jesse Marcel and son of Col. Jesse Marcel, Jr., MD gives testimony at the Citizen Hearing on Disclosure

"With the war over and life returning to sense of normalcy grandpa (Major Jesse Marcel) received a simple order an order that would change his and most of our lives forever. The heavens would open up and send us a visitor that would establish alien and flying saucer in the English vernacular and it was him they sent to investigate it."

- Jesse Marcel III

Transcript of Jesse Marcel III's testimony below from Episode 11, Roswell Part I at
https://vimeo.com/ondemand/chd courtesy of **http://citizenhearing.org**, beginning at 42:40

Senator Mike Gravel: I want to clear up something, because we've got three Marcel's here. We're talking about your father who was a major, intelligence officer, is that correct?

Dr. Jesse Marcel, Jr.: Yes sir.

Senator Mike Gravel: OK, then you're a colonel, and a medical doctor in addition to that, and then you've got your son. You'd be Marcel number 2, he's Marcel number 3... and then we've got Denice who I presume is your....

Jesse Marcel III: Sister.

Denice Marcel: Sister. I'm a daughter also.

Senator Mike Gravel: We got the whole family here and we're going to get testimony from all of you....

Moving ahead to Jesse Marcel III's testimony.

Senator Gravel: We move now to your son Jesse, the 3rd

Jesse: The 3rd, yep.

Senator Gravel: Marcel is what a French name?

Jesse: Yes.

Jesse: Thank you distinguished members of the committee. I'm here today to speak as an expert witness to what I've heard and researched about Roswell but simply to tell you about two great men, my grandfather, Major Jesse Marcel, Sr., and my father, Dr. Jesse Marcel. My grandfather was a simple man who simply wanted to live a simple life. He started at a very early age when he wasn't helping the family with the farm. He would sneak away and find parts to build radios.

Later in his life before entering the war he would use these skills to build a ham radio that would become a lifetime passion. He would spend endless hours chatting with people from around the world. Things would change rapidly as we were pulled into the Second World War.

On his own accord he left his job as a civilian draftsman to join the war effort where he excelled in his duties from the very beginning. His superiors recognized his aptitude for problem solving and sent him to intelligence school. Again he excelled in his courses and was asked to teach the next incoming class.

He would eventually end up at Roswell Air Force Base working on the nuclear armament program, the 509th deposit. With the war over and life returning to sense of normalcy grandpa received a simple order an order that would change his and most of our lives forever. The heavens would open up and send us a visitor that would establish alien and flying saucer in the English vernacular and it was him they sent to investigate it.

Chapter 16

Testimony of Roswell investigator Dr. Kevin Randle at the Citizen Hearing

"Every member of Colonel Blanchard's staff, Blanchard being the commanding officer at Roswell at the time, who was later aligned to be Chief of Staff of the Air Force, gave us a variation of that. Major Jesse Marcel Sr., the Air Force intelligence officer at the time said, on video tape, 'It seems it was something that came to Earth, but it was not something made on Earth.'"

- Kevin Randle

Transcript of Dr. Randle's testimony below from Episode 11, Roswell Part I at
https://vimeo.com/ondemand/chd courtesy of http://citizenhearing.org, the oath is at the beginning and Lt. Col. Kevin Randle's testimony begins at 21:14

Announcer: So, we'll be beginning the hearings with an oath. I'll go ahead and read it so you know what you're about to promise and I'll ask you to stand and repeat after me. So the oath is that I hereby affirm that I will tell the truth and nothing but the truth to this committee today. So, if you want to do that go ahead and stand. (pause as they stand) And Stan (Friedman) you can go ahead and do it a second time. (laughs) I do hereby affirm.

Denice Marcel, Jesse Marcel III, Colonel Jesse Marcel, Jr., MD, Kevin Randle, Stanton Friedman: I do hereby affirm.

Announcer: That I will tell the truth.

Denice Marcel, Jesse Marcel III, Colonel Jesse Marcel, Jr., MD, Kevin Randle, Stanton Friedman: That I will tell the truth.

Announcer: And nothing but the truth.

Denice Marcel, Jesse Marcel III, Colonel Jesse Marcel, Jr., MD, Kevin Randle, Stanton Friedman: And nothing but the truth.

Announcer: To this committee today.

Denice Marcel, Jesse Marcel III, Colonel Jesse Marcel, Jr., MD, Kevin Randle, Stanton Friedman: To this committee today.

Announcer: Thank you.

(Clapping)

Moving ahead to Kevin Randle's testimony.

Senator Mike Gravel: Our next witness is also a military officer. I'd like to just point out one thing about the last several days of these hearings and that was the fact that non-disclosure were proffered that many people are forced to sign non-disclosure agreements. You take an oath in the military to the Constitution, not to the president, not to a general, not to an admiral, you take it to defend the Constitution and many times you have better judgment on what is defending our country than many of our leaders. So, Colonel, with that....

Kevin Randle: First of all let me point out that I prepared a document last night for you all that deals with Project Blue Book and how it was orchestrated to be closed by the military. It was a planned operation to defend Project Blue Book completely and that was circulated I think this morning.

My name is Kevin Randle and I'm a retired lieutenant colonel, with over 20 years' service with the Army, the Air Force and the National Guard. I served on active duty as a helicopter pilot in Vietnam and as an intelligence officer in Iraq. I served on both active duty and in the active reserve with the Air Force and ended my military career as a provost marshal in the Iowa National Guard.

I've published more than 20 books about UFOs starting with *UFO Casebook* in 1989 and currently ending with *Alien Mysteries, Conspiracies and Cover-Ups* just this last month. I've been working on a book about what can be found in government files about UFOs for the last several months. In 1988 I was at a science fiction convention and participated in a debate about UFOs with some of the top science fiction writers in the world, these included Frederik Pohl and I believe, George R. R. Martin, who I mention here I mention today just because of his success in recent months.

When it was over Don Schmitt talked to me about the Roswell UFO crash and said that the Center for UFO Studies was beginning to do some research into it. He thought my military background might be a benefit because many of the witnesses were retired military and of course many of the witnesses had been married to military at the time of the events. One of the first things I noticed was that Colonel Thomas DuBose, had been identified as General Roger Ramey's aid. Brigadier Generals don't have a full Colonel as an aid. Dubose was a chief of staff a much more important position. DuBose would later provide some very interesting testimony about what had been seen and done including transferring Roswell debris to staff headquarters in Washington, DC at the time, all documented on videotape.

We had our first trip to Roswell in February 1989. We started in Albuquerque and had a meeting with Frank Joyce, but when we arrived Joyce begged off saying that he was ill. We met with a group of UFO researchers in Albuquerque but they turned out to be a group of people more interested in New Age phenomenon and not exactly UFO researchers. At any rate they had nothing of interest for us and had no insight into the Roswell case. We headed to Roswell and met with Cliff Stone. He knew a great deal about UFOs, but was unable to shed any insight in the Roswell case other than the crash site was beyond twin windmills.

We thought this might be a really good clue until we saw how many twin windmills there were in New Mexico. Our last interview was with Bill Brazel, son of Mac who had found the debris. I didn't hold out much hope for this when we met with him in Carrizozo New Mexico. He was able to provide us with some very interesting information. We chatted for a few minutes and then Brazel said to us 'My dad found this thing' and we were

off. Bill told us what had happened to his father Mac, how he had been held at the base in Roswell for a number of days, how he was asked not to talk about it. I suppose you could say he was sworn to secrecy and there didn't seem to be any threats made to him nor documents signed. Mac didn't even tell Bill much about what he had seen. Bill told us that he was out on the ranch in the next couple of years where the object had crashed or at least touched down briefly, where his dad had found this debris and he would look for some of it.

He described for on audio tape three items that he had found over the years, a piece of wood like material that was so tough he couldn't get a sliver on it when he started carving on it with a pocket knife which he said he used to cut barbed wire. He said also that it was very lightweight, brown, and it seemed to be like balsa wood. He found a bit of wire but he said you could shine a light into one end and it would come out the other which of course is fiber optics. And he had a piece of foil the famous foil that could be crushed into a ball and unfold itself without a sign of a wrinkle or a crease.

Bill showed it to his father who said, 'That looks like some of the contraption I found.' At this point we realized it was more than a misidentified weather balloon as the Air Force had suggested in 1947. It was clear from the descriptions of the material that Brazel himself had held, what he had described for us was not something that had been manufactured on Earth. We knew there was a lot more work to be done.

I located former Major, later retired Colonel, Edward Easley, who was a provost marshal in the base in 1947. A provost marshal is similar to the Chief of Police in a city, but a provost marshal also has a number of other duties revolving around security. Easley, because this was an atomic strike force, they had greater responsibility of officers of a similar grade at other military installations. He told me on audio tape several times that he'd been sworn to secrecy. Finally, in somewhat exasperation to my questions he said, 'I can't talk about it. I promised the President that I wouldn't. I don't know whether he talked to President Truman personally or a representative of the president, which is about the same thing but whatever the circumstance he believed he had promised the president he wouldn't talk about it.

Skeptics ask, 'Would the president talk to a major?' And I say, 'A scared lieutenant colonel talked to the President and the Doolittle Raid was born.

Easley confirmed that Brazel had been held on the base for several days. He said that Brazel was held in a guest house which is not exactly jail but if you have a guard at the door and you're not allowed to leave it really doesn't matter how comfortable quarters are, it still qualifies as a jail.

I will note that we can prove that Brazel was in Roswell after he first reported the find based on the documentation we have. Neighbors tell us he complained about being held there. Marian Strickland, one of the neighbors said on video tape that Brazel had been gone for several days and he was mad about it. So Easley confirmed part of the story for us. Easley was also asked by me if the craft was extraterrestrial. What happened precisely is that I asked him if we were following the right path. He said 'What do you mean?' I said 'We think it was extraterrestrial' and he said 'Well, that's not the wrong path.'

Every member of Colonel Blanchard's staff, Blanchard being the commanding officer at Roswell at the time, who was later aligned to be Chief of Staff of the Air Force, gave us a variation of that. Major Jesse Marcel Sr., the Air Force intelligence officer at the time said, on video tape, 'It seems it was something that came to Earth, but it was not something made on Earth.'

Let me say here that the skeptics have attempted to slander the memory of Blanchard by suggesting he was a loose cannon, which explains his handling of the discovery and the press release that he ordered issued. But his ratings not long after (the) Roswell crash by his superior officers, he was rated quite high and there was nothing mentioned about the Roswell case. A loose cannon is not promoted to General and is not destined to be the Chief of Staff.

Major Patrick Saunders, the base adjutant wouldn't talk much about the Roswell case when I interviewed him, did leave some documentation for us. He wrote on the fly leaf to the book *UFO Crash at Roswell*, 'Here's the truth and I still haven't told anybody anything' and he signed it 'Pat.' This page is called damage control and it tells that files were altered, that they changed personnel records and the code words and that the bodies of the craft were removed from Roswell. In a letter to his daughter, (which she) sent to me Saunders talked about how they had successfully hid the paper trail.

Walter Haut the man who wrote the press release announcing that they had captured a flying saucer signed an affidavit about what he had seen including craft and bodies. Haut said that as his position as PIO (Press and Information Officer) that he often operated as Colonel Blanchard's aide-de-camp, the Colonel not being authorized to have an aid. There has been some controversy about Haut's statement because after 20 years that I knew him he always said that he just wrote the press release. He didn't know anything beyond that. He didn't see anything beyond that. Then the affidavit signed and released after his death said that he'd seen the bodies in direct contradiction of what he'd claimed.

Ten years before that I interviewed a fellow named Richard Harris. He was a finance officer at Roswell Army Air Field and he helped Patrick Saunders bury the expenditure of money. Let me digress here for just a moment. Everything has to be paid for by the military, through the military and all expenditures must be accounted for. You can't send an aircraft on a training flight for example without needing a funding source for that flight. Of course you can have a cross country training flight from Roswell to Wright Field in Dayton, Ohio, a perfectly legitimate expense and you could always put the records of an alien craft with the bodies on the flight without having to notice it, or note it. The flight is paid for out of the training budget and there is no need to mention the genesis of the mission, which is to take the stuff to Ohio.

So Harris confirmed some of what Saunders had said and more importantly he told me that he had almost seen the bodies. According to Harris he was in a hanger where a body was temporarily located and Haut asked him if he wanted to see it. Harris said he put his hand on the door knob but he didn't turn it. This said to me, given the chance I would've opened the door. But that's today not 1947. Harris said that he didn't want to see that. But it confirms to an extent what Walter Haut said about seeing the bodies and as I said Harris told me this ten years before Walter Haut mentioned anything like that.

Now I have, noticed that I have just a minute left and I have some interesting things that I wanted to cover but let me just say this - The Air Force claimed this was Project Mogul The documentation suggests it was flight number 4. When we look at the diary created by Dr. Albert Crary, who was the leader of the project, he said flight number 4 had been cancelled. There was no flight number 4.

There is a note that they made some kind of a test flight but it's not part of the official record of the project in New Mexico. Mogul by the way was not highly classified. The equipment was off the shelf. What they were doing in New Mexico was published in the newspapers, and worse still, according to the documentation, these flights had to be announced in the FAA NOTAMS. These "Notices to Airmen" were items that could affect their navigation. An array of balloons some 600 feet long drifting along at tens of thousands of feet fit that definition. Moore was aware of that and in 1995 wrote that they had not contacted the FAA because they didn't expect this mythical flight number 4 to leave the restricted area.

I wanted to mention one final thing and I see my time is expired but on July 8th they made the press release. On July 9th according to the newspapers, the United Press reported the reports of flying saucers whizzing through the sky fell off sharply today because the army and navy began a concentrated campaign to stop the rumors. The question is what happened to make them stop on July 9th when they had published everything else?

I will say this that in 1947 the Air Force said what fell out of Roswell was a weather balloon. When they made their investigations in the mid 1990s they said they lied about that and what they said was a weather balloon was a weather balloon. They just changed the name. It was just a cluster of balloons. There was nothing special about them they were just weather balloons tethered together in a long train but it did not ask the question, why did the search members at Roswell Field identify it as such? Why could they not identify a weather balloon no matter what name you apply to it? Thank you very much.

Applause

Chapter 17

Further Testimony from Col. Jesse Marcel, Jr., MD at the Citizen Hearing

"He said that in reality, and these are his words that 'There's a black government,' which, I'm not really conspiratorial but that's what he said. He said they have control over the debris and they answer to no one, they are not elected and they have unlimited funds to spend. And he said that they're the ones who have it. They have control over it. So, you tell me what that meant but that's what he said."

- Colonel Jesse Marcel, Jr., MD

Transcript of Dr. Jesse Marcel's testimony below from Episode 11, Roswell Part I at
https://vimeo.com/ondemand/chd courtesy of **http://citizenhearing.org**, beginning at 01:02:14

Col. Marcel: Years ago I was called to Washington, I was going to a meeting and there was a gentleman by the name of Dick D'Amato who wanted to interview me when I got to Washington. And he was in the Capitol Building, Center Room 228 if I remember right. He said he wanted to talk to me about what I saw in Roswell. So, I went up to the Capitol Building and a very friendly, very nice gentleman, he said, I want to talk to you about what you saw in Roswell. And he asked me, did I want to talk in a secure room. And I said, well, sir, I'm not going to say anything I haven't said publicly already. He said, but I might tell you something and so we'll talk in a secure room.

So, we went down into the basement, several floors down below the Capitol Building and there's this beautiful meeting room there, with a big table there, with a picture of our founding fathers (motions with hand indicating it was quite large). When we sat down he sat down at the head of the table. I sat to his right. He had a legal pad to take notes on and there was a book on the table too, it was called Majestic. It was a book by Whitley Strieber that actually is a fiction account of an established fact there, and he said, this is not fiction.

So, he admitted to me right there – 'This is not fiction. This is a story about Roswell, only fictionalized.'

Questioner: So, it's a conclusion you came to after you've had a chance to listen to some people and analyze some of that material, am I correct?

Col. Marcel: Yes.

Questioner: I'm not saying necessarily whether you'd be right or wrong about it I just wanted to know how you arrived at your decision that you believe it is from non-terrestrial sources or extraterrestrial?

Col. Marcel: Well, you know this is the first time someone in the inner sanctums? of our government admitted to me that this is not fiction - Roswell. And I said I know it isn't so when are you guys going to tell the public about this. And he said, well, if it was up to me I'd of done if yesterday, but he said - it's not up to me. I'm just here to investigate the costs of keeping this secret and all that. He said that in reality, and these are his words that there's a black government, which, I'm not really conspiratorial but that's what he said.

He said they have control over the debris and they answer to no one, they are not elected and they have unlimited funds to spend. And he said that they're the ones who have it. They have control over it. So, you tell me what that meant but that's what he said.

Questioner: I obviously don't (know), but thank you very much.

Applause

Chapter 18

Testimony of Linda Moulton Howe at the Citizen Hearing

"I encountered truth embargoes repeatedly as I investigated the bloodless, trackless animal mutilations in Colorado and the surrounding region for my TV documentary special 'A Strange Harvest' beginning in September 1979 and I provided for you a letter from United States Senator Harrison Schmitt dated March 14, 1979. It is attached to my statement. It was a letter that Apollo astronaut then US Senator Harrison Schmitt of New Mexico had sent to constituents announcing the conference in Albuquerque to be held on April 20, 1979 to discuss the ongoing persistent problem of animal mutilations and he wanted the Department of Justice and the Federal Bureau of Investigation to investigate it."

- Linda Moulton Howe

Transcript of Linda Moulton-Howe's testimony below from Episode 18, Truth Embargo at
https://vimeo.com/ondemand/chd courtesy of http://citizenhearing.org, beginning at 27:02

Linda Moulton Howe: (I entered the session after it had already started) ...Blocking truth, that we're calling the 'Truth Embargo' has been the intent of the American government's official policy of denial since 1947 when the President Truman administration decided that all information about non-human intelligences interacting with this planet to be kept from the public and media, and that includes Congress and the Supreme Court and all the machinery of our government except for those designated as having quote-unquote 'a need to know' and the prowords and numbers that have gone with the few people who have had total access in MJ-12.

I encountered truth embargoes repeatedly as I investigated the bloodless, trackless animal mutilations in Colorado and the surrounding region for my TV documentary special *A Strange Harvest* beginning in September 1979 and I provided for you a letter from United States Senator Harrison Schmitt dated March 14, 1979. It is attached to my statement. It was a letter that Apollo astronaut then US Senator Harrison Schmitt of New Mexico had sent to constituents announcing the conference in Albuquerque to be held on April 20, 1979 to discuss the ongoing persistent problem of animal mutilations and he wanted the Department of Justice and the Federal Bureau of Investigation to investigate it.

And that 1979 meeting was held five months later in September 1979 as Director of Special Projects for a CBS station in Denver I began what became a nine month, eighteen hour a day, seven days a week investigation. I went to Santa Fe and did an interview with Senator Schmitt and one of the most important things that he told me was, to my question 'Are you aware of any intelligence committee or any agency that you have communicated with who has told you that we're dealing with extraterrestrial biological entities as perpetrators of worldwide animal mutilations as law enforcement repeatedly had told me?' And I remember the pause and look on his face when he said, 'No.' And I remember his next words were 'But I'm not surprised at your question or the implications.'

His request as a United States senator to have the Department of Justice and the Federal Bureau of Investigation formally investigate animal mutilations was blocked. He told me that firsthand.

The rest of the pages of the statement that I have submitted to you occurred after I was contracted with Home Box Office in March 21, 1983 to do an hour special that would follow up *A Strange Harvest* about the animal mutilations and they had a working title in the contract that I would produce for them an hour special called *UFOs, the E.T. Factor*. At the time there was an attorney in New York named Peter Gersten. He was the first attorney to file against the CIA, the NSA, National Reconnaissance Organization, the Defense Intelligence Agency and other military agencies under the brand new Freedom of Information Act, FOIA, for documents that those agencies have.

What Peter Gersten found was, initially the Central Intelligence Agency denied that it had any information about them, but that the National Security Agency had a hundred and eighteen. So, he would send the Central Intelligence Agency's formal letter to the National Security Agency asking for the documents referenced by the CIA. And the National Security Agency would send him a formal letter referencing the fact that the Central Intelligence Agency had thirty-five documents shared with the National Security Agency! Eventually he assembled dozens of documents that came from those agencies each one pointing the finger at the other.

It went to the Supreme Court. The Supreme Court denied to hear what essentially was a New York attorney representing Citizens Against UFO Secrecy in what was called Ground Saucer Watch under the first Freedom of Information Act, simply asking for information from our government about documents that they all said they had.

Even though the Supreme Court denied the carrot that they would take on that lawsuit. Out of it came many pages of blacked out information that has been held up by Stanton Friedman and others overs of us over the years, that agencies that are not allowed to speak and have been responsible for counterintelligence since World War II to convince us that there's nothing to this phenomena.

[Moderator interrupts stating there is one minute left]

They are the very agencies who have the information and have been interlinked with Majestic 12, appointed by Harry S. Truman, who within a very short period of time, after the crash retrievals in July of 1947. And Majestic 12, MJ-12, whatever the numbers and letters are in 2013, the same kind of inner sanctum agency still exists interacting with other inside inner sanctum black agencies. There is a parallel black budget. There is a parallel government. This is how the truth this gentleman (referring to a previous filmed testimony) described and that many people in our government have known since at least 1941 when there was another crash retrieval from Missouri and an instrument called the utronic propulsion unit was hand delivered to Oppenheimer for his use in developing and researching what became the atomic bomb.

And finally the Truth Embargo said that you would have reference to the two agencies that in the beginning had the most information, the Atomic Energy Commission and the Department of the Navy. All of those documents of all of the truth that he (pointing, again to someone interviewed and shown on video earlier) has said, that I have tried to report about now for thirty-three years. They are essentially off limits to any access by Congress or even the President, because they are classified as only under a need to know and probably the Suitland, Maryland archive has them.

Moderator: Thank you.

Applause.

Chapter 19

More testimony by Linda Moulton Howe at the Citizen Hearing

"... to get those people, law enforcement and ranchers to stand up in front of a camera and tell the world what they've seen with their own eyes is the biggest difficulty of my entire career because we are on a planet where humans are more afraid of humans and their ridicule than they are of extraterrestrials."

- Linda Moulton Howe

Many thanks to Steve Bassett (pictured above) of the Paradigm Research Group (PRG) for the following testimony - Transcript of Linda Moulton-Howe's testimony below from Episode 9, Various Issues at **https://vimeo.com/ondemand/chd** courtesy of **http://citizenhearing.org**, beginning at 46:18

Linda Moulton Howe: ...The first global media report about this phenomena was in September of 1967 when a female horse named Lady was found dead on a ranch near Alamosa in southern Colorado. The horse's entire scull and long neck had been stripped of flesh and every organ in the chest of that horse had been surgically excised according to a medical doctor. There was no blood anywhere, not in the animal, not around the animal and nowhere nearby. And there were no tracks of the animal. It was powdery soil and the animal is lying there stripped of flesh, but there were no tracks around the body, not even the own horse's tracks. But a hundred and some feet away there were horse tracks in a circle, as if the horse had been caught in something in which the feet had gone around in a circle. And then a hundred and some feet away the body was found.

At that same time, [and Jennifer image 00] on July 15, 1984, *The Sunday Times* in Australia headlined quote "Cover-up Alleged over UFO linked to Animal Slaughter - Many reports of UFOs and strange lights in the sky." Farmers in the Adelaide Hills have discovered mutilated animal corpses and burn marks on the ground. In one incident researches say a farmer discovered four cows with holes drilled into their skulls and the brains removed.

Adelaide UFO researcher Colin North said "I have been told the army asked the farmer to remain quiet about the animals and that the army would cover the whole thing up." Mr. North said pod marks in the ground and burnt tree tops indicated the UFO craft had landed.

They had a journal from 1911 that had been published about a hundred four sheep being found in an Australian billabong, the ear, eye, tongue, genitals cored out. A hundred and four all in one billabong with no blood and no tracks around those animals either.

....with a specimen collected via electrosurgical excision. It is not possible to tell whether this lesion was caused by a laser. It does appear does appear consistent with a heat induced injury." But Lynn Louder called me at KMHTV in Denver after the broadcast of my TV documentary *A Strange Harvest* and he said that he had seen my documentary and he was calling me because, and this is what he said to me, he knew that something from outer space was involved in the mutilations that the RCMP in Canada had investigated.

When I asked him why then have you told the media the perpetrators are satanic cults? He said, the reason was because he felt the truth was too difficult to report publicly. And to get those people, law enforcement and ranchers to stand up in front of a camera and tell the world what they've seen with their own eyes is the biggest difficulty of my entire career because we are on a planet where humans are more afraid of humans and their ridicule than they are of extraterrestrials.

I am hoping that in this Citizen Hearing, I kind of exercised what I hope will take place. All of this should be presented in formal executive official congressional hearings. Why has the agencies of the United States government, the Department of Justice, the FBI, the CIA, the NSA, the DIA, the NRO, they've all been studying this, they have more data than I do. Why shouldn't this country get back on the track of being of and by and for the people?

Chapter 20

We're in deep #@*&! Where do we go from here?

"We're at a tipping point..., and it's not clear which way it's going to go, but **WE** *are the ones that are going to determine which way it's going to go, and it's up to us."*

- Dr. Edgar Mitchell, April 19, 2008

In a nutshell here's the deal. We have an unelected secret government who aren't investigated or held accountable for anything they do. No conspiracy theory here, just a review of history beginning with the enactment of the National Security Act of 1947. With elections for federal and state governor being censored by the corporate media, we're stuck with two different brands of puppets, but not serious representation in many key respects and certainly not people who will so much as question the secret government no matter what atrocities they commit.

If we had informed caring people as representatives then things would be put in the hands of the people, not special interest groups' puppeteers. We're talking about 545 people as per Charlie Reese's famous column referred to in the introduction to this manuscript.*

*See, http://articles.orlandosentinel.com/1984-02-03/news/os-ed-charley-reese-545-people-1984-073111_1_tax-code-president-vetoes-con-game

The point is there are not many people who are allowing this insanity to continue in proportion to the 320,000,000 they're not truly representing. What we have is a disproportionate minority of censors misguiding most at the height of the Information Age at an extreme cost to human beings both within the USA and outside our borders as well as being a considerable threat to the continued existence of humans on this planet. How would we explain our insane behavior of allowing them to get away with such an easily decipherable yet destructive plan to an outside intelligence if given a chance?

I'm proposing that we overcome the election censors and choose candidates who are not puppets of huge campaign contributors. Unlike other nations, we don't have a single member of any political party except Democrats and Republicans in all national positions discussed by Charlie Reese. We should push for fair open televised debates in which all candidates who are on the ballot, or in the case of the presidency enough ballots to win, are invited to participate. if they don't include them, then I suggest we take a good look at who they censored and vote according to common sense and decency, not who advertised more. I also propose openly proclaiming to those in power that the gag's up, we know they're creating problems in major areas and they need to stop it now.

Also, we need to get people registered to vote. We're missing enough right there to damn near turn this thing around. But for those of you who've lost your voting rights due the Drug War and other bogus reasons, always remember that there is far more power in informing others than via a single vote. No election has ever come down to a single vote.

"What about the Libertarian Party?"

Some aspects of the Libertarian Party are fabulous, and make total sense, as per this video of Paul Jones who I ran against in the 2014 election and I consider a good friend. So, I would say vote Green if you can, and if it's either one of the two branches of what Chomsky has referred to as "The Business Party," then at least contact the Libertarian first before the election to discuss social issues with her or him to see if headway can also be made in these areas. If you're planning on running for office yourself and can best get on the ballot as a Libertarian, then do so but run as a Libertarian-Socialist, which you'll see further on is not an oxymoron. I doubt they'd let you run for US Senate* adopting such values, but you might get to run for congress and each and every voice of reason we get in there will be one more than we have now.

* I don't know how Kevin Zeese would describe himself, but he did get the nomination of both the Greens and the Libertarians when running for US Senate from Maryland, so maybe you could run for Senate or even the presidency itself as a Libertarian-Socialist under the banner of the Libertarian Party. Either way, we need candidates and my first choice if given but one would be to run as a Green. There really isn't a national party I'm completely satisfied with and have thought we should eventually start "The Rational Party," but we'll see, perhaps that won't be necessary.

Above: Libertarian congressional candidate Paul Jones makes an excellent point
about the absurdity and harmfulness of United States Drug War in just a few seconds.

Below, what I titled **Paul Jones hits the nail on the head** posted on my YouTube channel specifically at **https://www.youtube.com/watch?v=TMEpslxldjs&feature=youtu.be.**

Paul Jones: You take these innocent kids and adults that are law abiding citizens in every way, but if we catch them with a little too much weed on them, they go to prison, for years! What the hell's the sense in that? Then we support their family, because they can't work because they're in prison. It's insane. It is insane.

Adults should be treated like adults. They should have a right to do what they want with their body as long as it doesn't harm someone else and the government's gotta quit this pretending they're our nanny ... That's all I'll say.

Audience applauds, including me. When do you see that sort of thing in a televised political debate or forum?

There is a lot of agreement with how the Libertarians feel about the Drug War and our overseas wars. The disagreement seems to be about taxes and issues of social welfare safety nets, among other things discussed with Noam Chomsky in the following chapter. In personal talks Paul and I didn't disagree in thinking we need to make sure the hungry are fed, especially since so many are children.

I think it's possible that we could make some changes to the US Libertarian Party and make it far better, by focusing more on the roots of libertarianism as will be discussed shortly. If that happens I doubt you'll be hearing rumors about the Koch brothers supporting their candidates anymore.

Chapter 21

Discussing the US Libertarian Party with Noam Chomsky

"What the so-called libertarian movement in the United States, which incidentally I have friends I don't agree with about things, but their policies, whatever their goals may be, their policies tend to drive people under the control of the worst possible form of tyranny, unaccountable, private tyranny and that's the opposite of libertarianism."

- Noam Chomsky

Transcript of Noam Chomsky video below titled *Noam Chomsky on the US Libertarian Party, Part I* posted at **http://youtube.com/drkenhildebrandt** specifically at **https://www.youtube.com/watch?v=Bf9TLzSnd9M&feature=youtu.be**.

Ken Hildebrandt: Greetings, we're here with Professor Noam Chomsky at MIT, who's the most cited living author and the reason I bring that up all the time is because I want to bring attention to how often he's NOT seen on TV. If he's the most cited living author, what don't they want you to hear that he has to say?
Well anyway, the reason that I'm here today Noam is that, I've run for congress a couple of times as you know and what I've seen, and what's a disturbing factor I've seen is the rise of the Libertarian Party in the United States. And I want to ask you to give us a little background on the history of how libertarianism in the US has strayed from its origins in Europe.

Professor Noam Chomsky: Well, libertarian conceptions basically come out of classic liberalism, 17th, 18th century classic liberalism. The core principles of classic liberalism were opposition to illegitimate authority. People should be free from constraints and controls by authoritarian structures which have no inherent legitimacy, basically one or another form of tyranny or domination. So, in the early days they were concerned with feudalism with tyrannical states and so on. By the late 19th century on through the 20th century, some of the major authoritarian illegitimate structures are the corporate system, private tyrannies. A corporation is basically a tyranny, dominated from the top, take orders from above given down below, at the bottom you can rent yourself. You have no, I mean it doesn't even pretend to have anything like popular democratic control.

What the so-called libertarian movement in the United States, which incidentally I have friends I don't agree with about things, but their policies, whatever their goals may be, their policies tend to drive people under the control of the worst possible form of tyranny, unaccountable, private tyranny and that's the opposite of libertarianism.

Ken: Going back to 2004 Vice-Presidential debate, it was interesting because they had a Green there and also had a Libertarian and the Libertarian whenever it came to social issues he was like, 'Well, we leave that up to the community.' They had it right with the Drug War. They had it right with not being, the US getting involved with all these interventions, to get out of those. But when it comes to social policy it's like 'We leave that up to the community. Communities aren't doing a very good job. We leave it up the community now.

Noam: Who's the community? The community is not a collection of people who are equal in opportunity and power. The community, the society consists of a highly inegalitarian structure, with extreme wealth and power concentrated in a very small sector and most people disempowered. That's the community. So, if you leave things up to the community what you're in effect saying is 'Let's let the top fraction of one percent in wealth and power determine everything. And what are they going to determine? Well...

Ken: In their favor.

Noam: In their interests. I'm not saying that whoever this speaker was believes this, but the implications, the consequences of this pretense that you're leaving things to a community of equal participants is just wildly off base. You're leaving it to a community of people within, a group within which a tiny percentage, actually literally a fraction of one percent have overwhelming power and opportunity and as you move down the scale, less and less and most of them are simply disempowered.

Ken: What I'm worried about is we're coming up on (an election). Charlie Reese wrote an article entitled *545 People.* In this he made an argument that you've got the Senate, you've got the congress and you've got the president and nine Supreme Court members. So, other than that, 536 of those people we choose.

Noam: Shakes his head 'no.'

Ken: Well, sort of, I mean with the electoral process (being what it is). We all know that.

Noam: We don't actually choose them. For one thing a large part of the population doesn't even bother to vote. There are good reasons for it.

Ken: But you know my struggle against all odds has been to get these elections, incidentally actually last time I was included in the debate. But the Republican didn't show, so they didn't televise it (on corporate TV). So, if it's not put over the propaganda box it's like it didn't even happen. But what I fear is that with the rise of the third party it seems that the Green Party, in the US, the Libertarian Party is rising and the Green Party is lessening. And I just want to see more.

Noam: Well, there's a reason for that. The Libertarian Party, whatever the goals and intentions of the individuals is a party whose programs favor concentrated wealth and power.

Ken: But they're fooling a lot of regular folks.

Noam: ...relatively acceptable.

Ken: They're fooling a lot of regular folks though, that's what I'm saying.

Noam: That's what I'm saying, perfectly nice people. Many of these people say I really believe in freedom, liberty, equality and so on, but take a look at their policies, their policies say for example, remove regulation on financial institutions. What does that do? It frees them to concentrate power, to punish the rest of us and of course in the background is something that's not said, take say financial institutions. The government actually in many ways designs policies which ensure that the taxpayer subsidizes those institutions.

Ken: Oh, of course.

Noam: And that's not discussed.

Ken: No, that's not discussed.

Noam: Incidentally that's not a joke. There recently was an IMF study, International Monetary Fund study of the profits of the major, I think half dozen major US banks and to trace them almost entirely to a tacit government insurance policy that is a tacit commitment that they won't be allowed to crash. Now that's not just the bailouts. That's a small part of it. They get access to cheap credit. They get inflated credit ratings. They have the opportunity of making very risky and hence profitable investments because if they collapse the taxpayer will step in and bail them out. All of that contributes enormously to their profits.

The business press, Bloomberg, estimated the implicit taxpayer subsidy at about over 80 billion dollars a year.

Ken: Right.... Now what do you say to the person who says, 'libertarian socialism' is an oxymoron?

Noam: In the United States because in the United States libertarian means support for capitalist autocracy and yes, it would be an oxymoron to talk about socialist support for capitalist autocracy. But that's a US term. ... in the world, the legacy of classic liberalism which is quite different.

Ken: Worker's struggles.

Noam: Like say John Stewart Mill, outstanding figure of classic liberalism was in favor of worker ownership of enterprises.

Ken: Wow, because when you talk about some of these things I'm making it so the average Joe or Jane can understand.

Noam: In the United States.

Ken: Yeah, in the United States.

Noam: But the US is off the spectrum. This is a business run society to an unusual extent.

Ken: Well they got funding, supposedly, well not the race, the guy I was running against, but somebody else I heard that he got funding from the Koch brothers...

Noam: I wouldn't be surprised. Yeah, the Koch brothers call themselves libertarians.

Ken: Yeah. (laughs)

Noam: Meanwhile they've lavished with huge government subsidies, protected in all sorts of (ways). I mean even the Pentagon is to a substantial extent a subsidy for the energy corporations.

Ken: Oh, of course.

Noam: Their pipelines, sea lanes, the energy system working for them and so on. That's a small part of it.

Ken: I'm hoping that the Green Party can be seen as something apart from tree hugging, ah, not that that's bad, tree huggers or whatever.

Noam: The phrase is interesting. See, in a highly indoctrinated society like ours if you're trying to protect the commons from attack from private power you're denounced as tree hugging. If you can't answer the arguments you use invective.

Ken: I know, and they use it, and it's powerful. I mean they can change, like green can become a bad word. I remember the AYDS appetite suppressant candy and then all of the sudden you don't see commercials for that after AIDS came around.

Noam: The effect of propaganda is pretty dramatic. One interesting case is a great current concern is the health system. There have been polls in the United States for decades which show that the population, most people are in favor of some kind of national health care.

Ken: Yeah, they've had it in other countries for...

Noam: Of course it's never even been considered.

Ken: Well, public option was, but not...

Noam: The public option, when Obama produced his Affordable Care Act, initially there was a proposal for public option. It was favored by a large majority of the population. It was dropped without discussion.

Skipping a few minutes of our discussion, the conclusion of my talk with Noam Chomsky continues below in what's titled *Noam Chomsky on the Libertarian, Republican and Democratic parties* and posted at **http://youtube.com/drkenhildebrandt** specifically at **https://www.youtube.com/watch?v=FnY7lNpLBpA&feature=youtu.be.**

Ken: From what I understand 19 out of 20 (people) are covered (under the Affordable Care Act). Shouldn't we live in a society where 20 out of 20 are covered?

Noam: Well, that's why I said it's a small step.

Ken: And it (public option) would've been cheaper.

Noam: It's a small (step). It would've been much cheaper.

Ken: We could've covered everybody, thrown out the middlemen.

Noam: It would've been much cheaper just to extend Medicare to the whole population.

Ken: Exactly.

Noam: But let's be clear it's a small step. In the United States government funding of medical care is about at the level of other industrialized countries, but that's about half of the total cost. Since we have to go through a privatized system costs are heavily inflated.

Ken: It's so wasteful.

Noam: So it's roughly twice the per capita cost of other countries and pretty poor outcomes. That's because of the privatized element. There's a ton of bureaucracy. In fact the costs are vastly underestimated. Even this figure of twice as high as other countries, standard figure, that's an underestimate for ideological reasons. Economists do not count the costs to individuals. So if, suppose you say, originally my wife had to get, go through this system to get insurance. Well, you know it takes days of work. You have to work through a maze of bureaucracy. You try to use the web, it crashes.

Ken: Oh, it's crazy. (Remember, I worked with insurance companies as a self-employed chiropractic physician for 13 years, so have had a fair bit of exposure to how the various insurances work.)

Noam: You call somebody; you're waiting like an hour before you can speak with them. (Not only that but more than once it's happened when your call finally goes through and then it somehow gets cut off before the transfer happens and you have to call back and start all over again.) All of these are costs.

Ken: Right.

Noam: These are huge costs but to individuals so they're not counted. Same is true quite generally. Suppose you get a bank statement and there's a mistake in it and you want to get the bank to fix it, so you call the number, you get an automated response with a menu that doesn't have what you want. You push another button.

Ken: Try to talk to a person.

Noam: Then you sit there for half an hour listening to music while very once in a while an automated voice says, you know, 'We appreciate your...' Finally you get some human being, maybe you solve it. That's a cost to you and that cost is spread over to huge numbers of people, but those are not counted by economists. What they count is the cost to the business. So, this may be profitable to the business so it's called efficient but it's costly for the population, but that's not called inefficient.

These are ideological decisions. If we included them then the cost of US medical care would not be twice as high as other countries it'd be far beyond that. It's an extremely inefficient system for people, quite efficient for the rich, and that's the way policy's designed. And if you follow the Libertarian proposals, so-called 'libertarian' proposals, that's what the world would be like even more so than today.

Ken: So, now what do you think now, libertarians when it comes to, I mean they're against the ACA, but what are they...?

Noam: What are they in favor of?

Ken: I don't know.

Noam: We know what they're in favor of. Take say Rand Paul, who's a doctor of some kind.

Ken: Yeah he's...

Noam: Something. But he said at one point that he's opposed in any government involvement in health care because it's the same as slavery. He said 'I'm a doctor and if the government orders me to take care of someone that's slavery.' Yeah, that's libertarianism. In other words,
If you can pay for it maybe I'll do it for you. If you can't, I'm not going to do it. Why should I bother?'

Ken: If we had public option the doctor would still be paid.

Noam: Yeah..., but he would be compelled to do something at a cost below what someone else would pay him.

Ken: Well that's, I'll tell you when I was interviewed (on WDBJ7 a major Roanoke, Virginia television station that broadcasts a couple of hours away from Roanoke in all directions)

Noam: You work only for the rich. You don't have to take care of the people who come in. Same with an emergency room at a hospital. If somebody comes in..., we actually have national health care in the United States. It's called emergency rooms. And if you can get into an emergency room they have to take care of you. And that's extraordinarily costly even from the point of view of say economist's measures and for human beings it's tremendously costly. You sit in the emergency room for hours and days and you know, so on and so forth.

But Rand Paul's position was 'I don't want to be forced to take care of people. I don't want emergency rooms to exist. I want to just do what I choose for the rich...'

Ken: So, here we are in the US and we rank I think it's in the, like around 35 or something like that in life expectancy. I remember you criticized this in Manufacturing Consent when it was in the low 20s and now the rankings are up there I think the last I saw was 36.

It's funny because in the debate (which was our second US congressional candidate forum, this one held by the League of Women Voters in Charlottesville, Virginia in late October 2014) I mentioned, I said in the high 40s because there are different figures you see.

Noam: Yea.

Ken: And the guy twisted it around in the paper and he said that i said that people lived to be in their high 40s. (laughs)

Noam: (laughs)

Ken: And we're not doing that great with the system here. I remember as a chiropractor when I left the office Medicare was good. When i started it was bad but it became one of the better insurances because all the rest had gotten increasingly worse...

Noam: Well, Medicare is interesting. It's much more efficient than the private system but it is expensive because it has to work through the private system. Those are the extra costs of Medicare. Like, I have Medicare because of my age and it does work through the private system. You still have to pick a private insurance policy.

Ken: As a secondary (to cover expenses Medicare doesn't cover, since Medicare pays 80% of one's bill leaving another 20% for the patient which can be astronomical if one is unfortunate enough to have an operation and/or a hospital stay.)

Noam: All of those are costs.

Ken: Now when you say 'public option' and 'Medicare for all' I mean you said that we should really do away with the other, with the co-pay.

Noam: We should do away with private insurance altogether.

Ken: Altogether.

Noam: Altogether. In most countries in the world. My wife happens to come from Brazil. If you're ill in Brazil you go to a doctor, you go to a hospital. Now actually that's a little bit misleading because in many countries the public system is underfunded so the wealthy will go to private doctors and private hospitals.

Ken: Right.

Noam: So it's still kind of two tiered but in a different way, but at least for the general population you're guaranteed some level of health care with no costs.

Ken: Well I certainly hope that with these, the upcoming elections I mean people are fed up if you look at what the Republicans and Democrats are putting out there for the presidency it's really terrible. I hope that we have the...

Noam: Take a look at the figures on respect for the political system.

Ken: Way down there.

Noam: Congress it's single digits.

Ken: Single digits.

Noam: The president maybe, you know, 15%. Even the Supreme Court which used to be high up I think is in the low 20s now.

Ken: Well, people are getting aware but they still consider outsiders as spoilers and we don't have time to get into that. That's actually the book I'm writing is called *Election Spoilers* and I'm saying that the spoilers are the media who censor the candidates, not the candidates who challenge the system. And there's not much difference between the two as time goes on I mean they're both corporate funded parties.

Noam: Well, what's happened is that over the years both parties have shifted to the Right.

Ken: Exactly.

Noam: And the Republicans have shifted so far that they're simply off the spectrum.

Ken: Off the spectrum.

Noam: They're not a parliamentary party anymore.

Ken: No.

Noam: In fact one of the leading conservative commentators Norman Ornstein, very respected conservative political analyst at American Enterprise Institute, he simply described the modern Republican Party as a radical insurgency which has abandoned any commitment to the parliamentary process. And you can see that in the last ten years.

Ken: And they get away with it.

Noam: Yeah, they're getting away with it.

Ken: So far.

Noam's assistant Bev comes in so Noam can prepare for a skype interview that didn't work due to it having to have seventy some odd updates and taking too much time. I think they planned on giving up entirely on skype interviews after this. Anyway, I had been told beforehand we would be interrupted but then would have a few more minutes after his interview was over. Below we continue.

Ken: You've said and I've said, this is the reason I'm doing this, our planet's future's at stake right now. If we don't turn this thing around...

Noam: Actually, this is the first time in human history when we have to make decisions which will determine whether our grandchildren have a decent world to live in. We're advancing towards a precipice which we might fall over in which the chances for decent human survival are finished.

And there are basically two crucial problems, one is nuclear weapons.

Ken: Yep.

Noam: We've, by a miracle, a virtual miracle we've survived the last 70 years without destroying ourselves. And it's always, always a chance. The other is simply climate catastrophe.

Ken: Right.

Noam: Which is coming along and we can try to deny it if we like but that's determining the fate of future generations.

Ken: I hope people wake up at election time. That's what i hope because...

Noam: Well, actually the population is in favor of stronger actions, but the decision making classes are not. So you read say the newspapers they tell you about the marvels of, of the great expansion of fossil fuel production, it's going to lead to a century of energy independence, whatever that means. Oil companies are prepared if the current glut declines to pour new oil into the market is just wonderful except that it's destroying ourselves.

Ken: It's unbelievable what people do for profit. Well, I hope that things do turn around in the next election. I mean those 545 people who Charlie Reese bought up I mean basically, I mean well, governors have a little say (all the others discussed by Reese are in the federal government).

Noam: Well, take say Congress, Mitch McConnell, his chief priority is to insure that we maximize the use of the most destructive fossil fuels, namely coal, because his rich constituents can make profit from it.

Ken: Profit over people at the expense of the world.

Noam: In this case it's really lethal.

Ken: And Germany is shutting down their nuclear facilities. We could get to solar, we could get to geothermal, we could get to hemp. We could deal with this.

Noam: That's the most successful economy in the world and they're moving towards sustainable energy.

Ken: Wow, well I hope we end up doing the same because we don't have much time.

Noam: Nods in agreement.

Noam: Gotta keep fighting.

Ken: Definitely.

Conclusion:

"Blessed are the Censors, for they shall inhibit the Earth!" – Alfred E. Neuman, MAD Magazine, June 1970

As stated in Chapter 20, I'm proposing we overcome the election censors and choose candidates who are not puppets of huge campaign contributors. Additionally I'm proposing we tell the others who do have wealthy campaign contributors that their scam has been revealed, and we realize how they're shafting the people. We're hardly setting the bar too high in asking them to stop the Drug War, the wars overseas, the illegality of useful plants such as industrial hemp, and revert the tax structure to something like it was in the 1960s, with modifications as discussed.

I also would like to see UFO/ET disclosure, which if anyone thinks is out there, how do you explain why the government openly investigated it from the end of 1947 to the end of 1969? Was it all for nothing? Do you really think that? In this manuscript I drove home one case, that of Roswell. All it takes is one case to open up this can of worms, though I did add another in which retired Captain David Schindele of the Air Force testified about something he'd seen and was even discussed in the December 17, 1966 issue of the *Saturday Evening Post*, but what the Post article didn't mention was what its writers had no way of knowing, that the widely reported UFO took all the nuclear missiles offline, meaning it just shut them all down, or coincidentally they all shut down as the UFO appeared, though nothing like that had ever happened before. It was rare for even one to go offline. Um, don't you think that has a wee bit to do with national security? Captain Shindele testified that he didn't tell anyone about it for over 39 years, not even his wife!

Concerning something else in the sky that has been identified yet hasn't been explained, wouldn't it be nice to know what the aerial spraying is all about we're seeing these days? Jet aircraft don't leave trails that go across the entire visible sky and then spread out from there. This is not jet fuel exhaust. If it was then we would've been seeing this all through the jet age, not just the last 20 years or so. Is it helping to counter global warming? If so, then why all the secrecy? We need disclosure about this as well.

Autism seemed to pop out of nowhere, around the same time we started seeing these trails, which reportedly contain aluminum, barium and strontium. Excuse me, but we aren't supposed to be breathing metals, nor are we designed to consume these things, but if they're dumping it in the sky it's falling to earth. Therefore, there is no such thing as organic anymore, unless it's grown in a green house. Otherwise, it's been sprayed.

Once you see this it's beyond comprehension that it hasn't created more of a public outcry. I can't help but think of the words of a former high school teacher of mine Mr. Louis Couche who used to say, *"The best way to keep a secret is to mimeograph it and hand it out."* I used to think his statement was foolish, until I saw this happening and most people not having a clue that this astronomically expensive military campaign was happening right over their heads.

SOAP – Subjective, Objective, Assessment, Plan

Everyone wants a better world but few have a plan. In medicine there's an acronym, SOAP, Subjective – the patient's complaint(s), Objective – the doctor's findings, Assessment – what's it called and Plan – what can be done to treat the malady? No doctor practices without a plan, yet most who struggle for a better world have no plan, at least here in the US. The plan is to replace political puppets with people and pressure the ones who haven't been replaced to finally do what's reasonable instead of cowing to their puppeteers.

None of this is rocket science. We're all being royally scammed and the caring and brave who are informed have certainly had enough. Are there enough of us? Only time will tell, but I'm not going to give in to being shafted by a small proportion of humans who are scamming and endangering the world. It's up to each person to either try or side with the disproportionate minority of the nation's and world's insane oppressors.

Unlike other industrialized nations with similar governmental structures, we don't have a single member of any political party except Democrats and Republicans in all national positions discussed by Charlie Reese. We should push for fair open televised debates in which all candidates who are on the ballot, or in the case of the presidency enough ballots to win, are invited to participate. If they don't include them, then I suggest we take a good look at who they censored and vote according to common sense and decency, not who advertises more, or has more charisma.

As this book goes to print it looks like it's going to be a four way race for President of the United States in 2016, Trump as the Republican, Dr. Jill Stein for the Green Party, former New Mexico Governor Gary Johnson, a Libertarian and long time outspoken critic of the Drug War, and Hillary Clinton on the Democratic side.

Regarding Trump, suppose he stops Muslims from entering the country, what's to stop someone from being a radical Islamic terrorist posing as a born-again Christian? Did not Soviet spies infiltrate the CIA? Surely that was a lot more difficult than posing as a Christian. It's best we get at the roots of these problems, not cause more of them by fighting fanaticism with fanaticism.

In one of the debates Trump openly proclaimed the Iraq War should've never happened, cost us some two trillion dollars, and much loss of lives and limbs. What I don't understand is if he knows this, why does he want to bomb ISIS, which doesn't even have its own country, knowing that these tactics lead to further destabilization?

In my opinion considering what I learned in Harlem as discussed in Part I, Chapters 2 and 6, platform matters most. And when it comes down to platform, Dr. Jill Stein comes out ahead in many areas, though not all. I have problems with her stated stance on the rights to gun ownership, saying the "mentally ill" should not have gun access. Everyone alive has some classification in the DSM, the bible of mental illnesses. Lincoln got severely depressed and thus would not be able to own a gun under this criteria.

As for the other races, I suggest helping Greens and like-minded independents by supporting their candidacies, so we can join the rest of the civilized world in having a variety of people in Congress, not merely factions of what Noam Chomsky has called "The Business Party," who aren't for you, aren't for your loved ones, not for the world, and if they really thought things through not even for themselves, since they too live in a more dangerous world than need be just a few button pushes away from changing forever.

If your only other choice is a Libertarian, then please bring up social issues to that candidate. Ask specifically if she or he would like to see the end of unnecessary infant and childhood deaths at a rate of about 700* per hour worldwide for what just a fraction of the Pentagon budget could stop.

- There has been an improvement in this area, yet the tragedy continues. It's still outrageous, but has for whatever reasons come down from the 1000 per hour talked about elsewhere in this manuscript.

If we don't get to elect people outside the two aspects of "The Business Party," then we need to let those who are in office realize fully that we want the inefficiencies and barbarism discussed herein stopped immediately. Each of us is making history at this critical time of human existence. In the opinion of a politically enlightened friend of mine who's of the ripe age of 21, it's the time to live if you think about it. We're the deciders regarding which way things are going to tip. Will reason prevail? "It's up to us," as Dr. Edgar Mitchell stated as per the conclusion of Part 1. Let's do this. If enough of us try we'll win. We have the internet. We have social media. We can break through the lies and spread the truths.

We don't need a revolution. We need an INFORMolution. We need to elect people over political puppets based on common sense, not on who spent more, or who was or was not included in televised debates. We also need to pressure the puppets to stop the insanity. Remember, we're not setting the bar very high here and none of this is rocket science. It's all easy to understand. We're all in this together. May WE prevail, together, now.

My hope is that enough come away from this book understanding the following:

1) US federal elections are a farce that comes at an enormous expense, not limited to just those in the United States, but also those in many other places throughout the globe. Their scam is hardly complicated. Candidate debates are held and televised omitting candidates who are on the ballot, or in the case of the presidency, enough ballots to win the election. The media simply pretend the others don't exist. One of my earlier titles for this book was "Same Old Scam." With the internet the scam can be overcome, which has been my simple message since the year 2000.

It's even easier now, and finally happened with the Sanders campaign in March 2016. His supporters bombarded Twitter with tweets about why he still very much had a chance to win the Democratic nomination and they said why. The media had been trying to claim it was over for the Sanders campaign. Well, his supporters helped overcome the media with this tweet bombardment. He went on to have crushing defeats over Hillary Clinton in Alaska, Hawaii and the state of Washington immediately afterwards. In the end of course he threw in the towel, much to the chagrin of many, if not most, of his supporters.

2) It seems that one aspect of Bernie Sanders' idea of socialism is to raise the taxes only for the wealthy back just a tiny bit higher than what Ronald Reagan had first lowered them to, which was 50%, but had been 91% when Republican Dwight D. Eisenhower left office in 1961. That's hardly socialism in my opinion, and does nothing to lessen the burden on the poor and middle classes.*

*Even Sanders himself admitted that he was less of a socialist than Republican Dwight D. Eisenhower here http://www.ontheissues.org/2016/Bernie_Sanders_Tax_Reform.htm

What apparently seemed to be understood in Eisenhower's day but not now is that people only make money via two avenues, Earth and human resources, since we're not importing either from Mars. The top one percent of income earners are paying just 39.6% now, which is no doubt no small part of why we've seen this vast divide between the ultra-wealthy and everyone else over the last few decades, instead of having the tide rise for all as it should've as we improved technologically in leaps and bounds.

It stands to reason that the top one percent should now be broken down further since someone making half a million dollars a year is not anywhere near the same as someone making a billion, or billions of dollars a year. When Eisenhower left office, there was no such thing as a billionaire, only millionaires. Howard Hughes is the one I remember most from my youth. The bottom line is, if the ultra-wealthy paid their fair share, or closer to their fair share, things could be a lot better for the rest of us. I know plenty of people who've been overburdened due to taxes, and that just shouldn't be. These are not people living high on the hog. They are people who are struggling like far too many in order to give those who've figured out a way to get everyone else to do their work for them, or have used Earth's resources, or both, a break.

If it's true that the Bush tax cuts cost the nation trillions, with him lowering the rate for his favorite one percent of the population from 39.6% to 35%, imagine how much cuts that went from 91% to 39.6% have cost us. And please, if anyone runs into Ann Coulter, who will likely bring up that the uppermost of income earners pay a disproportionate share of the overall taxes, ask Ann how they make their money. They skip that part don't they? One case I've talked about is about someone who was called a "self-made billionaire" by the major media who made his money from oil. Please, did he create the oil? Did he make the steel the ships that transported it were made of? Did he make the ships? Did he drill for the oil? Did he navigate the ships that delivered the oil? How then, can anyone explain, is he a "self-made billionaire?"

3) Hemp reportedly has over 25,000 uses according to the February 1938 issue of *Popular Mechanics*, yet it's illegal. How can any sane beings claim that making an Earth given plant illegal is the right thing to do, much less such a useful one, but really any plant? How would we explain our behavior to a superior intelligence if given the chance? Hemp's uses are vast. One of its uses is for fuel. Its seeds can be crushed and its stalks fermented to make fuel. Henry Ford had a car that ran on hemp seed oil. Not only that but it was used to make the exterior of an automobile, reportedly making it several times stronger than steel, as anyone can see by

doing a search on YouTube for the Ford hemp car. There's a guy hitting the trunk with an ax will all his might and not making a dent. Don't believe me, check for yourself.

To have this plant illegal is absolutely insane. This is one area Elaine and I have been told we made an impact here in Virginia, since a bill to legalize hemp just passed unanimously, and being that both of us ran as the first married couple to do so in the history of Virginia, we got enough media coverage for the hemp issue to take off. It was something we could say with concision, which Chomsky correctly argues is what's required when dealing with today's US corporate media. So, we talked about it, a lot. We can push issues, even with puppets in office, and this is why I encourage everyone to do just that, in addition to trying to get marginalized candidates on the ballots for every federal office possible and demanding they be included in televised debates.

4) The Drug War has resulted in the "Land of the Free" becoming the "Land of the Caged," with more incarcerates per capita and even in total than any nation on Earth. Are we any safer? No. When stats were first taken in the 1960s, 90% of homicides were reportedly solved in the US. Now it's 64%, meaning whereas it used to be that just one in ten got away with murder, now more than one of three do! Of course this also means there will be more criminals of every real kind at large because law enforcement can't do two things at the same time. This is taking away from them finding more murderers, pedophiles, rapists, thieves, along with every other real crime as well as missing people including children.

So, if you're for the Drug War, you're for having more murderers at large, having more missing people not found, and so forth. And that's not all. I know a woman who was told that the person who raped her would do his entire five year sentence, yet they let him out two years early in order to snitch on people for marijuana! How sick is that! I saw some of the impact this had on loved ones when I practiced and it wasn't pretty. What about the children whose parents are taken from them when sent to live in cages for illegitimate reasons? If they only have one parent they become orphans. If they have two sometimes both are busted and they still become orphans. Either way losing one parent is abusive. Is this not state sanctioned tax funded child abuse?

Elaine does a lot with animal rescues. How many pet owner turn ins" are due to the Drug War? No one knows.

Below: From Sad to Glad

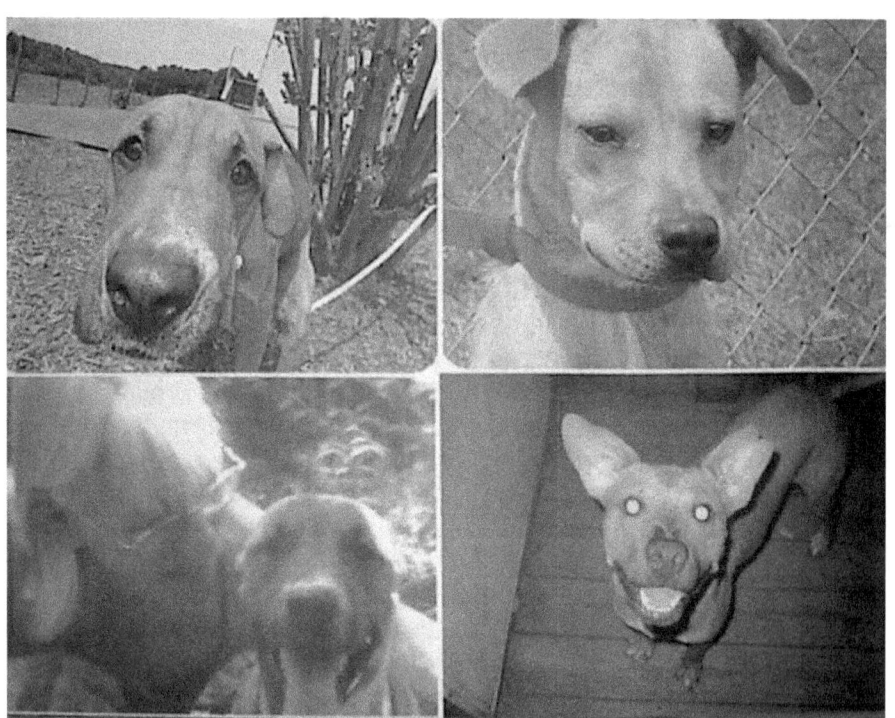

These are two of our thirteen dog rescues, Gomer is pictured on the left top before his rescue and on the bottom afterwards with Elaine, and that's Maverick on the right, before and after. They were both owner surrenders for reasons we were not told. They are both wonderful dogs. Aren't they all?

Again, we end up with more unjustified misery due to this continued insanity where bad medicine is purposefully administered to the masses, not only children, but also on pets, and of course adults as well.

Every arrest for this nonsense is a crime whose tentacles are not reported on television or newspapers, but they're real all right. How do the people involved live with themselves? Well, some don't. Some have seen the light. Please take the time to check out LEAP, Law Enforcement Against Prohibition, to see I'm hardly alone saying we need to stop this ongoing insanity. http://leap.cc

Please take a moment to read LEAP's mission statement about wanting to heal and help normalize the relationship between police and the general population, which is something that's decayed enormously throughout this unjust war against people's rights to liberty. Furthermore, if the nation thought drugs were a crime then Obama would not have been elected, because he admitted to doing cocaine and not getting caught. Imagine if he said he held up a convenience store but didn't get caught, or he had mugged or raped someone. So, clearly the nation knows the difference between crimes and non-crimes. No victim, no crime. It's not very complicated. How will future historians, if there are any, look back at this time when we locked people up in violent cages en masse for invalid reasons at such an enormous expense?

5) On July 08, 1947, ABC radio reported that a "flying disc" had crashed and been recovered by the Army Air Force on a ranch outside of Roswell, New Mexico. They later reported that it was all a mistake and what had been thought of as being something from out of this world was actually just a weather balloon.

Roswell was home to the 509th, the ones who bombed Hiroshima and Nagasaki. I ask the reader to think about this; why would they leave people in charge of nuclear weapons who were so inept they didn't know the difference between a weather balloon and something not made on Earth? Hundreds of witnesses to aspects of the case have come forward and we have our choice, to believe them or the government's view of what happened.

There are plenty of other solid cases. This book mostly focuses on one of them. If it happened once, it can happen more than once. And it has. If you don't think this is important ask yourself this, why would the government go to such lengths to hide this from us for going on 70 years if it wasn't? Surely you don't think in light of everything else discussed it's for our own good, do you? I trust there is more than enough evidence to convict regarding Roswell in this book thanks to the 2013 Citizen Hearing in Washington, DC, of which I was close enough to attend three of the five days by driving back and forth for the parts I was most interested in hearing and filming.

6) Less than 3 weeks after the crash reported above, the National Security Act of 1947 was enacted. This created a "secret government" according to the respected journalist Bill Moyers in his famous special, *The Secret Government: The Constitution in Crisis*, who are not elected and answer to no one. During the Iran-Contra hearings, Senator Daniel Inouye stated,

"There exists a shadowy government with its own air force, its own navy, its own fund raising mechanism, and the ability to pursue its own ideas of national interest, free from all checks and balances, and free from the law itself."

What "fund raising mechanism?" They aren't having bake sales, but they have been linked to the drug trade. Can it get any sicker? Yes, it can actually. Guess who Colonel Jesse Marcel, Jr., MD said was at the heart of the whole ET issue, having the entire thing in its hands? That's right, the secret government. And please don't anyone bring up anything about conspiracy theories. The National Security Act of 1947 is not a conspiracy theory. Admittedly their link to the Drug War is a theory, but I can't think of any other and I doubt seriously that outside this county the CIA earning the name, Cocaine Importing Agency, has not been without cause.

7) *"WE'RE DOING SOMETHING ABOUT THE WEATHER!,"* was a feature article in the April 1972 issue of *National Geographic* magazine, and they are. Don't you think we should have a right to know what it is they're using to seed clouds, or are they using the same old techniques from the 60s discussed in this article? Surely they're doing something because jet trails didn't spread across the sky until the last couple of decades or so, other than in some kind of experimentation in the 40s everyone likes to cite, and I'm sure they experimented elsewhere here and there.

The way I discovered this "nugget" was by looking back in *National Geographic* magazines trying to find the oldest one in which I'd see a proliferating trail like we see today. I found it, but they called it a contrail. If that was the case then how come there aren't tons of photos of proliferating trails from that time period? Proliferating trails were not generally seen in the 60s, 70s, 80s, and roughly half way through the 90s in most places, though they reportedly did tinker with things in some areas during that period, so one might come up with a photograph or two but nothing like today's crisscrossed lines and all the other abnormal patterns we see.

Weather manipulation is old hat. Exhaust fumes under any atmospheric conditions do not proliferate while maintaining an uninterrupted line from horizon to horizon, period. What impact this is having on global warming is anyone's guess. Is it helping? Is it harming? We know Emergency Rooms get overwhelmed with respiratory patients following reported sprayings. That much was even admitted in the 2007 *Chemical Contrails* documentary on the *Discovery Channel*. Reportedly there are increased levels of barium, aluminum and strontium after these sprayings in soil samples. We're not supposed to be breathing in metals. That's not a normal part of our atmosphere's chemical composition.

8) Every hour approximately 700 children die worldwide of preventable causes that just a fraction of the Pentagon budget could completely stop. In other words they die of neglect. No shores of Normandy Beach need be invaded to save them. They just need to be seen as real and the people demand that they be given the medicine(s), the food and/or the clean water they need.

9) We all have a common ancestor out of Africa who was dark skinned and thus we're all, as Jimi Hendrix sang in his song *Machine Gun*, "families apart." In the 1960s I grew up as we got away from the term "colored people," yet now people are separated anew and called "people of color." Excuse me, but I've never met a colorless person in my life. Let's get over bogus divisions, OK?

10) There could be peace in the Middle East between Israel and Palestine if the US and Israel weren't blocking it from happening.

11) Everyone who's on enough state ballots to win, meaning almost surely Trump, Clinton, Stein and Gary Johnson of the Libertarian Party for 2016, should have a right to debate the others under fair conditions on television for all to see. No one should be left out. The fifteen percent inclusionary rate is far from democratic, especially since the media have shoved two of the candidates in our faces for over a year, and refused to give us a fair look at the others.

No matter what happens in the 2016 Elections, we need to "Keep pushing ahead" to borrow the words of the late Jimi Hendrix from his final song *Straight Ahead*. We have to push for these truths to be uncovered and demand that we cease doing harmful things to our society, outlawing solutions and having overall insane inefficiency. It must stop, and we must also demand that we have fair federal elections, which we have every two years, or we will continue in the downward spiral we're in quite possibly past the point of no return.

12) We're all making history at this critical time of human existence on Earth, one way or the other.

//

I sincerely apologize if I didn't catch every mistake in this book. At some point I felt it would never be good enough and I'd better hurry to try to get it out there to enough to matter in time. I hope it's clear enough and little things are overlooked. Please forgive me for jumping from first to third person at times. Sometimes it felt best the one way, sometimes the other.

First and foremost I would like to thank my overwhelmingly supportive wife Elaine. Without her help this book would not exist. I would also like to thank Noam Chomsky, his assistant Bev Stohl, Fran Forstadt for her countless hours of helping us edit a much earlier edition, most of which is still in Part I, everyone who's featured in the book, Mark Achbar and (unfortunately, the late) Peter Wintonick, neither of whom I've ever met or even corresponded with but were the makers of *Manufacturing Consent: Noam Chomsky and the Media*, which introduced me to Professor Chomsky and got me started on this path.

Many thanks to Steve Bassett of the Paradigm Research Group for helping organize the Citizen Hearing on Disclosure as well as to Jeremy Corbell and Reuben Landon for giving me permission to use some key excepts of that historic event for this book. Thanks also to Dr. Joe Buchman for helping me with some words and names in the transcriptions.

Thanks also to Brandon Stanway for the long talks and up to date information I've relied on him heavily for especially surrounding the 2016 Presidential Election, Jake Kettle for his friendship and support, and our friend J. J. Denson who's helped enormously with technical issues, literally keeping us up and running.

Additional thanks go to my friend Mark Brown for both keeping our vehicles on the road and helping with some last minute editing.

I'd especially like to thank every rational person who helps spread these truths to enough to matter in time as we all make history together at this most critical time of human existence on the crust of this rock we call Earth.

"Pass it on. Pass it on, to the young and old."

- Jimi Hendrix, from his final song, Straight Ahead

Addendum:

I guess I never liked what I considered illegitimate authority, at least from age nine I didn't, as per the above. I don't know how others can submit and look themselves in the mirror, or even enjoy life at all. Why would anyone willingly hand their lives over to their oppressors once they understood what was happening.

"You were a born radical, bucking the system, questioning authority at age 9. Awesome!"

– Dr. Stephen Saunders, regarding the comic above

"Look, you have two choices, you can say 'I'm a pessimist. Nothing's going to work. I'm giving up. I'll help ensure that the worst will happen.' Or you can grasp onto the opportunities that do exist, the rays of hope that exist and say, 'Well, maybe we can make it a better world.' It's not much of a choice."

- Noam Chomsky

Election 2016 update, August 2016, just before this book goes to print:

If Hillary only has to face Trump from here on in and the media successfully censor the other candidates who are on enough ballots to win, or will be, meaning Jill Stein of the Green Party and former New Mexico Governor Gary Johnson for the Libertarians, then I can't say one way or the other who would win. I honestly don't know, nor would I even venture to guess. Both Clinton and Trump are terrible, so the only choice is what flavor of terrible do you want? The point is that this should not be another media election. I'm not saying whether this book will make a difference at all, but I am putting it out there with close to a quarter lap around the Sun before the 2016 Election. At the height of the Information Age, I'm just saying, yes, it certainly COULD be done and in my opinion would be in a world that's even remotely reasonable.

On the surface we kind of know what to expect from Hillary, as Obama said himself when debating her eight years ago, 'If you're happy with the way things are now then Senator Clinton's your candidate.' We don't know what to expect from Trump, and when one considers things like nuclear bombs and nuclear holocausts, that kind of gets a bit worrisome. I'm not saying I would vote for Hillary. I would be incapable of casting my vote in her favor. If there was no one else but those two I'd write in Donald Duck. I'm voting for Stein, period. She's the best of the four who are, or will almost certainly be, on enough state ballots to win the presidency. If I have to write her name in, big deal.

Gary Johnson has reportedly backed the TPP, so that really leaves him out even more so than before, because in comparison to Jill Stein when it comes to platform his is just not near as fair. So, I don't care if Dr. Stein only gets on say 40 ballots, as opposed to Johnson's 51 including DC, then that means she could get 80% of the vote, and if people realized this was like choosing whether to get smacked with a 32 oz hammer or with a feather, she'd get that 80%, or close to it anyway.

Is it not insane to vote for pain, suffering, oppression, lack of safety and rights, all because you're scared of someone even worse, especially since employing this tactic has arguably done us zero good since first employed in 2000? Here we are sixteen years later. Should we try it one more time?

Who would vote in disfavor of themselves in so many ways if they only knew?

If enough would rather have someone who is for peace in the Middle East verses someone who isn't, who would tax the rich more over someone who won't, and would work towards ending the Drug War that leaves more real criminals at large vs. someone who won't, then Jill Stein can win the presidency.

If with 3 days to go or so Jill saw it wasn't happening, well then she could call a press conference and do what she wanted, so no one could accuse her of assisting a horrible person to obtain the most powerful known position of any human being on Earth. How's that sound? What if Trump says he'll adopt more of Stein's platform than Hillary will? I wouldn't be at all surprised. There was a recent article by John Pilger giving some pretty sound reasons in arguing the case that Hillary is worse than Trump.*

- See, **https://newmatilda.com/2016/03/23/john-pilger-why-hillary-clinton-is-more-dangerous-than-donald-trump/?utm_campaign=shareaholic&utm_medium=facebook&utm_source=socialnetwork**

Of course, in an informed world Dr. Stein would take away votes from both Clinton and Trump, enough so to win easily. Remember the online vote of 2000 at Time Magazine discussed early on in Part I, in which over a million people had responded and Nader got 58.77% the last time I checked, with Bush getting about half as many and Gore getting less than 10%. I'm not saying that it was a scientific study but it does stand to reason that someone reasonable in major ways her opponents are not would not have a rough time winning.

An important point I want to make is that no matter how this election goes, we've GOT to keep pushing these issues until enough understand them. Then the gag will be up. If say 2/3 of the population understands even just half of the few hidden elementary truths presented in this book, how could the leaders and the corporate TV continue to misguide us on a highly destructive course all to satisfy the insatiable greed of a small percentage of cowardly psychopaths? I don't think Jill Stein or anyone is qualified to take on all that's been presented here. Whoever gets in must be backed by the people regarding these concerns.

Forget about so-called swing states and safe states. People in all states have been voting against themselves, which is why you'll never hear me discuss in depth this nonsense that has worked like a charm since 2000 to keep us focused on the lesser of evils, instead of where we should be. Even if we're going third party, though not an evil choice, I doubt very seriously that Dr. Stein knows about a lot of what's been covered in the second half of Part II of this book.

The Drug War is likely related to the "Secret Government*" (I mean, something's funding them and if it's covert it sure isn't legit), which is almost certainly related to the massive aerial sprayings (who else could it be?) and IS reportedly related to the ongoing cover-up of ET interactions with Earth humans as per the testimony of the late Colonel Jesse Marcel, Jr, MD above in Chapter 17 of Part II.

- It is highly recommended everyone see the Bill Moyers special entitled, ***The Secret Government: The Constitution in Crisis***, from 1987 disclosing once again that Noam Chomsky's statement about elementary truths being easily buried is in fact true.

This is not the time to focus on so-called "safe" and "swing" states, especially when it's arguable as to who is worse, is it? Do we not want someone reasonable for president? Is that asking too much? Let's face it, Bill Clinton's embargo against Iraq killed over half a million children. While it's true no one is responsible for anyone else's actions, Hillary was Bill's wife during this entire atrocity, and there were no objections I'm aware of. Trump is scary in some ways, yet he's never overseen an operation that resulted in half a million horrible deaths of little children and babies over a prolonged period of time, has he? So, who's worse? Do we know for sure?

Our message and these issues need to permeate the red and blue so everyone realizes they were and are getting shafted in monumental ways.

All we're requesting is they end this insanity. We're not setting the bar very high here. Let the INFORMolution begin and the insanity begin to end. Life is hard enough without adding all this manufactured harmfulness and risk to the short time we have here. Enough is enough. We ought to be living life, not wasting it due to a minority of cruel people and a majority of duped ones, not at the height of the Information Age.

Index

A World of Ideas (Bill Moyers), 54

A Strange Harvest (documentary by Linda Moulton-Howe), 137 - 138, 140

ABC radio, July 08, 1947, 119

Abu-Jamal, Mumia, 12 - 13

Achbar, Mark, 14, 22, 35, 65, 159

Afghanistan, 58, 69, 96, 107, 110

Africa, 60, 83, 91, 158

Air Force, 110, 115, 117 - 118, 120 - 125, 130 - 134, 157 - 158

Albright, Madeleine, 38

alcohol, 16, 22, 33, 48, 53, 61, 74, 83, 85, 101

Alderman, Ellen, 48

Alford plea, 28

American Broadcasting Company (ABC), 112, 119 -120, 157

Americans, 10, 13, 18-19, 22, 34, 60, 69, 74-75, 82-83, 98, 101

animals, 139-140

Anti-Semitism, 93

Apartheid, 51

Apollo astronaut, 35, 87, 137

Armed Services Committee, 54

Army Air Force, 119-120, 157

Associated Press, 15, 22, 40, 43

Attenborough, David, 86

Auschwitz, 93

Austin, Texas, 22

automobiles, 11

ballots, 7, 11, 21, 31, 33, 46, 52, 57, 68, 71, 81, 141, 154-156, 159

Bassett, Steve, 139, 159

Ben-Gurion, David, 93

Best, Darrel, 24

Best, Wanda, 24-29

Biden, Joe, 50

Biko, Steve, 12, 51

Bill of Rights, 22

Bloomberg, Michael, 146, 154

Bolkestein, Frits (Dutch Minister of Defense), 46

Borregard, Eric, 52-55, 57-58, 61

Brazel, Bill (William), 123, 132

Brazel, W. W. "Mac", 124, 133

Brown, Mark, 159

Buchman, Dr. Joe, 159

Burke, Edmund, 47

Bush, George Herbert Walker (Sr. Bush), 38, 50, 82

Bush, George W., 4, 11, 13, 15-16, 20-21, 32-34, 38, 50, 56-57, 63, 70, 78, 82, 156

Butler, Nicholas Murray, 44

C-Span, 34

cages, 22, 47, 50, 61, 104, 106, 156-157

California, 78-79

Campbell, Douglas, 52, 55-57

Campbell, Carey, 84, 154

Canada, 6, 19, 32, 140

cannabis, 10, 29-30, 47, 49, 79, 82-83, 96, 101-102, 105

Carlson, Tucker, 56

Carnahan, Jean, 60

cars, 9-10, 49, 71, 110

Carter, Jimmy, 7, 15, 33, 73

Central Intelligence Agency (CIA), 138

Charlottesville, Virginia, 90-91, 107, 110-113, 149

Cleland, Max, 60

Cheney, Dick, 34, 56

chemtrails, 102, 110-111

China, 32, 39, 45, 74, 76, 96, 105

Chomsky, Noam, 1, 4, 6, 8, 14-15, 19, 22-23, 30-31, 33-35, 46, 54, 57-58, 65, 72, 76-77, 80, 85-86, 88, 92-94, 99, 105, 110, 115, 143-144, 147, 154, 156, 159-160

Christ, 10, 20, 28, 56, 127, 154

Chrysler, 55

CIA (Central Intelligence Agency), 138

cigarettes, 49, 101

Citizen Hearing on Disclosure, 121, 124, 126, 129, 159

Clinton, Bill, 13, 32, 38, 50, 82, 92-93

Clinton, Hillary, 70, 73-74, 154-155, 159, 161

Congress, 6, 12, 18, 59-60, 63, 70, 75-76, 84, 94-95, 104-106, 137-138, 142, 144-145, 150-151, 154

congressional, 7, 18. 30, 35, 49, 58, 62, 81, 85, 90-91, 104, 107, 110-112, 140, 142 149

Corbel, Jeremy, 159

corporate media, 14, 19, 46, 62, 64, 141, 156

corporation, 55, 60, 74, 144

corporations, 16, 62, 67, 74, 78, 97, 103, 146

corporate welfare, 13

Corso, Philip, Col., 112

CNN, 69, 71, 73

Curry, Dayna, 20

Daily News, The (New York City), 56, 118

Dashiell, Joe, 94, 99-100

DEA (Drug Enforcement Agency), 32

Dean, Howard, 73, 75-76

Dean Scream, 73

Democrats, 36, 38, 50, 58, 62, 66, 69, 78, 141, 150, 154

Democratic Party, 59-62. 66. 69-70, 73, 75

Denson, J. J., 159

Drug Enforcement Agency (DEA), 32

Drug War, 15-16, 20, 22, 30, 45-46, 48, 50, 63, 74, 85, 96, 105-106, 110, 113, 142-143, 145, 153-154, 156

Dubose, Thomas, 123, 132

Dutch Minister of Defense (Frits Bolkestein), 46

East Timor, 7, 14-15, 33

Economist, 22, 148-149

ElectElaine.com, 105, 110

ElectKen.com, 105-106

Eighth Amendment, 22

Eisenhower, Dwight D., 34, 72, 82, 105, 112, 155

Extraterrestrial, 112, 133, 135-137, 139-140

Faulkner, Police Officer Daniel, 12

FBI (Federal Bureau of Investigation), 140

Federal Bureau of Investigation (FBI), 137-138, 140

fetal alcohol syndrome, 53

Flight 93, 11

flying disk, 119-120

flying saucer, 114, 119-120, 122-125, 127, 129-130, 134

foo fighters, 114

foreign aid, 112

Forstadt, Fran, 159

Fortunato, Joe, 49-50, 59, 62-64

Friedline, Doug, 40, 42-43, 49

Friedman, Stanton, 121-123, 127, 131, 138

Friedman, Sue, 90-91, 107, 110-111, 113

Fulbright, Bill, 73

Gates, Bill, 10, 59, 61, 64

Gaughan, Lawrence, 91, 107

Gaza, 92-93

GE (General Electric), 73

General Electric (GE), 65

Germany, 16, 20, 45, 151

Gersten, Peter, 138

Gandhi, Mahatma, 18

Giuliani, Rudy, 70

Glick, Ted, 36-38, 40-45, 49, 58-59, 66-68

Goebbels, Joseph, 58, 69

Gore, Al, 11, 13, 15-16, 59

Government Intelligence Committee, 54

Graham, Gary (Shaka Sankofa), 56

Granny D (Doris Haddock), 62

Grant, Taylor, 119-120

Gravel, Mike, 18, 69-77, 83, 102, 121, 123-126, 129, 132

Green, Dr. David Michael, 30

Green Party, 12, 36,-37, 45, 49, 52, 55, 58-60, 62, 64, 66-68, 78-79, 81-82, 84, 94-95, 100, 105, 145-146, 154, 159

Greer, Emily, 113

Greer, Steven, MD, 112-113

Gross National Product, 19

Gutenberg, Johann, 14

Haddock, Doris (Granny D), 62-63

Harkin, Tom, 60

Hamas, 93

Harlem, 16, 34, 55, 64, 154

hemp, 8, 10, 32-33, 52-54, 79, 82, 95-97, 99-101, 104-105, 107-108, 110, 151, 153, 156

hemp oil, 10

Hendrix, Jimi, 60, 83, 85-86, 91. 158-159

Herer, Jack, 11, 53-54

Hibler, Dr. Neil, 127

Hildebrandt, Elaine, 31, 50, 53, 59, 77, 94, 99, 104, 109-110, 113-114, 154, 156

Hillary, 70, 73-74, 154-155, 159

Hiroshima, 38, 112 119, 124, 157

Hitler, 19, 34, 58, 69, 93

Hofstra University, 30

Holt, Rush, 60

Holzer, Dr. Hans, 91

House of Representatives, 105

hunger, 19, 31, 38

Hume, David, 70, 85-86

Hussein, Saddam, 38, 69

Hurst, Chris, 94-103

Hynek, Dr. J. Allen, 115, 117, 122

Inauguration Day, 92

Independent Green Party of Virginia (Indy Greens), 84, 105

Indonesia, 15

Industrial hemp, 8, 32, 79, 95, 97, 99-101, 104, 107-108, 110, 153

Indy Greens (Independent Green Party of Virginia), 84, 105

Information Age, 1, 5, 11, 13, 19-20, 22, 30, 57, 65, 70, 80, 85, 141

Inouye, Senator Daniel, 110, 158

internet, 6, 11, 13-15, 18-19, 21, 23, 31, 34, 39, 46, 55, 64-65, 70, 74-75, 85, 100, 117, 119, 123, 127, 155

Iran, 39, 70, 73-74, 76, 93, 158

Iraq, 4, 15-16, 36, 38-39, 54, 69, 96, 123-124, 132, 154

ISIS (Islamic State of Iraq and Syria), 38, 154

Israel, 54, 88, 92-93, 154, 158

Israel/Palestine, 88, 92-93, 154

Iraqi Embargo, 15-16, 38

jail, 16, 21-22, 26-28, 36, 38, 40, 45, 47-48, 53, 57, 74, 83, 133

Jeffries, Ken, 127

JFK (John F. Kennedy), 38

Johnson, Gary, 154, 159, 161

Johnson, Tim, 60

Jones, Paul, 91, 107, 142

Kennedy, 48, 82,

Kennedy, Caroline, 48

Kennedy, John F. (JFK), 38

Kerry, John, 11, 21, 33

Kettle, Jake, 159

Koch brothers, 143, 146

Kucinich, Dennis, 60, 70, 77, 103, 110

Langdon, Reuben, 159

law enforcement, 20, 22, 30, 50, 53, 74, 85, 104, 107, 138-140, 156-157

Law Enforcement Against Prohibition (LEAP), 157

League of Woman Voters, 113

LEAP – Law Enforcement Against Prohibition, 157

Lieberman, Joseph (Joe), 73

Levin, Carl, 52, 54-55

Libertarian Party, 71, 142-145, 159, 161

libertarianism, 143-145, 149

Los Angeles Times, 94

Machine Gun, Jimi Hendrix, 83, 91, 158

MajorMediaBypass.com, 32, 72

MANUFACTURING CONSENT: NOAM CHOMSKY AND THE MEDIA, 6, 99,159

Marcel, Denice, 126, 129, 131

Marcel, Jesse III, 129-131

Marcel, Jesse, Jr., MD, 124-126, 129-131, 135, 158

Marcel, Jesse, Sr., 119, 121-123, 126, 129-131, 133

marijuana, 10, 32, 49, 53, 57, 74, 79, 81, 83, 86, 96, 100-101, 104-105, 110, 154, 156

Mars, 10, 34, 39, 85, 97, 155

Mayer, Carl, 33, 58-61

MBNA, 55

McCain, John, 20, 70

McClousky, Pete, 73

McGaa, Ed, 58

McGovern, George, 73

McKinney, Cynthia, 12, 68

media, 5-11, 13-15, 18-23, 30-37, 39, 43, 45-48, 50-52, 55-57, 62, 64-65, 68-72, 74-77, 80, 85-88, 90, 94, 98-99, 137, 140-141, 150, 155-156, 159

Medicare, 54, 97-98, 148-150

military-industrial complex, 72-73, 76, 110, 112

Milton, John, 24

Minot Air Force Base, North Dakota, 115

missing children, 105-106

Mitchell, Dr. Edgar, 35, 87, 141, 155

moon, 35

Moulton-Howe, Linda, 159, 161

Moyers, Bill, 22, 54, 88, 110, 157, 162

MRI (magnetic resonance imaging), 49, 56

MSNBC, 69-70, 73-74

murder, 12, 22, 29, 56, 70, 104, 156

murderers, 10, 30, 47, 50, 57, 63-64, 74, 86, 105-106, 156

Nagasaki, 112, 119, 124, 157

Nader, Ralph, 9-11, 13, 15, 21-22, 32-34, 50, 52, 55, 67-68, 82, 104-105, 110

National Geographic, April 1970, 109, 111, 158

National Reconnaissance Organization, 138

National Security Act of 1947, 89, 110, 141, 158

National Security Agency (NSA), 138

NBC (National Broadcasting Company), 73-74

NSA (National Security Agency), 138, 140

Neptune, 88-89, 115

Nelson, Gaylord, 73

New Hampshire Primary, 18, 33, 77

New York Times, 14-15, 29, 59

nicotine, 16, 22, 33, 48-49, 61, 85, 101

Northern Alliance, Afghanistan, 20

Northwestern University, 122

nuclear power, 52, 60

Obama, Barack, 12-13, 20, 50, 70, 74, 87, 91-92, 97, 107, 147, 157

ObamaCare, 97

opium, 61

organize, 19, 65, 86

Orwell, George, 9

overcomethemedia.com, 77

PAC (Political Action Committee), 52, 54, 60

Palestine, 88, 92-93, 154, 158

Palestinian, 92-93

Paradigm Research Group (PRG), 124, 139, 159

Patriot Act, 95

Paul, Rand, 148-149

Paul, Ron, 70, 77, 109

Pauling, Linus, 5

pedophiles, 10, 30, 47, 50, 57, 63, 86, 105-106, 156

Peltier, Leonard, 13

Pentagon, 19, 31, 36, 38-39, 90, 112, 146, 154, 158

Pentagon Papers, 69, 71-72, 76

pillory, 22-23

Pilger, John, 161

plants, 107, 110, 153

Popular Mechanics, 79, 95, 100, 104, 156

Poppies, 107

Poppy, 107

ppbnj.com, 66

presidency, 7, 10, 21, 33-35, 46, 55-56, 70, 74, 141-142, 150, 154-155

presidential pardon, 12

Prince of Peace, 11

PRG (Paradigm Research Group), 139

prisoners, 20, 22, 38, 45, 47, 74, 83, 96, 102, 104-105, 113

Project Blue Book, 121-122, 132

proliferating jet trails, 33

racism, 91

Ramey, Brigadier General Roger, 120, 123, 125, 132,

Randle, Kevin, 131-132

rape, 22, 47, 50

raped, 20, 48, 74, 102, 156-157

rapes, 38, 47, 83

Reagan, Ron, 22, 38, 50, 78, 82, 96, 107, 155

receptor sites, 49, 61

Reese, Charlie, 7, 18, 141, 145, 151, 154

Republican Party, 61, 75, 150

Republicans, 36, 38, 61-63, 66, 70, 78, 141, 150, 154

Revere, Paul, 20, 64

Right to Privacy, The (by Ellen Alderman and Caroline Kennedy), 48

Romania, 32

Roswell, New Mexico, 112, 119-126, 128, 130-136, 153, 157-158

Russell, Bertrand, 4, 88

Russia, 39, 74, 76

Sanders, Bernie, 154-155, 159

Sankofa, Shaka (Gary Graham), 56

Saturday Evening Post, December 17, 1966, 115, 117, 153

Saunders, Dr. Stephen, 160

Schindele, David D., Captain, US Air Force, Retired, 115, 117, 153

Schmitt, Don, 132

Schmitt, Harrison, 137

Secret Government: Constitution in Crisis (The), Bill Moyers, 1987, 88, 162

Senate, 10, 18, 36, 38, 40, 49-50, 52, 58-62, 66, 69, 110, 142, 145, 154

SOAP - Subjective, Objective, Assessment, Plan, 153

Social Security, 97

South Africa, 12, 51

Sr. Bush (George Herbert Walker Bush), 38, 82

Stahl, Leslie 38

Stanway, Brandon, 159

Stalin, Joseph, 11, 32, 76

Stanford Encyclopedia of Philosophy, 70

Stein, Jill, MD, 81-84, 95, 102, 150, 154, 159, 161-162

Stohl, Bev, 77, 159

Straight Ahead, (by Jimi Hendrix), 159

Suitland, Maryland, 138

Sumerians, 5

Sunday Times, The (Australia), 139

Syria, 74

Taba, Egypt, 93

Taliban, 20, 23, 69, 107,

Tele Mundo 74

THC (tetrahydrocannabinol),49,

The Secret Government: The Constitution in Crisis, Bill Moyers, 88, 158,

TIME magazine, 14-15

tobacco, 49, 61

Torricelli, Robert, 37-38, 42, 44, 47, 49-50, 62

Trenton Times, 44- 45

Tricomo, Ray, 58

Trinity Site, 122

Truman, Harry, 57, 133, 137-138

Trump, Donald, 154, 159, 161

Tucker, Karla Faye, 56

Twain, Mark, 19, 109

UFO(s), 3, 112-116, 118-119, 121-122, 126-127, 132, 138-139, 153

University of Colorado, 122

University of Texas, 9

Ventura, Jesse, 40, 42

Videomaker's Guide to PC Video, 19

Vietnam War, 13, 48, 72, 83

Wal-Mart, 10

WBAI radio, NYC, 59

WDBJ7, (Roanoke, Virginia), 94, 99, 149

Webb, Jim, 22, 83, 86-87

Wells, Laura, 78-80

Wellstone, Paul, 38, 58

White Sands Missile Range, 122

wind, 52-54, 106, 111, 118

Wintonick, Peter, 14, 22, 35, 65, 159

Wright Field, Ohio, 120, 134

York, Matthew, 19

YouTube Election, 19

Zeese, Kevin, 142

Znet Interactive, 13, 15

www.ingramcontent.com/pod-product-compliance
Lightning Source LLC
Chambersburg PA
CBHW051957280526
45793CB00005B/757